RESET

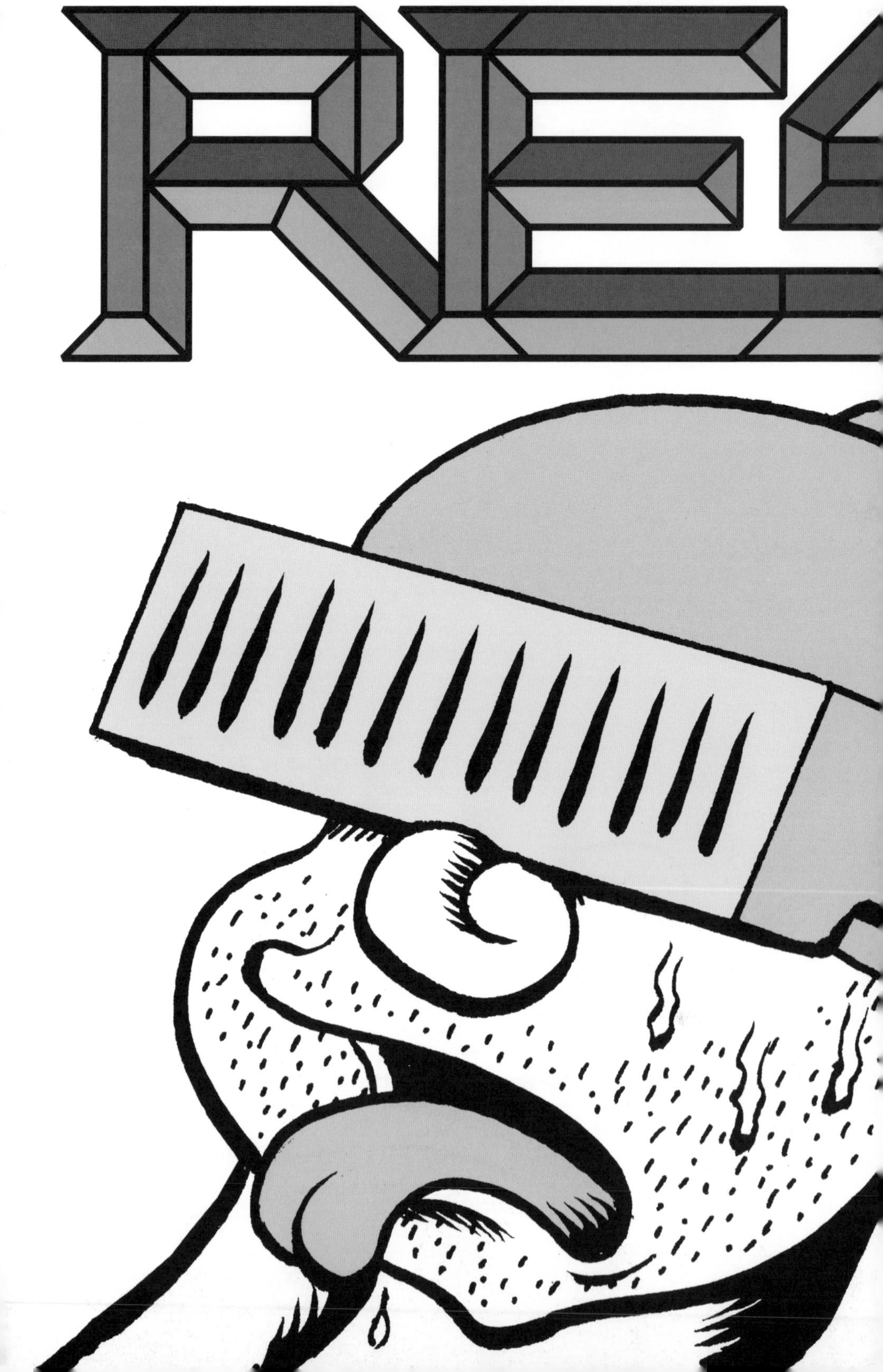

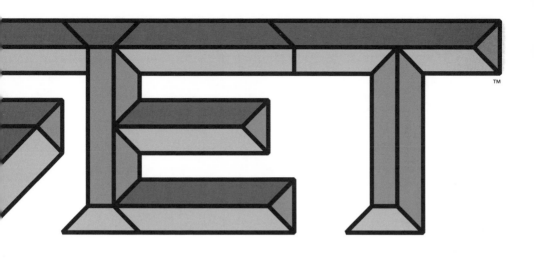

...OH BAY- BEE...

STORY AND ART BY
PETER BAGGE

COLORS AND GRAY TONES BY
JOANNE BAGGE

DARK HORSE BOOKS

President and Publisher
MIKE RICHARDSON

Editor
PHILIP R. SIMON

Designer
ADAM GRANO

Digital Production and Retouch
RYAN JORGENSEN

Special thanks to Rebecca Goodwin and Kari Yadro.

Published by Dark Horse Books
A division of Dark Horse Comics, Inc.
10956 SE Main Street
Milwaukie, OR 97222

DarkHorse.com
PeterBagge.com

To find a comics shop in your area, call the Comic
Shop Locator Service toll-free at 1-888-266-4226.

This volume collects issues #1 through #4 of Dark Horse Comics' *Reset* series.

First edition: January 2013
ISBN 978-1-61655-003-5

10 9 8 7 6 5 4 3 2 1
Printed at Shanghai Offset Printing, Guangdong Province, China

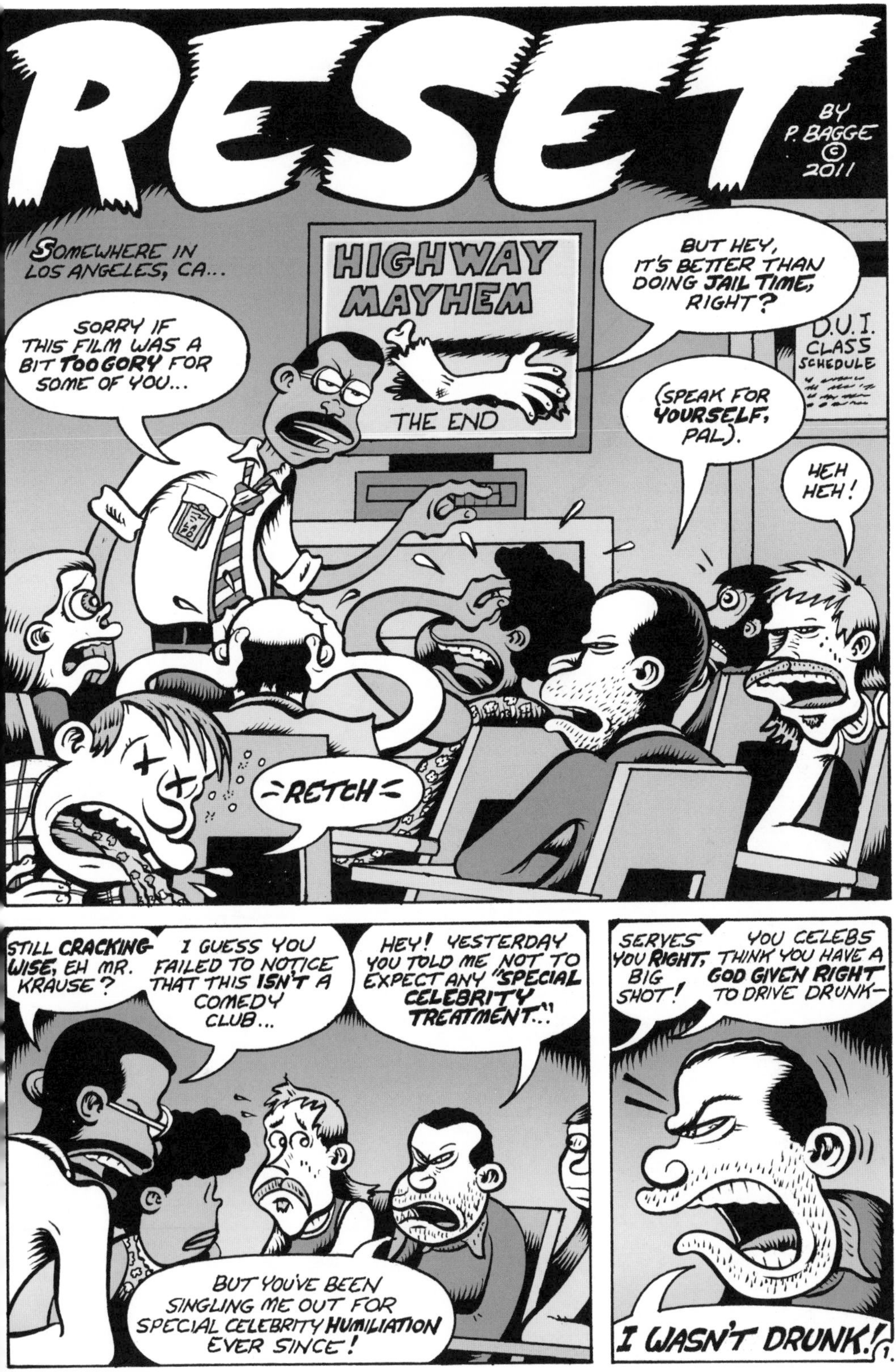
RESET
BY P. BAGGE © 2011
SOMEWHERE IN LOS ANGELES, CA...
HIGHWAY MAYHEM
THE END
SORRY IF THIS FILM WAS A BIT TOO GORY FOR SOME OF YOU...
BUT HEY, IT'S BETTER THAN DOING JAIL TIME, RIGHT?
D.U.I. CLASS SCHEDULE
(SPEAK FOR YOURSELF, PAL).
HEH HEH!
RETCH
STILL CRACKING WISE, EH MR. KRAUSE?
I GUESS YOU FAILED TO NOTICE THAT THIS ISN'T A COMEDY CLUB...
HEY! YESTERDAY YOU TOLD ME NOT TO EXPECT ANY "SPECIAL CELEBRITY TREATMENT."
BUT YOU'VE BEEN SINGLING ME OUT FOR SPECIAL CELEBRITY HUMILIATION EVER SINCE!
SERVES YOU RIGHT, BIG SHOT!
YOU CELEBS THINK YOU HAVE A GOD GIVEN RIGHT TO DRIVE DRUNK-
I WASN'T DRUNK!

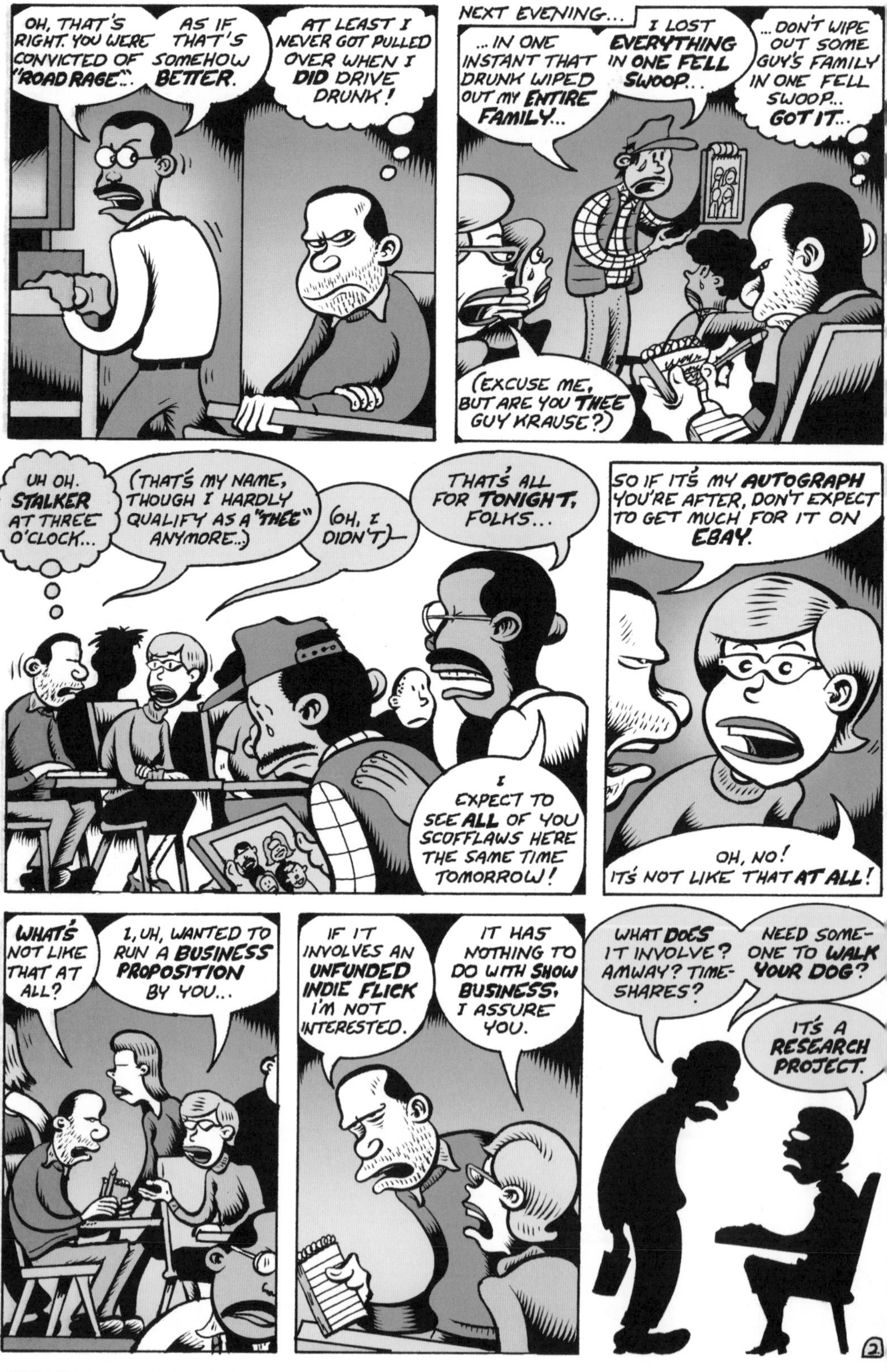
OH, THAT'S RIGHT. YOU WERE CONVICTED OF "ROAD RAGE"...
AS IF THAT'S SOMEHOW BETTER.
AT LEAST I NEVER GOT PULLED OVER WHEN I DID DRIVE DRUNK!
NEXT EVENING...
...IN ONE INSTANT THAT DRUNK WIPED OUT MY ENTIRE FAMILY...
I LOST EVERYTHING IN ONE FELL SWOOP...
...DON'T WIPE OUT SOME GUY'S FAMILY IN ONE FELL SWOOP... GOT IT...
(EXCUSE ME, BUT ARE YOU THEE GUY KRAUSE?)
UH OH. STALKER AT THREE O'CLOCK...
(THAT'S MY NAME, THOUGH I HARDLY QUALIFY AS A "THEE" ANYMORE...)
(OH, I DIDN'T)—
THAT'S ALL FOR TONIGHT, FOLKS...
I EXPECT TO SEE ALL OF YOU SCOFFLAWS HERE THE SAME TIME TOMORROW!
SO IF IT'S MY AUTOGRAPH YOU'RE AFTER, DON'T EXPECT TO GET MUCH FOR IT ON EBAY.
OH, NO! IT'S NOT LIKE THAT AT ALL!
WHAT'S NOT LIKE THAT AT ALL?
I, UH, WANTED TO RUN A BUSINESS PROPOSITION BY YOU...
IF IT INVOLVES AN UNFUNDED INDIE FLICK I'M NOT INTERESTED.
IT HAS NOTHING TO DO WITH SHOW BUSINESS, I ASSURE YOU.
WHAT DOES IT INVOLVE? AMWAY? TIME-SHARES?
NEED SOME-ONE TO WALK YOUR DOG?
IT'S A RESEARCH PROJECT.
2

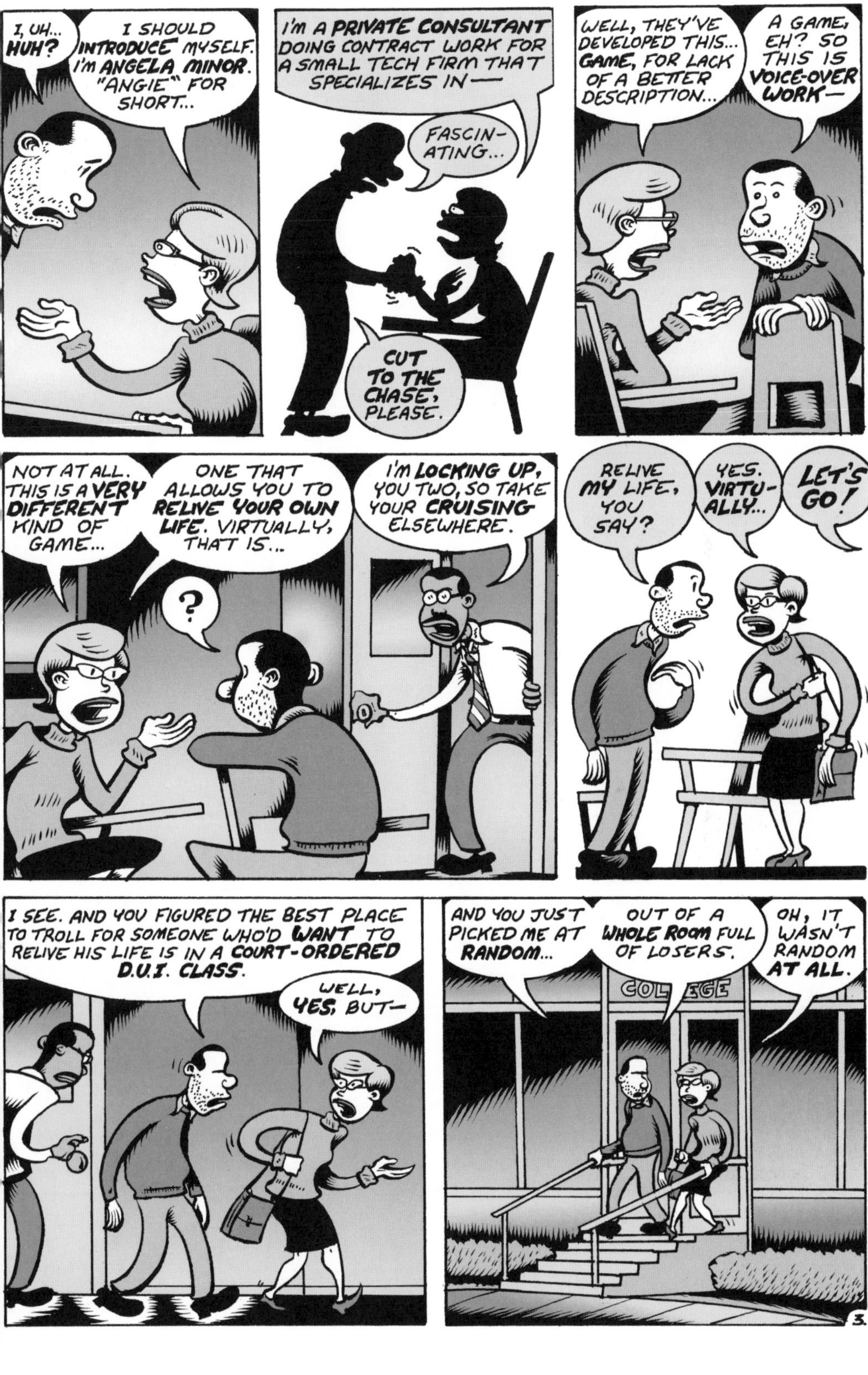
I, UH... HUH?
I SHOULD INTRODUCE MYSELF. I'M ANGELA MINOR. "ANGIE" FOR SHORT...
I'M A PRIVATE CONSULTANT DOING CONTRACT WORK FOR A SMALL TECH FIRM THAT SPECIALIZES IN—
FASCIN-ATING...
CUT TO THE CHASE, PLEASE.
WELL, THEY'VE DEVELOPED THIS... GAME, FOR LACK OF A BETTER DESCRIPTION...
A GAME, EH? SO THIS IS VOICE-OVER WORK—
NOT AT ALL. THIS IS A VERY DIFFERENT KIND OF GAME...
ONE THAT ALLOWS YOU TO RELIVE YOUR OWN LIFE. VIRTUALLY, THAT IS...
?
I'M LOCKING UP, YOU TWO, SO TAKE YOUR CRUISING ELSEWHERE.
RELIVE MY LIFE, YOU SAY?
YES. VIRTU-ALLY...
LET'S GO!
I SEE. AND YOU FIGURED THE BEST PLACE TO TROLL FOR SOMEONE WHO'D WANT TO RELIVE HIS LIFE IS IN A COURT-ORDERED D.U.I. CLASS.
WELL, YES, BUT—
AND YOU JUST PICKED ME AT RANDOM...
OUT OF A WHOLE ROOM FULL OF LOSERS.
OH, IT WASN'T RANDOM AT ALL.
COL EGE

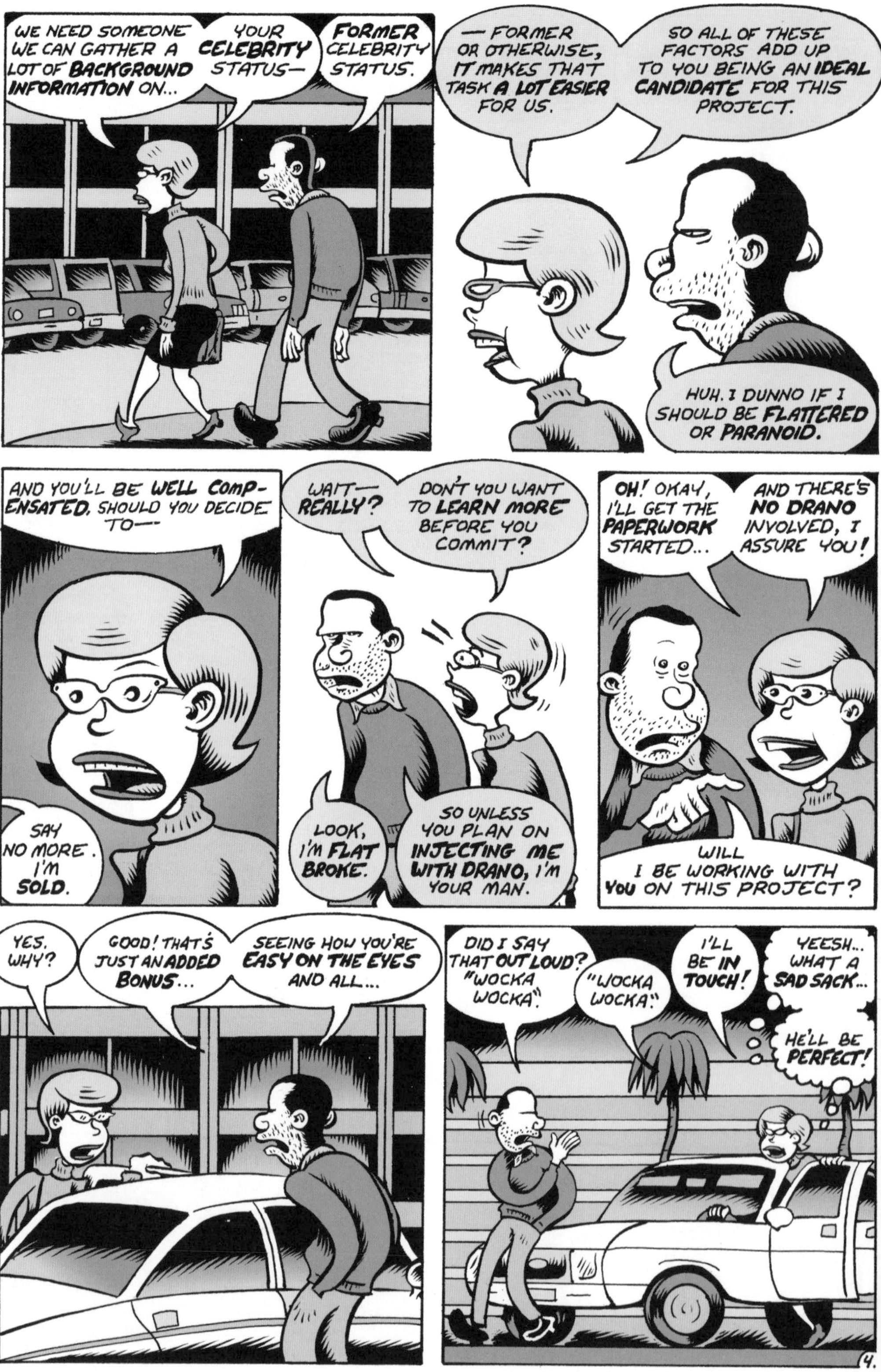
WE NEED SOMEONE WE CAN GATHER A LOT OF BACKGROUND INFORMATION ON...
YOUR CELEBRITY STATUS—
FORMER CELEBRITY STATUS.
— FORMER OR OTHERWISE, IT MAKES THAT TASK A LOT EASIER FOR US.
SO ALL OF THESE FACTORS ADD UP TO YOU BEING AN IDEAL CANDIDATE FOR THIS PROJECT.
HUH. I DUNNO IF I SHOULD BE FLATTERED OR PARANOID.
AND YOU'LL BE WELL COMPENSATED, SHOULD YOU DECIDE TO—
SAY NO MORE. I'M SOLD.
WAIT— REALLY?
DON'T YOU WANT TO LEARN MORE BEFORE YOU COMMIT?
LOOK, I'M FLAT BROKE.
SO UNLESS YOU PLAN ON INJECTING ME WITH DRANO, I'M YOUR MAN.
OH! OKAY, I'LL GET THE PAPERWORK STARTED...
AND THERE'S NO DRANO INVOLVED, I ASSURE YOU!
WILL I BE WORKING WITH YOU ON THIS PROJECT?
YES. WHY?
GOOD! THAT'S JUST AN ADDED BONUS...
SEEING HOW YOU'RE EASY ON THE EYES AND ALL...
DID I SAY THAT OUT LOUD? "WOCKA WOCKA"
"WOCKA WOCKA"
I'LL BE IN TOUCH!
YEESH... WHAT A SAD SACK...
HE'LL BE PERFECT!

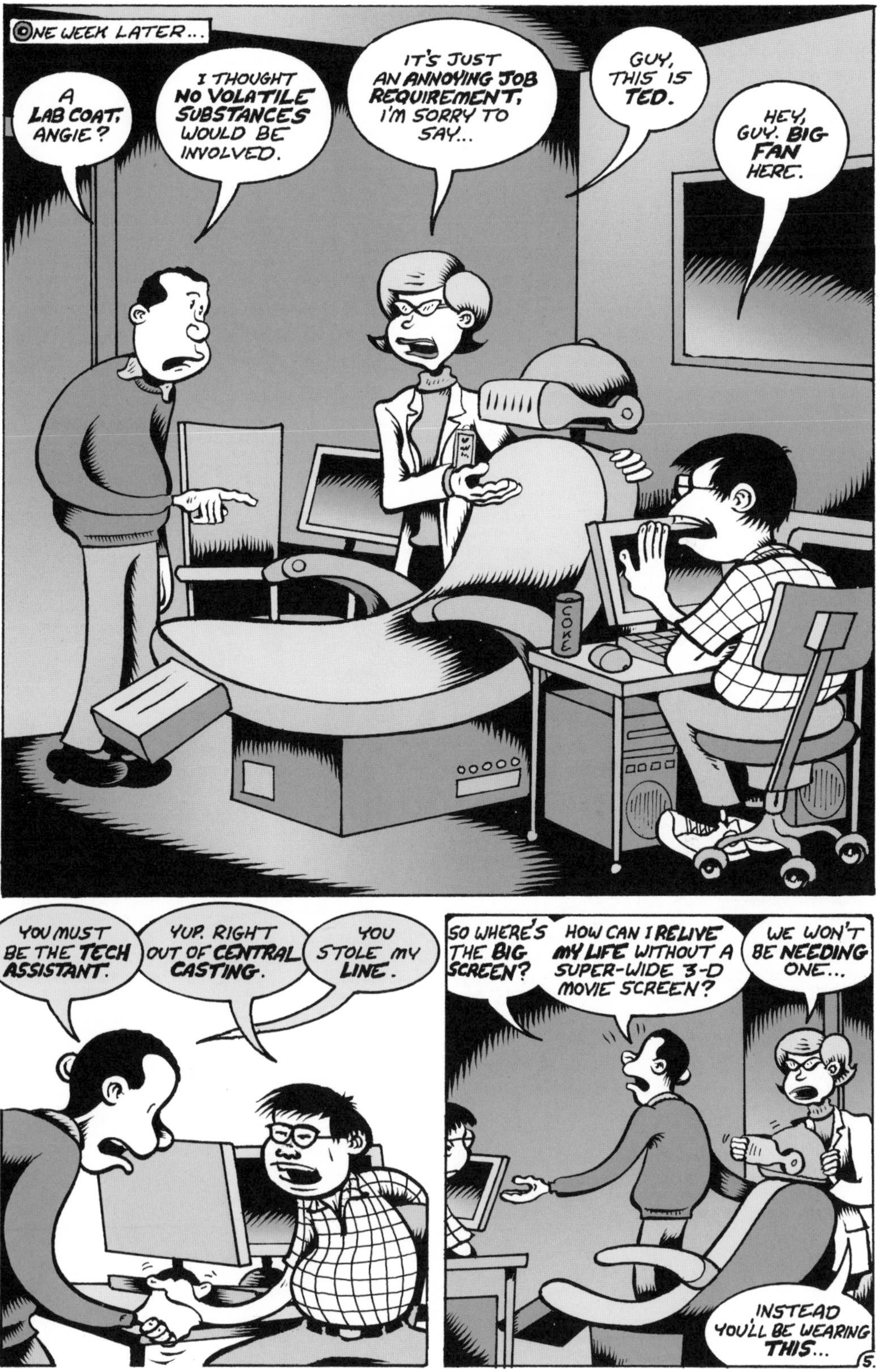
ONE WEEK LATER...
A LAB COAT, ANGIE?
I THOUGHT NO VOLATILE SUBSTANCES WOULD BE INVOLVED.
IT'S JUST AN ANNOYING JOB REQUIREMENT, I'M SORRY TO SAY...
GUY, THIS IS TED.
HEY, GUY. BIG FAN HERE.
COKE
YOU MUST BE THE TECH ASSISTANT.
YUP. RIGHT OUT OF CENTRAL CASTING.
YOU STOLE MY LINE.
SO WHERE'S THE BIG SCREEN?
HOW CAN I RELIVE MY LIFE WITHOUT A SUPER-WIDE 3-D MOVIE SCREEN?
WE WON'T BE NEEDING ONE...
INSTEAD YOU'LL BE WEARING THIS...

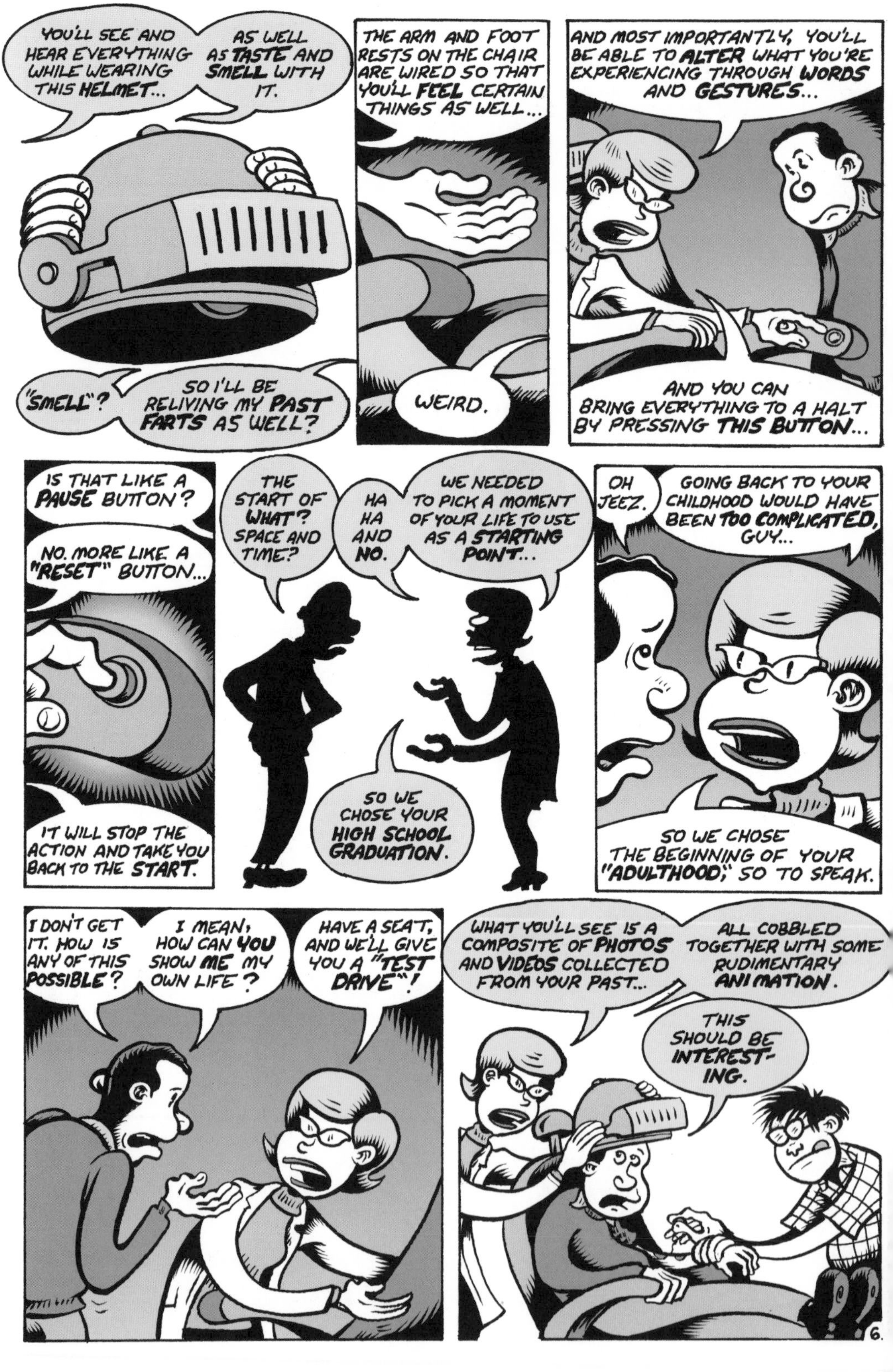
YOU'LL SEE AND HEAR EVERYTHING WHILE WEARING THIS HELMET...
AS WELL AS TASTE AND SMELL WITH IT.
"SMELL"?
SO I'LL BE RELIVING MY PAST FARTS AS WELL?
THE ARM AND FOOT RESTS ON THE CHAIR ARE WIRED SO THAT YOU'LL FEEL CERTAIN THINGS AS WELL...
WEIRD.
AND MOST IMPORTANTLY, YOU'LL BE ABLE TO ALTER WHAT YOU'RE EXPERIENCING THROUGH WORDS AND GESTURES...
AND YOU CAN BRING EVERYTHING TO A HALT BY PRESSING THIS BUTTON...
IS THAT LIKE A PAUSE BUTTON?
NO. MORE LIKE A "RESET" BUTTON...
IT WILL STOP THE ACTION AND TAKE YOU BACK TO THE START.
THE START OF WHAT? SPACE AND TIME?
HA HA AND NO.
WE NEEDED TO PICK A MOMENT OF YOUR LIFE TO USE AS A STARTING POINT...
SO WE CHOSE YOUR HIGH SCHOOL GRADUATION.
OH JEEZ.
GOING BACK TO YOUR CHILDHOOD WOULD HAVE BEEN TOO COMPLICATED, GUY...
SO WE CHOSE THE BEGINNING OF YOUR "ADULTHOOD," SO TO SPEAK.
I DON'T GET IT. HOW IS ANY OF THIS POSSIBLE?
I MEAN, HOW CAN YOU SHOW ME MY OWN LIFE?
HAVE A SEAT, AND WE'LL GIVE YOU A "TEST DRIVE"!
WHAT YOU'LL SEE IS A COMPOSITE OF PHOTOS AND VIDEOS COLLECTED FROM YOUR PAST...
ALL COBBLED TOGETHER WITH SOME RUDIMENTARY ANIMATION.
THIS SHOULD BE INTEREST-ING.

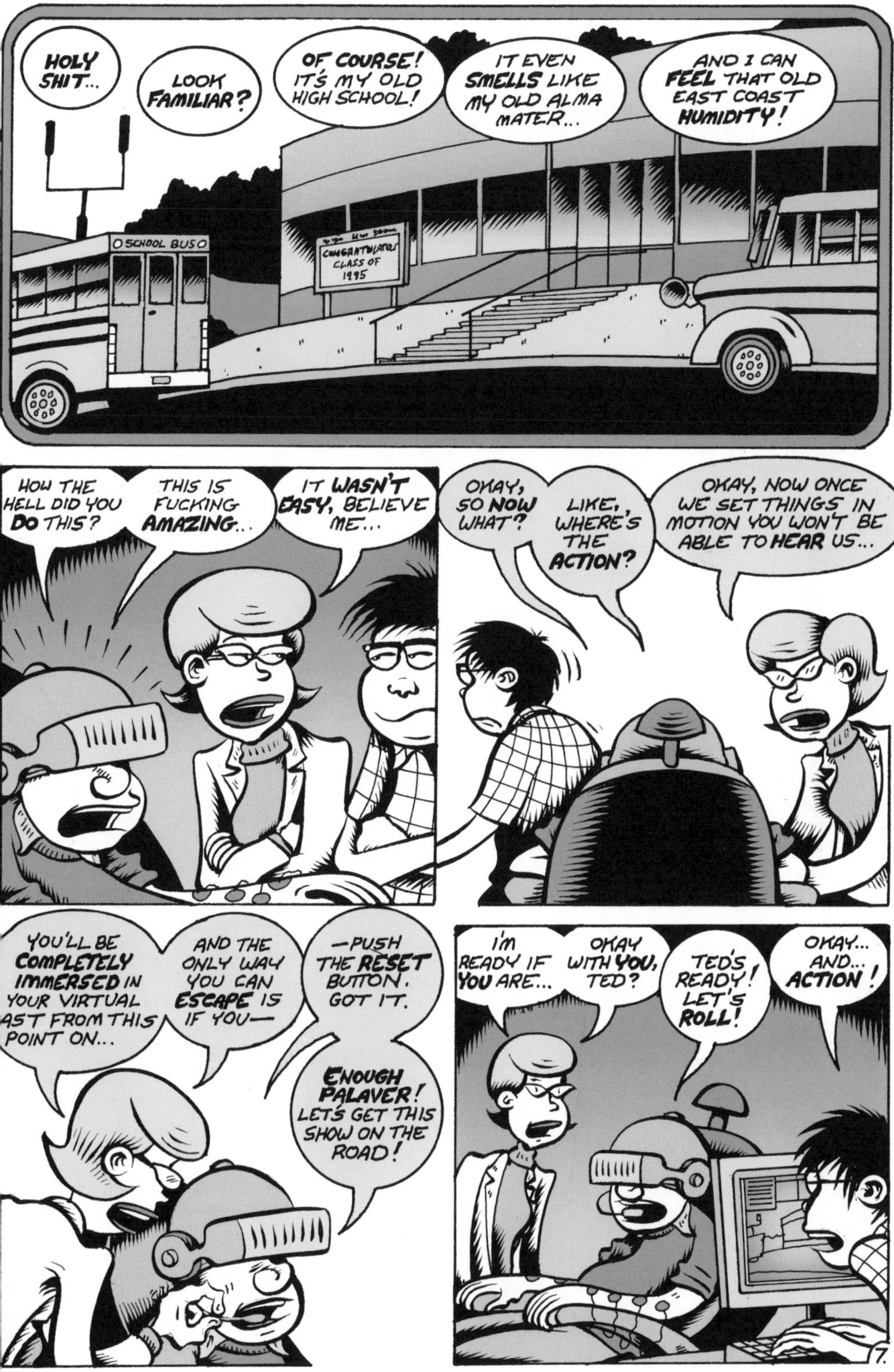
HOLY SHIT...
LOOK FAMILIAR?
OF COURSE! IT'S MY OLD HIGH SCHOOL!
IT EVEN SMELLS LIKE MY OLD ALMA MATER...
AND I CAN FEEL THAT OLD EAST COAST HUMIDITY!
SCHOOL BUS
CLASS OF 1995
HOW THE HELL DID YOU DO THIS?
THIS IS FUCKING AMAZING...
IT WASN'T EASY, BELIEVE ME...
OKAY, SO NOW WHAT?
LIKE, WHERE'S THE ACTION?
OKAY, NOW ONCE WE SET THINGS IN MOTION YOU WON'T BE ABLE TO HEAR US...
YOU'LL BE COMPLETELY IMMERSED IN YOUR VIRTUAL AST FROM THIS POINT ON...
AND THE ONLY WAY YOU CAN ESCAPE IS IF YOU—
—PUSH THE RESET BUTTON. GOT IT.
ENOUGH PALAVER! LET'S GET THIS SHOW ON THE ROAD!
I'M READY IF YOU ARE...
OKAY WITH YOU, TED?
TED'S READY! LET'S ROLL!
OKAY... AND... ACTION!

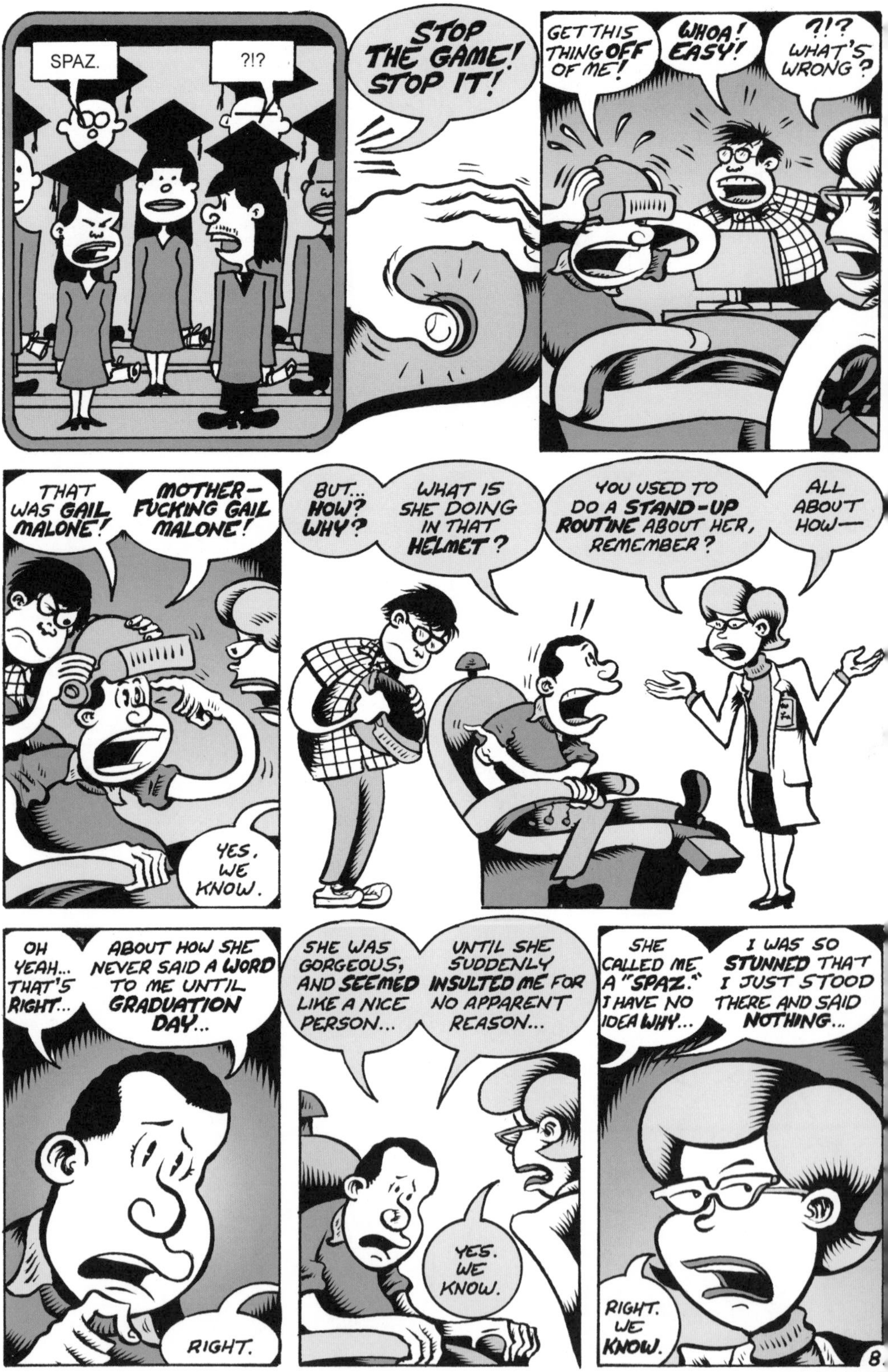
SPAZ.
?!?
STOP THE GAME! STOP IT!
GET THIS THING OFF OF ME!
WHOA! EASY!
?!? WHAT'S WRONG?
THAT WAS GAIL MALONE!
MOTHER-FUCKING GAIL MALONE!
YES, WE KNOW.
BUT... HOW? WHY?
WHAT IS SHE DOING IN THAT HELMET?
YOU USED TO DO A STAND-UP ROUTINE ABOUT HER, REMEMBER?
ALL ABOUT HOW—
OH YEAH... THAT'S RIGHT...
ABOUT HOW SHE NEVER SAID A WORD TO ME UNTIL GRADUATION DAY...
RIGHT.
SHE WAS GORGEOUS, AND SEEMED LIKE A NICE PERSON...
UNTIL SHE SUDDENLY INSULTED ME FOR NO APPARENT REASON...
YES. WE KNOW.
SHE CALLED ME A "SPAZ." I HAVE NO IDEA WHY...
I WAS SO STUNNED THAT I JUST STOOD THERE AND SAID NOTHING...
RIGHT. WE KNOW.

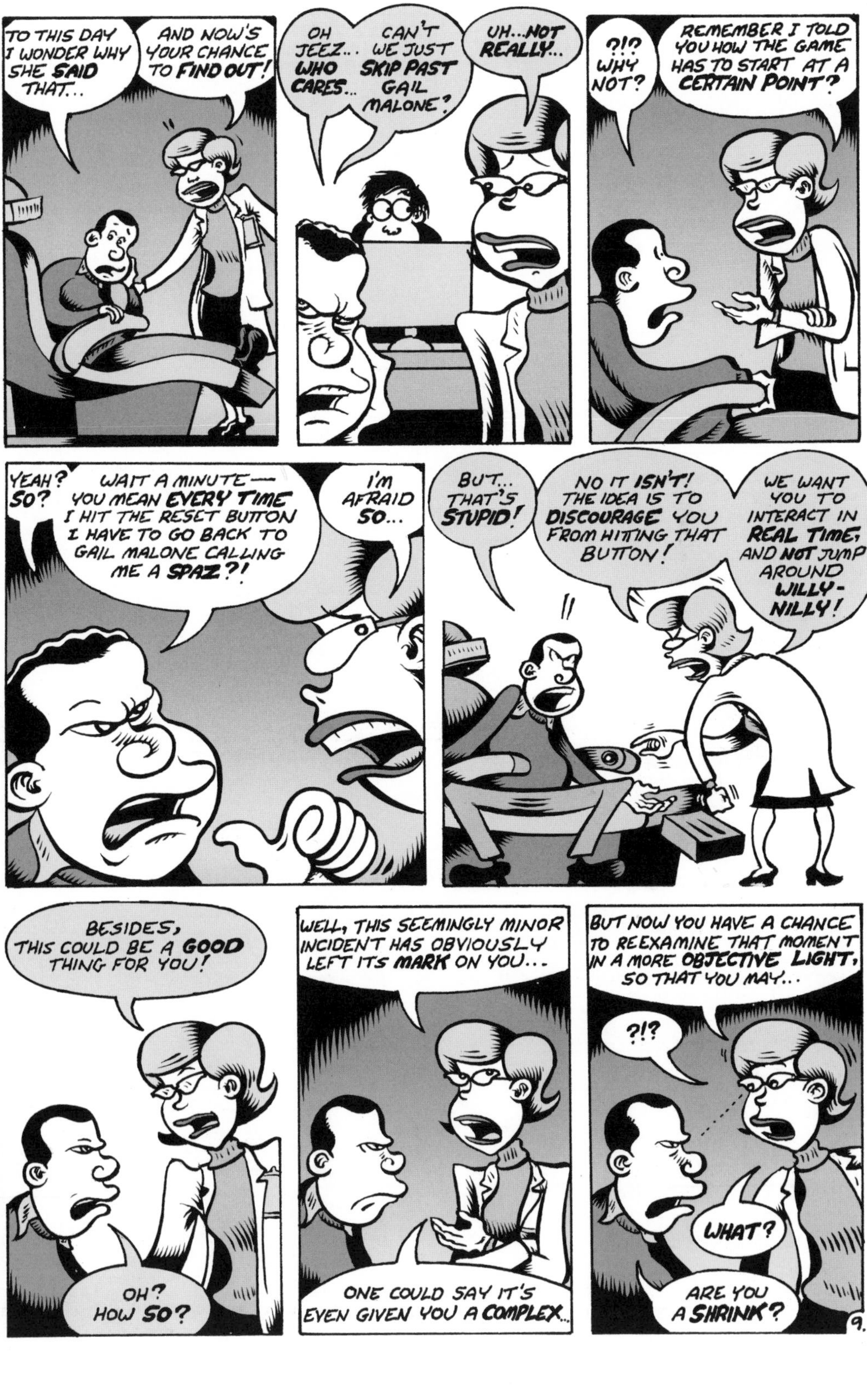
TO THIS DAY I WONDER WHY SHE SAID THAT...
AND NOW'S YOUR CHANCE TO FIND OUT!
OH JEEZ... WHO CARES...
CAN'T WE JUST SKIP PAST GAIL MALONE?
UH...NOT REALLY...
?!? WHY NOT?
REMEMBER I TOLD YOU HOW THE GAME HAS TO START AT A CERTAIN POINT?
YEAH? SO?
WAIT A MINUTE— YOU MEAN EVERY TIME I HIT THE RESET BUTTON I HAVE TO GO BACK TO GAIL MALONE CALLING ME A SPAZ?!
I'M AFRAID SO...
BUT... THAT'S STUPID!
NO IT ISN'T! THE IDEA IS TO DISCOURAGE YOU FROM HITTING THAT BUTTON!
WE WANT YOU TO INTERACT IN REAL TIME, AND NOT JUMP AROUND WILLY-NILLY!
BESIDES, THIS COULD BE A GOOD THING FOR YOU!
OH? HOW SO?
WELL, THIS SEEMINGLY MINOR INCIDENT HAS OBVIOUSLY LEFT ITS MARK ON YOU...
ONE COULD SAY IT'S EVEN GIVEN YOU A COMPLEX...
BUT NOW YOU HAVE A CHANCE TO REEXAMINE THAT MOMENT IN A MORE OBJECTIVE LIGHT, SO THAT YOU MAY...
?!?
WHAT?
ARE YOU A SHRINK?

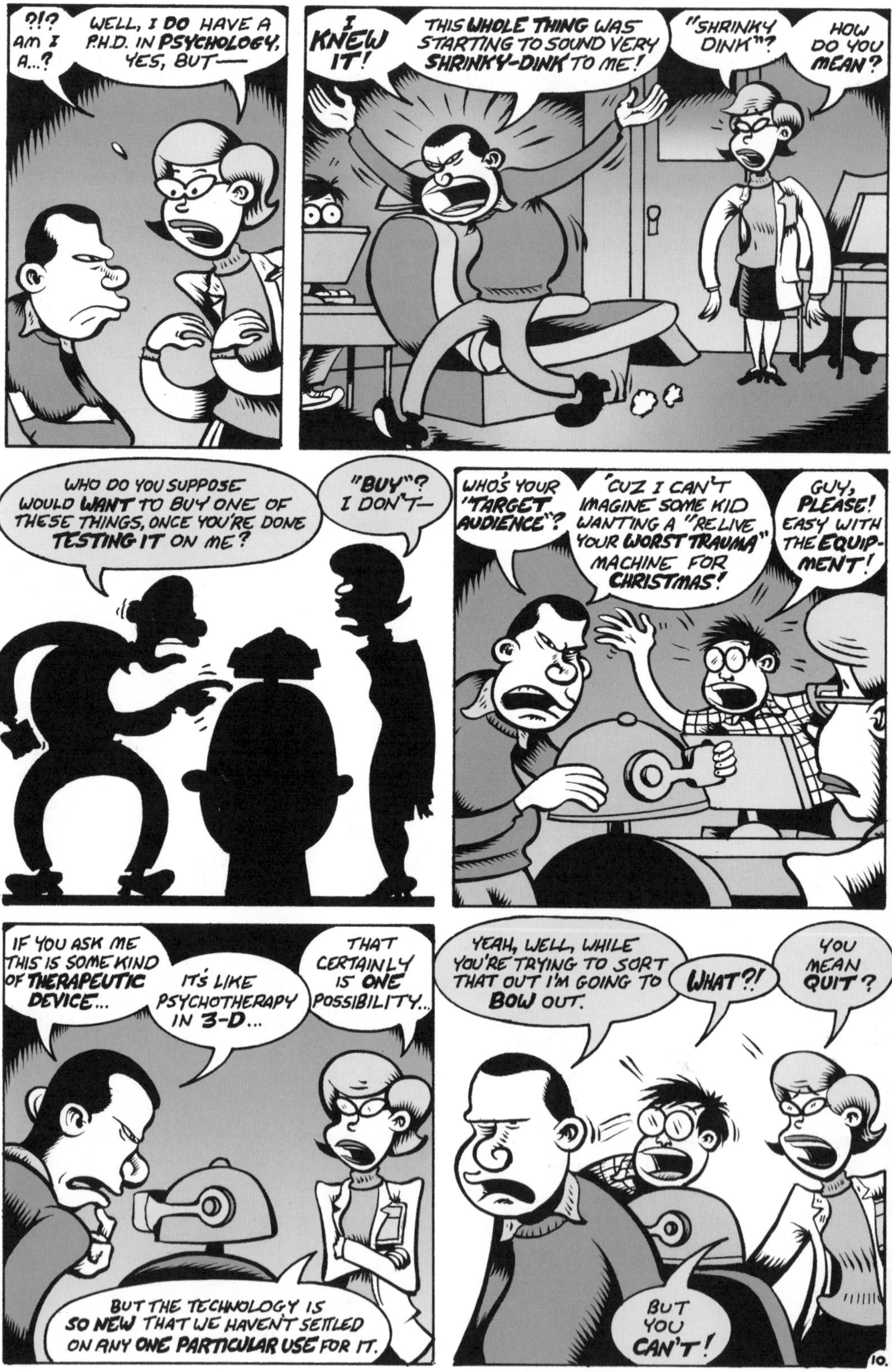
?!? AM I A...?
WELL, I DO HAVE A P.H.D. IN PSYCHOLOGY, YES, BUT—
I KNEW IT!
THIS WHOLE THING WAS STARTING TO SOUND VERY SHRINKY-DINK TO ME!
"SHRINKY DINK"?
HOW DO YOU MEAN?
WHO DO YOU SUPPOSE WOULD WANT TO BUY ONE OF THESE THINGS, ONCE YOU'RE DONE TESTING IT ON ME?
"BUY"? I DON'T—
WHO'S YOUR "TARGET AUDIENCE"?
'CUZ I CAN'T IMAGINE SOME KID WANTING A "RELIVE YOUR WORST TRAUMA" MACHINE FOR CHRISTMAS!
GUY, PLEASE! EASY WITH THE EQUIPMENT!
IF YOU ASK ME THIS IS SOME KIND OF THERAPEUTIC DEVICE...
IT'S LIKE PSYCHOTHERAPY IN 3-D...
THAT CERTAINLY IS ONE POSSIBILITY...
BUT THE TECHNOLOGY IS SO NEW THAT WE HAVEN'T SETTLED ON ANY ONE PARTICULAR USE FOR IT.
YEAH, WELL, WHILE YOU'RE TRYING TO SORT THAT OUT I'M GOING TO BOW OUT.
WHAT?!
YOU MEAN QUIT?
BUT YOU CAN'T!
10.

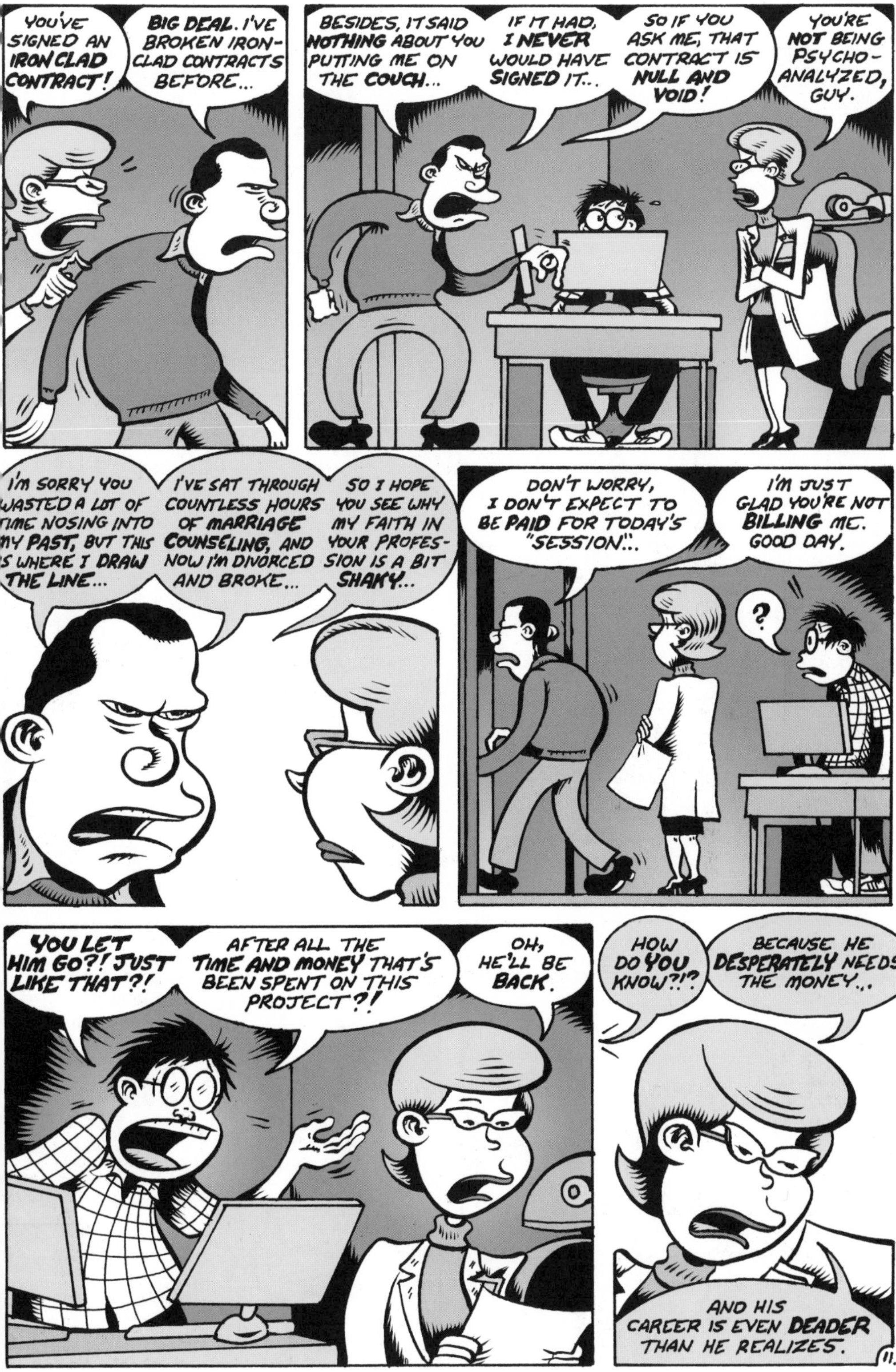

YOU'VE SIGNED AN IRON CLAD CONTRACT!
BIG DEAL. I'VE BROKEN IRON-CLAD CONTRACTS BEFORE...
BESIDES, IT SAID NOTHING ABOUT YOU PUTTING ME ON THE COUCH...
IF IT HAD, I NEVER WOULD HAVE SIGNED IT...
SO IF YOU ASK ME, THAT CONTRACT IS NULL AND VOID!
YOU'RE NOT BEING PSYCHO-ANALYZED, GUY.
I'M SORRY YOU WASTED A LOT OF TIME NOSING INTO MY PAST, BUT THIS IS WHERE I DRAW THE LINE...
I'VE SAT THROUGH COUNTLESS HOURS OF MARRIAGE COUNSELING, AND NOW I'M DIVORCED AND BROKE...
SO I HOPE YOU SEE WHY MY FAITH IN YOUR PROFES-SION IS A BIT SHAKY...
DON'T WORRY, I DON'T EXPECT TO BE PAID FOR TODAY'S "SESSION"...
I'M JUST GLAD YOU'RE NOT BILLING ME. GOOD DAY.
?
YOU LET HIM GO?! JUST LIKE THAT?!
AFTER ALL THE TIME AND MONEY THAT'S BEEN SPENT ON THIS PROJECT?!
OH, HE'LL BE BACK.
HOW DO YOU KNOW?!?
BECAUSE HE DESPERATELY NEEDS THE MONEY...
AND HIS CAREER IS EVEN DEADER THAN HE REALIZES.

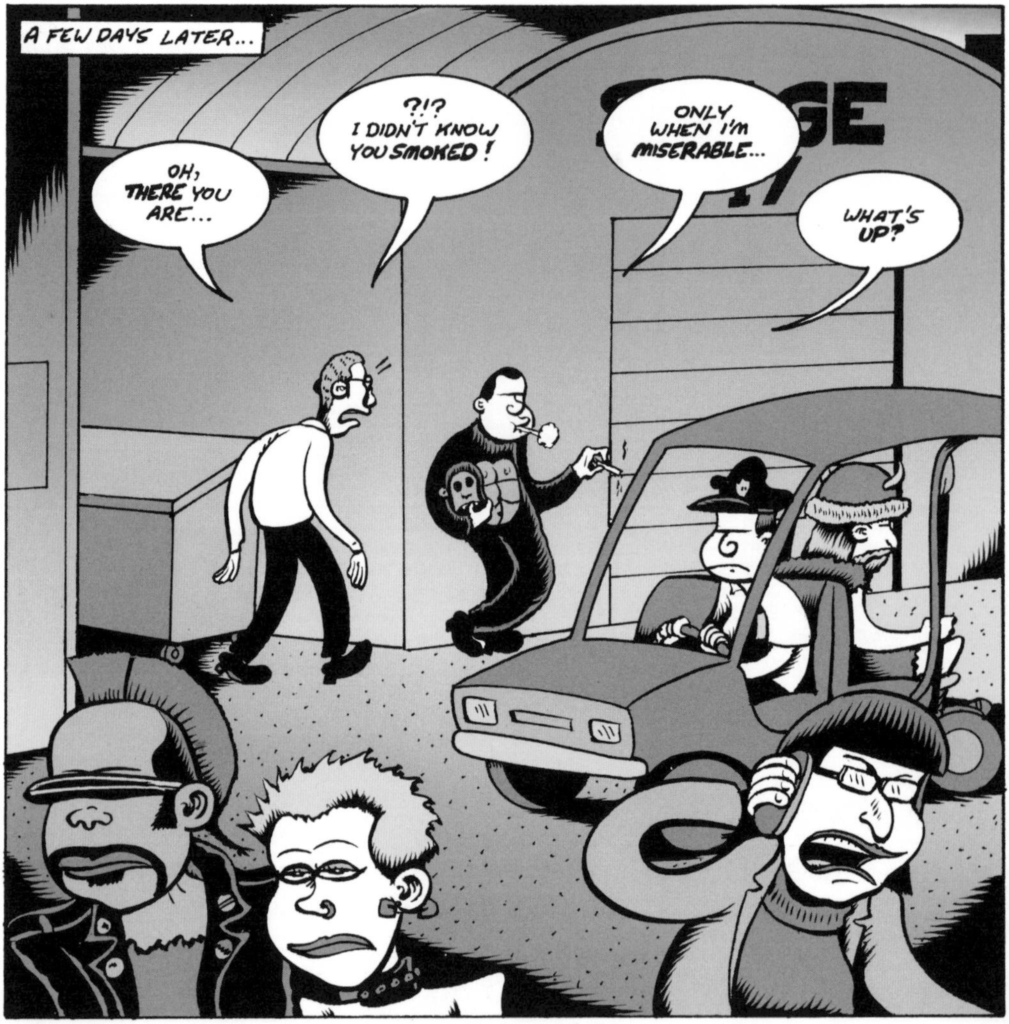
A FEW DAYS LATER...
OH, THERE YOU ARE...
?!? I DIDN'T KNOW YOU SMOKED!
ONLY WHEN I'M MISERABLE...
WHAT'S UP?

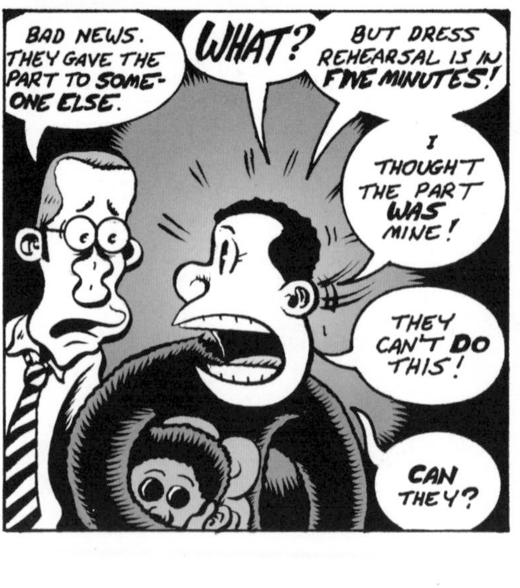
BAD NEWS. THEY GAVE THE PART TO SOME-ONE ELSE.
WHAT?
BUT DRESS REHEARSAL IS IN FIVE MINUTES!
I THOUGHT THE PART WAS MINE!
THEY CAN'T DO THIS!
CAN THEY?

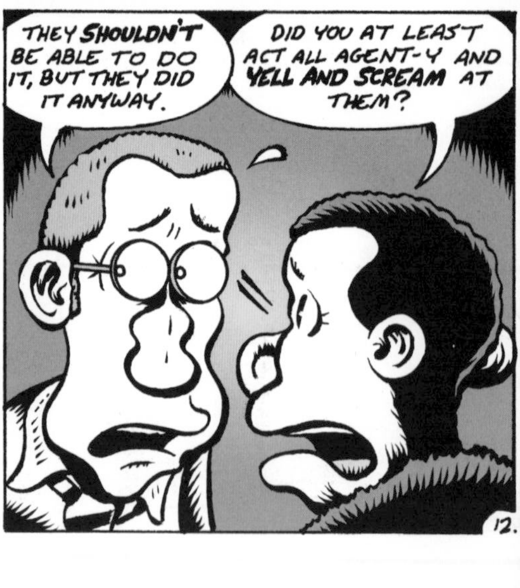
THEY SHOULDN'T BE ABLE TO DO IT, BUT THEY DID IT ANYWAY.
DID YOU AT LEAST ACT ALL AGENT-Y AND YELL AND SCREAM AT THEM?

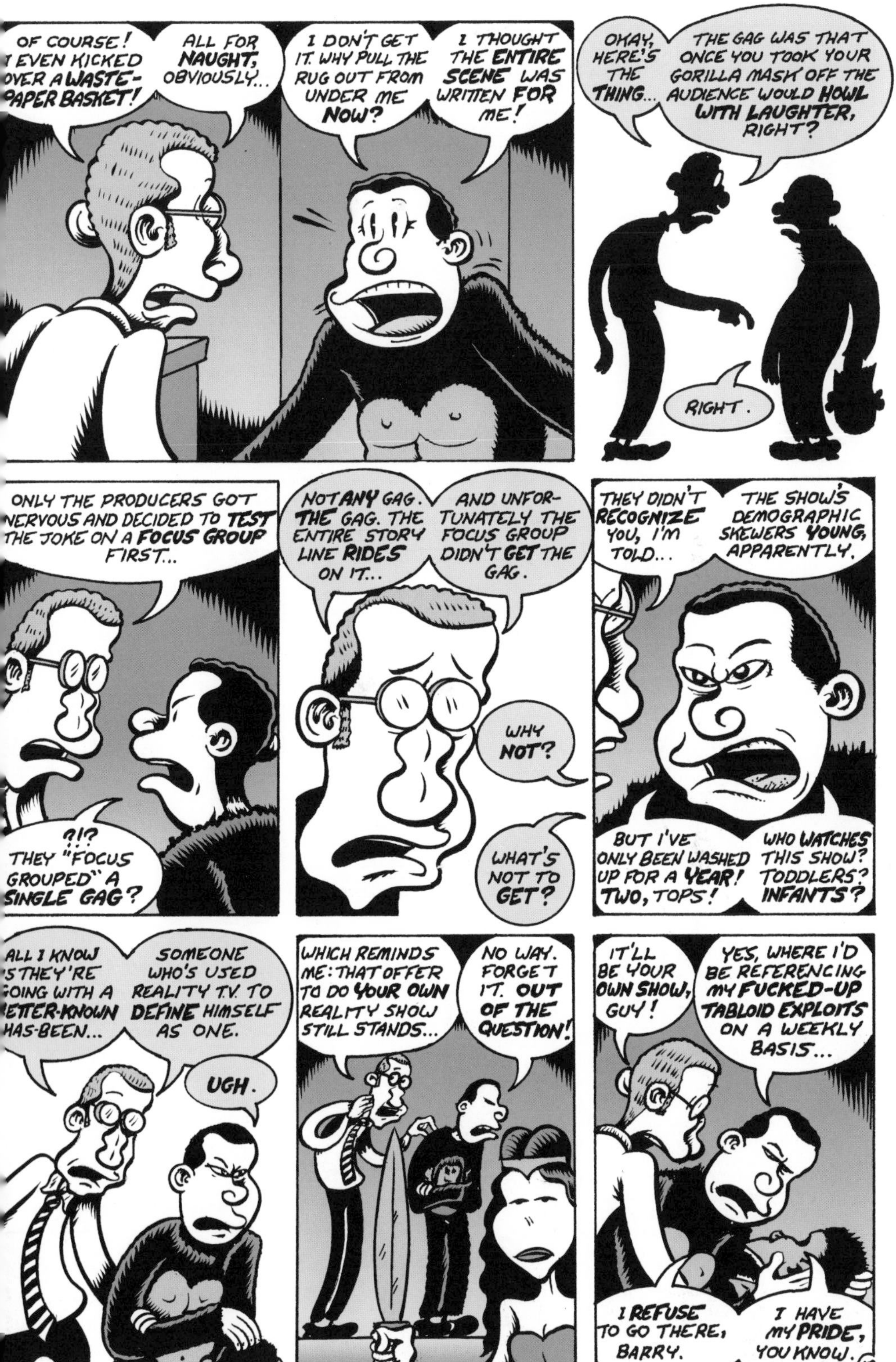
OF COURSE! I EVEN KICKED OVER A WASTE-PAPER BASKET!
ALL FOR NAUGHT, OBVIOUSLY...
I DON'T GET IT. WHY PULL THE RUG OUT FROM UNDER ME NOW?
I THOUGHT THE ENTIRE SCENE WAS WRITTEN FOR ME!
OKAY, HERE'S THE THING...
THE GAG WAS THAT ONCE YOU TOOK YOUR GORILLA MASK OFF THE AUDIENCE WOULD HOWL WITH LAUGHTER, RIGHT?
RIGHT.
ONLY THE PRODUCERS GOT NERVOUS AND DECIDED TO TEST THE JOKE ON A FOCUS GROUP FIRST...
?!? THEY "FOCUS GROUPED" A SINGLE GAG?
NOT ANY GAG. THE GAG. THE ENTIRE STORY LINE RIDES ON IT...
AND UNFORTUNATELY THE FOCUS GROUP DIDN'T GET THE GAG.
WHY NOT?
WHAT'S NOT TO GET?
THEY DIDN'T RECOGNIZE YOU, I'M TOLD...
THE SHOW'S DEMOGRAPHIC SKEWERS YOUNG, APPARENTLY.
BUT I'VE ONLY BEEN WASHED UP FOR A YEAR! TWO, TOPS!
WHO WATCHES THIS SHOW? TODDLERS? INFANTS?
ALL I KNOW IS THEY'RE GOING WITH A BETTER-KNOWN HAS-BEEN...
SOMEONE WHO'S USED REALITY T.V. TO DEFINE HIMSELF AS ONE.
UGH.
WHICH REMINDS ME: THAT OFFER TO DO YOUR OWN REALITY SHOW STILL STANDS...
NO WAY. FORGET IT. OUT OF THE QUESTION!
IT'LL BE YOUR OWN SHOW, GUY!
YES, WHERE I'D BE REFERENCING MY FUCKED-UP TABLOID EXPLOITS ON A WEEKLY BASIS...
I REFUSE TO GO THERE, BARRY.
I HAVE MY PRIDE, YOU KNOW.

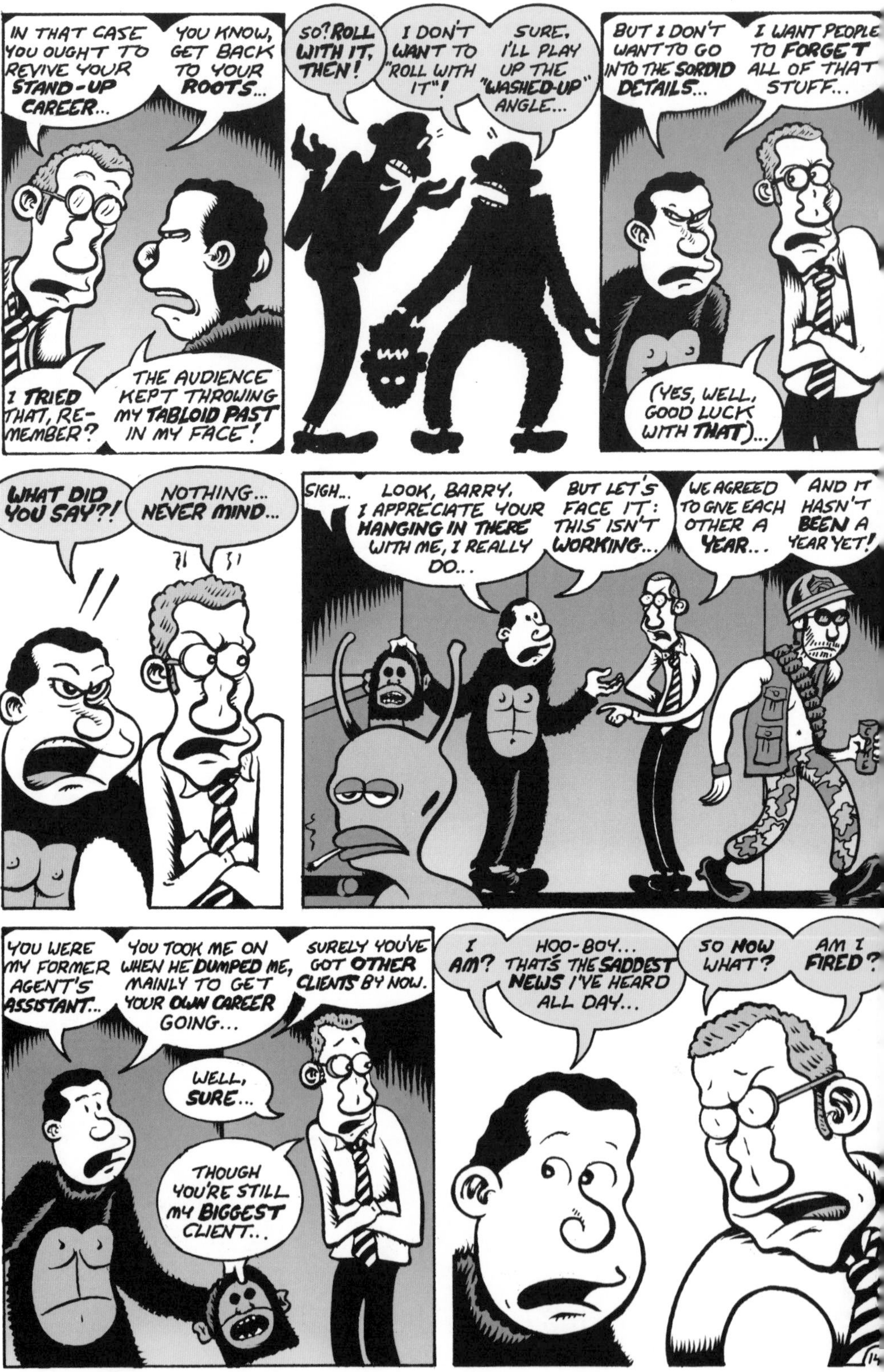
IN THAT CASE YOU OUGHT TO REVIVE YOUR STAND-UP CAREER...
YOU KNOW, GET BACK TO YOUR ROOTS...
I TRIED THAT, RE-MEMBER?
THE AUDIENCE KEPT THROWING MY TABLOID PAST IN MY FACE!
SO? ROLL WITH IT, THEN!
I DON'T WANT TO "ROLL WITH IT"!
SURE, I'LL PLAY UP THE "WASHED-UP" ANGLE...
BUT I DON'T WANT TO GO INTO THE SORDID DETAILS...
I WANT PEOPLE TO FORGET ALL OF THAT STUFF...
(YES, WELL, GOOD LUCK WITH THAT)...
WHAT DID YOU SAY?!
NOTHING... NEVER MIND...
SIGH...
LOOK, BARRY, I APPRECIATE YOUR HANGING IN THERE WITH ME, I REALLY DO...
BUT LET'S FACE IT: THIS ISN'T WORKING...
WE AGREED TO GIVE EACH OTHER A YEAR...
AND IT HASN'T BEEN A YEAR YET!
YOU WERE MY FORMER AGENT'S ASSISTANT...
YOU TOOK ME ON WHEN HE DUMPED ME, MAINLY TO GET YOUR OWN CAREER GOING...
SURELY YOU'VE GOT OTHER CLIENTS BY NOW.
WELL, SURE...
THOUGH YOU'RE STILL MY BIGGEST CLIENT...
I AM?
HOO-BOY... THAT'S THE SADDEST NEWS I'VE HEARD ALL DAY...
SO NOW WHAT?
AM I FIRED?

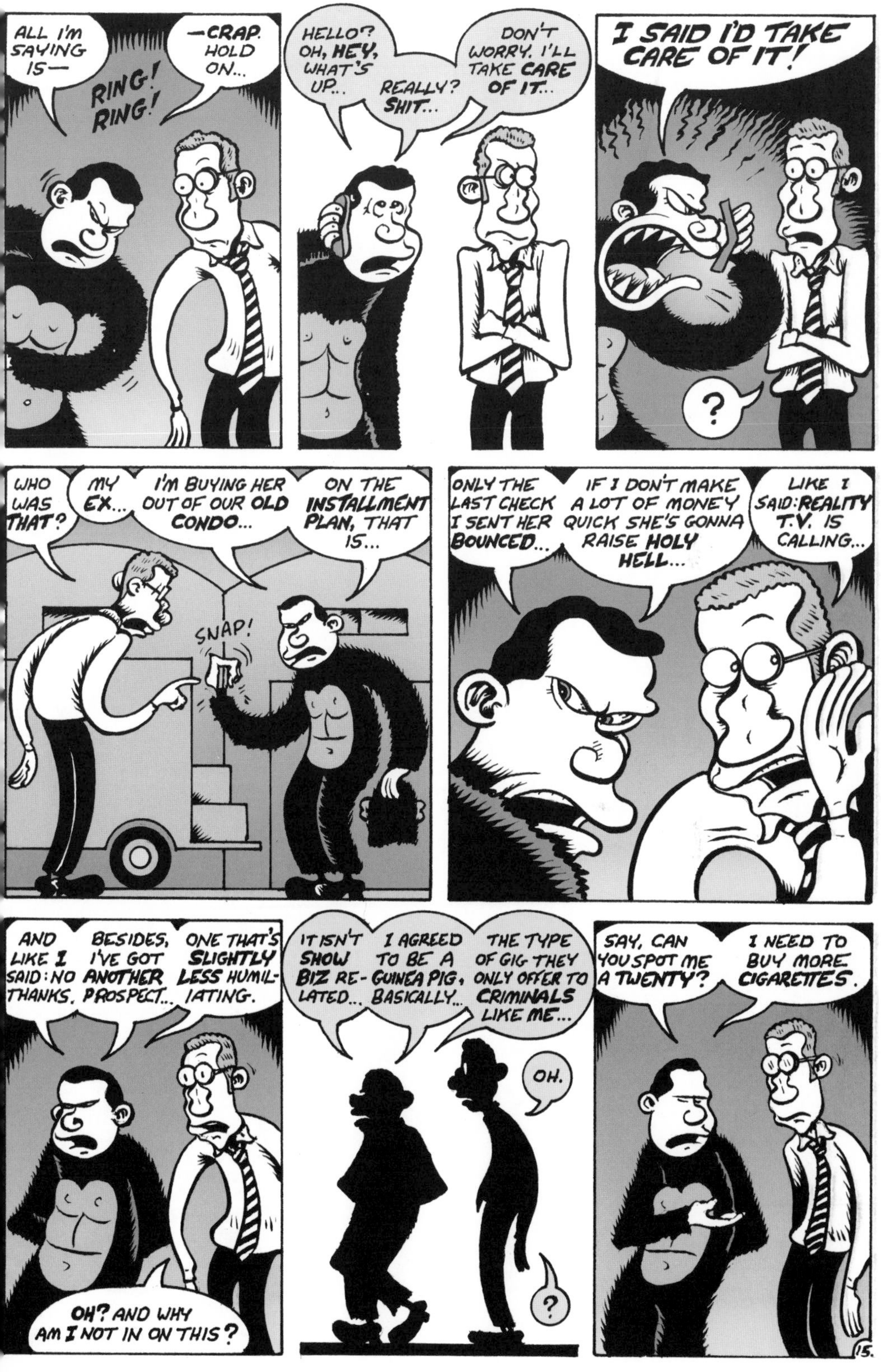
ALL I'M SAYING IS—
—CRAP. HOLD ON...
RING! RING!
HELLO? OH, HEY, WHAT'S UP...
REALLY? SHIT...
DON'T WORRY. I'LL TAKE CARE OF IT...
I SAID I'D TAKE CARE OF IT!
?
WHO WAS THAT?
MY EX...
I'M BUYING HER OUT OF OUR OLD CONDO...
ON THE INSTALLMENT PLAN, THAT IS...
SNAP!
ONLY THE LAST CHECK I SENT HER BOUNCED...
IF I DON'T MAKE A LOT OF MONEY QUICK SHE'S GONNA RAISE HOLY HELL...
LIKE I SAID: REALITY T.V. IS CALLING...
AND LIKE I SAID: NO THANKS.
BESIDES, I'VE GOT ANOTHER PROSPECT...
ONE THAT'S SLIGHTLY LESS HUMIL-IATING.
OH? AND WHY AM I NOT IN ON THIS?
IT ISN'T SHOW BIZ RE-LATED...
I AGREED TO BE A GUINEA PIG, BASICALLY...
THE TYPE OF GIG THEY ONLY OFFER TO CRIMINALS LIKE ME...
OH.
?
SAY, CAN YOU SPOT ME A TWENTY?
I NEED TO BUY MORE CIGARETTES.
15.

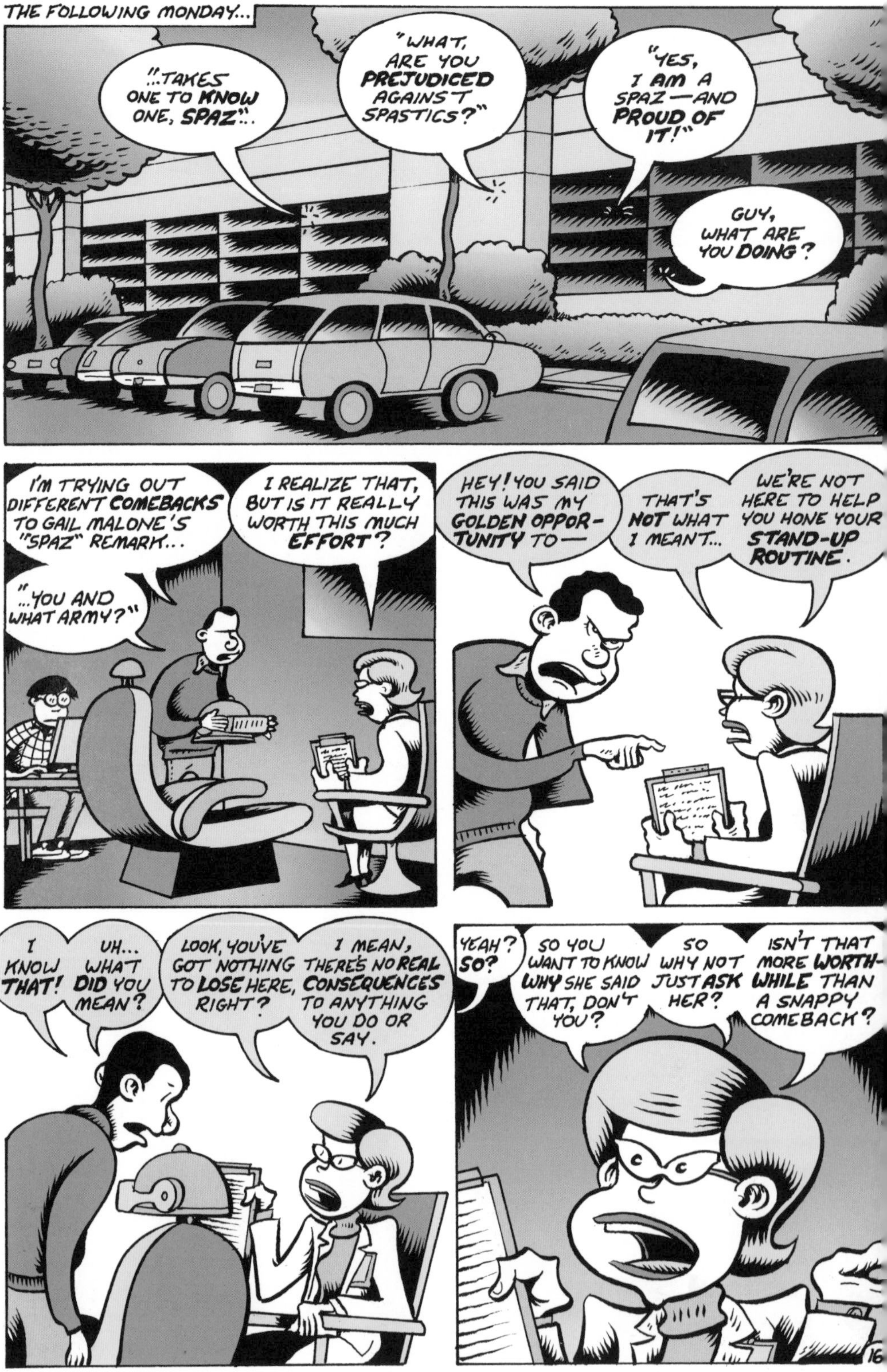
THE FOLLOWING MONDAY...
"...TAKES ONE TO KNOW ONE, SPAZ"...
"WHAT, ARE YOU PREJUDICED AGAINST SPASTICS?"
"YES, I AM A SPAZ—AND PROUD OF IT!"
GUY, WHAT ARE YOU DOING?
I'M TRYING OUT DIFFERENT COMEBACKS TO GAIL MALONE'S "SPAZ" REMARK...
"...YOU AND WHAT ARMY?"
I REALIZE THAT, BUT IS IT REALLY WORTH THIS MUCH EFFORT?
HEY! YOU SAID THIS WAS MY GOLDEN OPPORTUNITY TO—
THAT'S NOT WHAT I MEANT...
WE'RE NOT HERE TO HELP YOU HONE YOUR STAND-UP ROUTINE.
I KNOW THAT!
UH... WHAT DID YOU MEAN?
LOOK, YOU'VE GOT NOTHING TO LOSE HERE, RIGHT?
I MEAN, THERE'S NO REAL CONSEQUENCES TO ANYTHING YOU DO OR SAY.
YEAH? SO?
SO YOU WANT TO KNOW WHY SHE SAID THAT, DON'T YOU?
SO WHY NOT JUST ASK HER?
ISN'T THAT MORE WORTHWHILE THAN A SNAPPY COMEBACK?

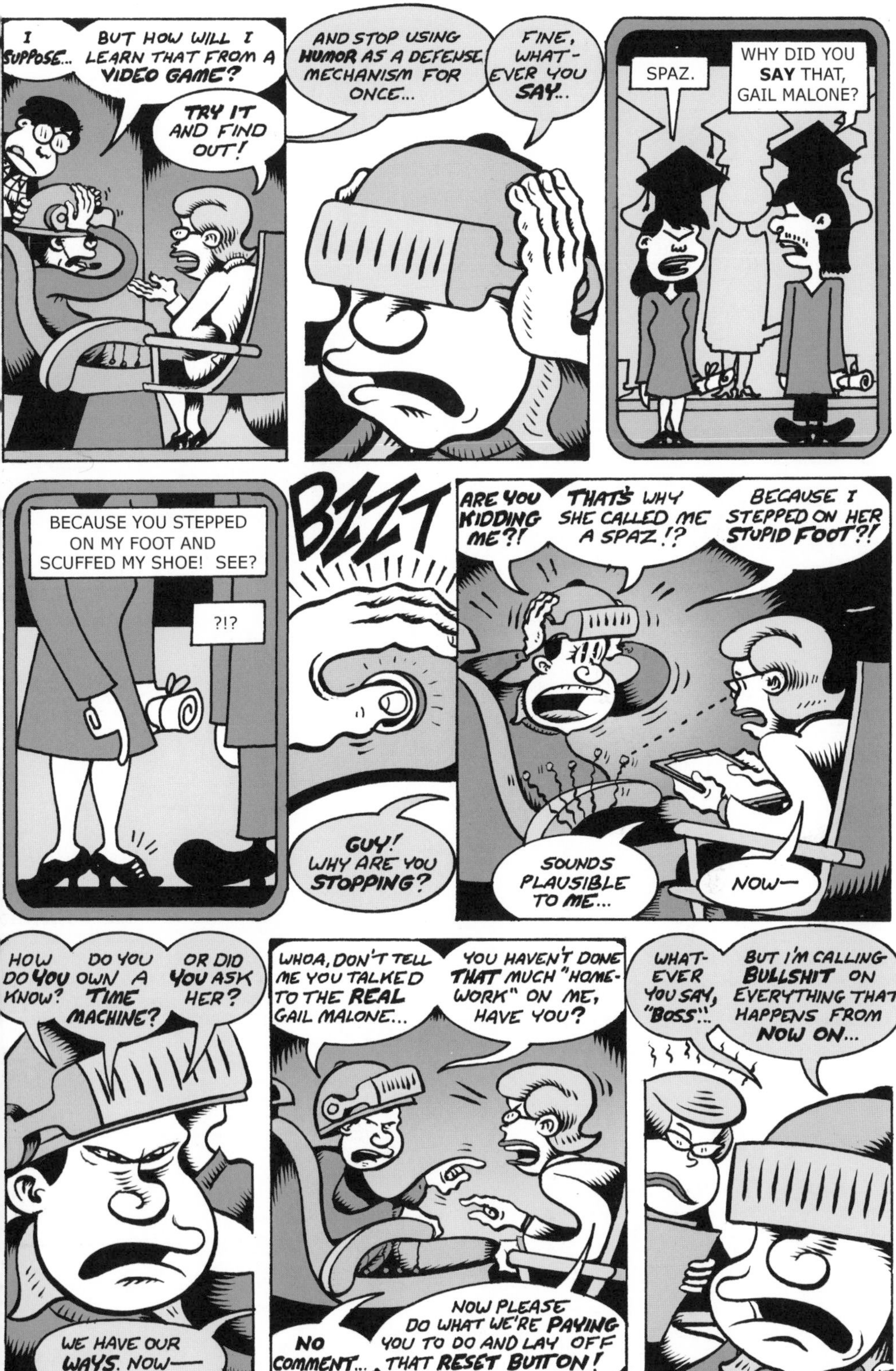
I SUPPOSE...
BUT HOW WILL I LEARN THAT FROM A VIDEO GAME?
TRY IT AND FIND OUT!
AND STOP USING HUMOR AS A DEFENSE MECHANISM FOR ONCE...
FINE, WHAT-EVER YOU SAY...
SPAZ.
WHY DID YOU SAY THAT, GAIL MALONE?
BECAUSE YOU STEPPED ON MY FOOT AND SCUFFED MY SHOE! SEE?
?!?
BZZT
GUY! WHY ARE YOU STOPPING?
ARE YOU KIDDING ME?!
THAT'S WHY SHE CALLED ME A SPAZ!?
BECAUSE I STEPPED ON HER STUPID FOOT?!
SOUNDS PLAUSIBLE TO ME...
NOW—
HOW DO YOU KNOW?
DO YOU OWN A TIME MACHINE?
OR DID YOU ASK HER?
WE HAVE OUR WAYS. NOW—
WHOA, DON'T TELL ME YOU TALKED TO THE REAL GAIL MALONE...
YOU HAVEN'T DONE THAT MUCH "HOME-WORK" ON ME, HAVE YOU?
NO COMMENT...
NOW PLEASE DO WHAT WE'RE PAYING YOU TO DO AND LAY OFF THAT RESET BUTTON!
WHAT-EVER YOU SAY, "BOSS"...
BUT I'M CALLING BULLSHIT ON EVERYTHING THAT HAPPENS FROM NOW ON...

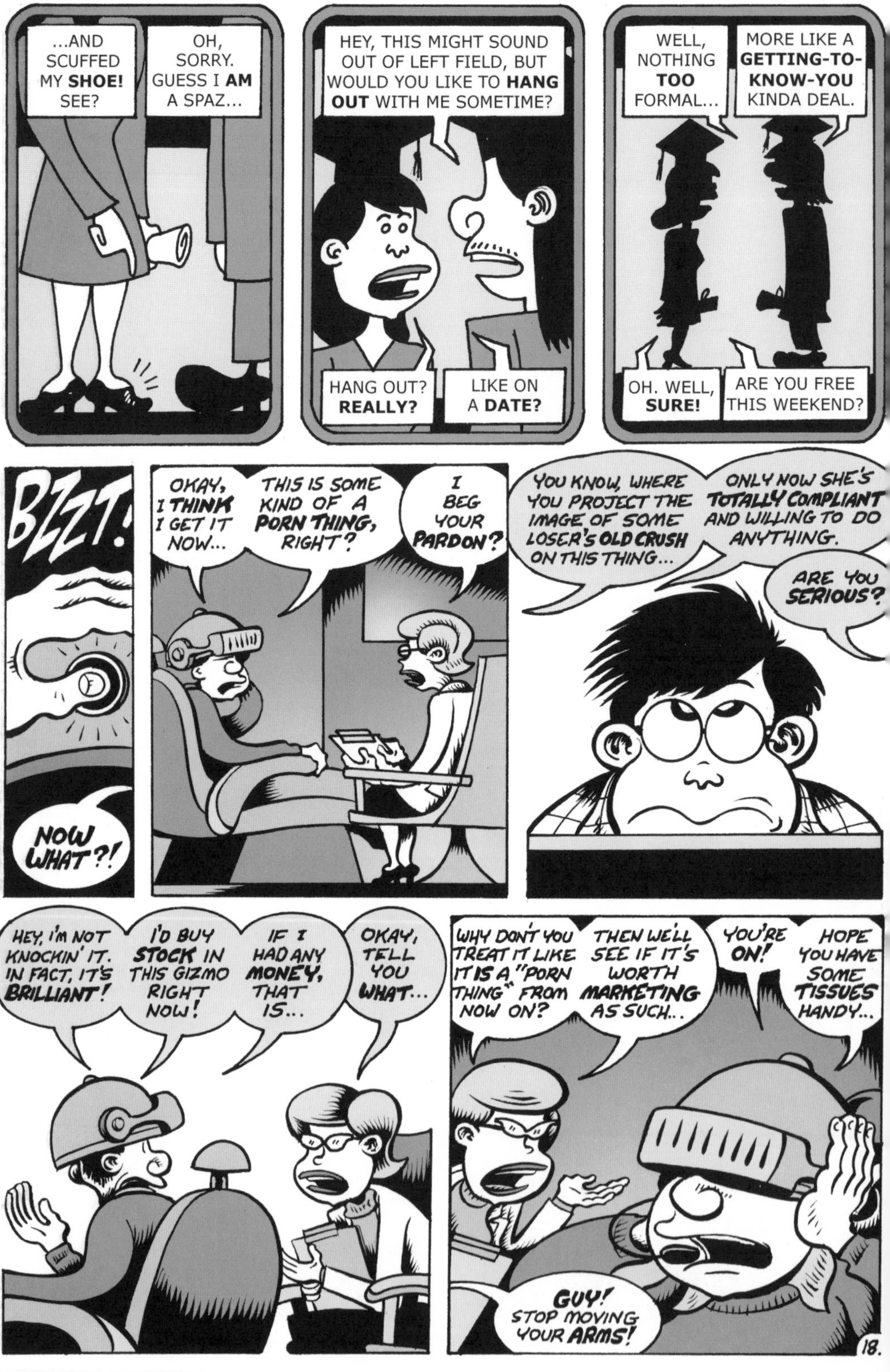

...AND SCUFFED MY **SHOE!** SEE?
OH, SORRY. GUESS I **AM** A SPAZ...
HEY, THIS MIGHT SOUND OUT OF LEFT FIELD, BUT WOULD YOU LIKE TO **HANG OUT** WITH ME SOMETIME?
HANG OUT? **REALLY?**
LIKE ON A **DATE?**
WELL, NOTHING **TOO** FORMAL...
MORE LIKE A **GETTING-TO-KNOW-YOU** KINDA DEAL.
OH. WELL, **SURE!**
ARE YOU FREE THIS WEEKEND?
BZZT!
NOW WHAT?!
OKAY, I **THINK** I GET IT NOW...
THIS IS SOME KIND OF A **PORN THING,** RIGHT?
I BEG YOUR **PARDON?**
YOU KNOW, WHERE YOU PROJECT THE IMAGE OF SOME LOSER'S **OLD CRUSH** ON THIS THING...
ONLY NOW SHE'S **TOTALLY COMPLIANT** AND WILLING TO DO ANYTHING.
ARE YOU **SERIOUS?**
HEY, I'M NOT KNOCKIN' IT. IN FACT, IT'S **BRILLIANT!**
I'D BUY **STOCK** IN THIS GIZMO RIGHT NOW!
IF I HAD ANY **MONEY,** THAT IS...
OKAY, TELL YOU **WHAT**...
WHY DON'T YOU TREAT IT LIKE IT **IS** A "PORN THING" FROM NOW ON?
THEN WE'LL SEE IF IT'S WORTH **MARKETING** AS SUCH...
YOU'RE **ON!**
HOPE YOU HAVE SOME **TISSUES** HANDY...
GUY! STOP MOVING YOUR **ARMS!**

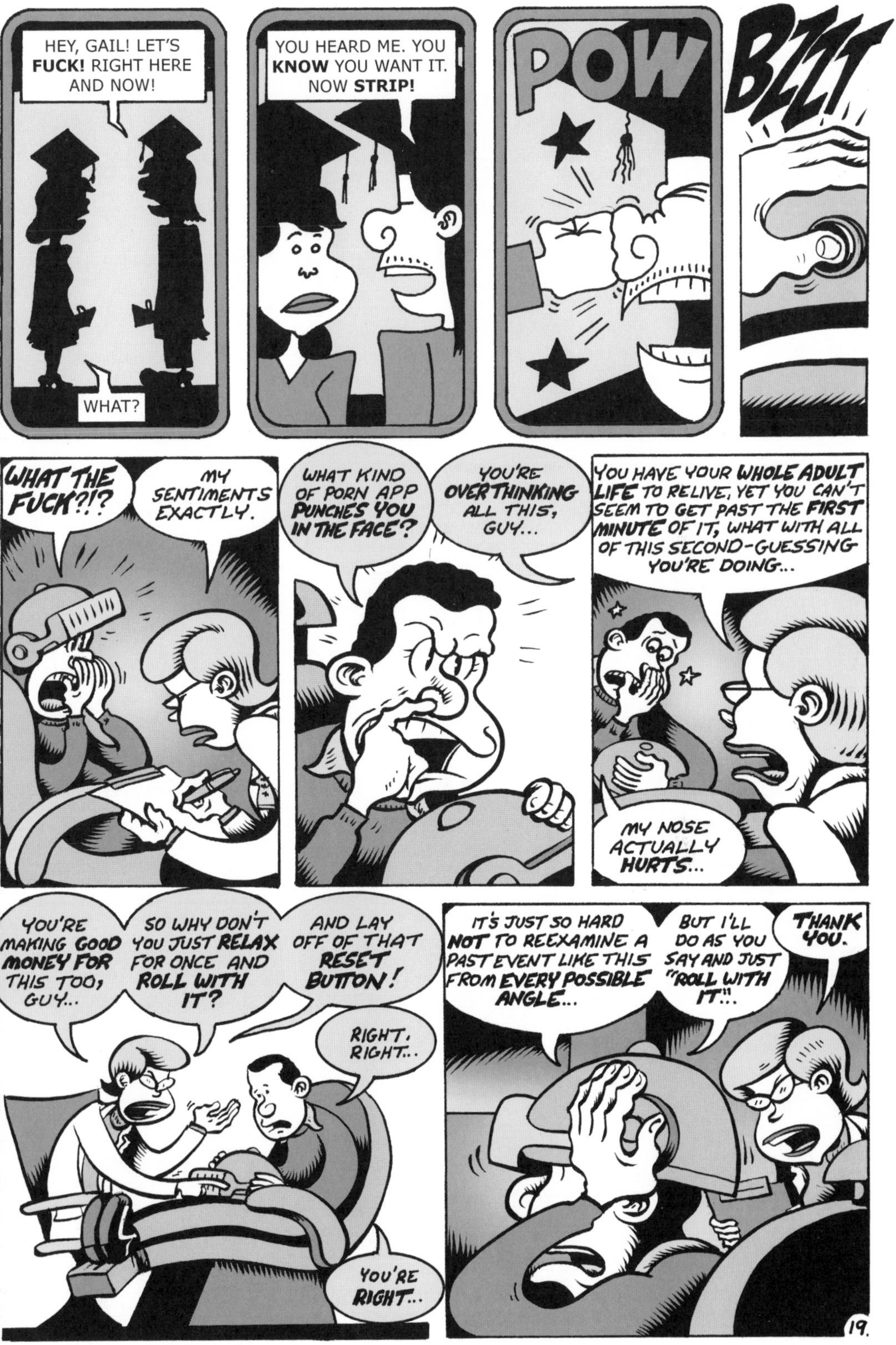
HEY, GAIL! LET'S **FUCK!** RIGHT HERE AND NOW!
WHAT?
YOU HEARD ME. YOU **KNOW** YOU WANT IT. NOW **STRIP!**
POW
BZZT
WHAT THE FUCK?!?
MY SENTIMENTS EXACTLY.
WHAT KIND OF PORN APP PUNCHES YOU IN THE FACE?
YOU'RE OVERTHINKING ALL THIS, GUY...
YOU HAVE YOUR WHOLE ADULT LIFE TO RELIVE, YET YOU CAN'T SEEM TO GET PAST THE FIRST MINUTE OF IT, WHAT WITH ALL OF THIS SECOND-GUESSING YOU'RE DOING...
MY NOSE ACTUALLY HURTS...
YOU'RE MAKING GOOD MONEY FOR THIS TOO, GUY...
SO WHY DON'T YOU JUST RELAX FOR ONCE AND ROLL WITH IT?
AND LAY OFF OF THAT RESET BUTTON!
RIGHT, RIGHT...
YOU'RE RIGHT...
IT'S JUST SO HARD NOT TO REEXAMINE A PAST EVENT LIKE THIS FROM EVERY POSSIBLE ANGLE...
BUT I'LL DO AS YOU SAY AND JUST "ROLL WITH IT"...
THANK YOU.

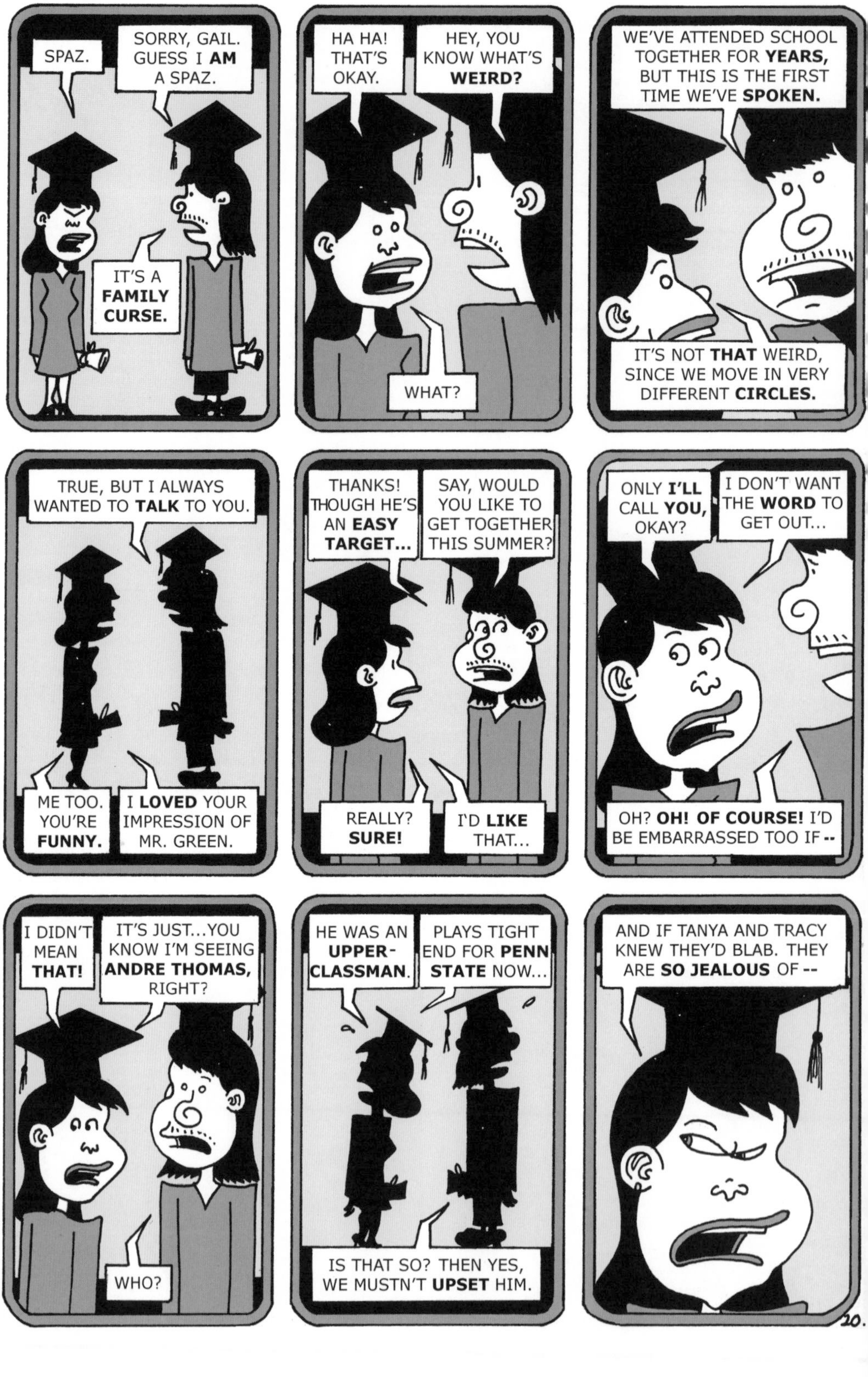
SPAZ.
SORRY, GAIL. GUESS I **AM** A SPAZ.
IT'S A **FAMILY CURSE.**
HA HA! THAT'S OKAY.
HEY, YOU KNOW WHAT'S **WEIRD?**
WHAT?
WE'VE ATTENDED SCHOOL TOGETHER FOR **YEARS,** BUT THIS IS THE FIRST TIME WE'VE **SPOKEN.**
IT'S NOT **THAT** WEIRD, SINCE WE MOVE IN VERY DIFFERENT **CIRCLES.**
TRUE, BUT I ALWAYS WANTED TO **TALK** TO YOU.
ME TOO. YOU'RE **FUNNY.**
I **LOVED** YOUR IMPRESSION OF MR. GREEN.
THANKS! THOUGH HE'S AN **EASY TARGET...**
SAY, WOULD YOU LIKE TO GET TOGETHER THIS SUMMER?
REALLY? **SURE!**
I'D **LIKE** THAT...
ONLY **I'LL** CALL **YOU,** OKAY?
I DON'T WANT THE **WORD** TO GET OUT...
OH? **OH! OF COURSE!** I'D BE EMBARRASSED TOO IF **--**
I DIDN'T MEAN **THAT!**
IT'S JUST...YOU KNOW I'M SEEING **ANDRE THOMAS,** RIGHT?
WHO?
HE WAS AN **UPPER-CLASSMAN.**
PLAYS TIGHT END FOR **PENN STATE** NOW...
IS THAT SO? THEN YES, WE MUSTN'T **UPSET** HIM.
AND IF TANYA AND TRACY KNEW THEY'D BLAB. THEY ARE **SO JEALOUS** OF **--**

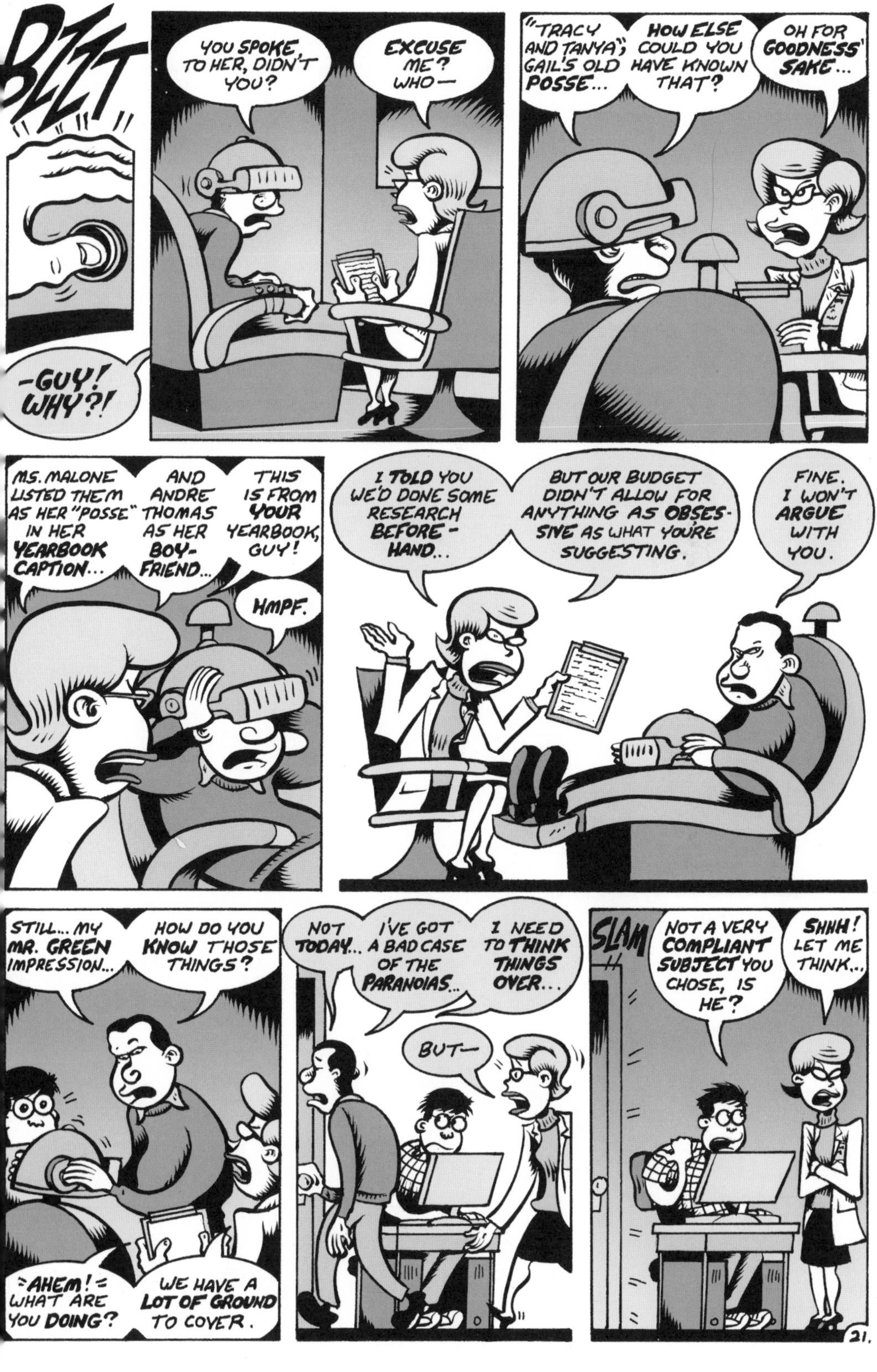
BZZT
-GUY! WHY?!
YOU SPOKE TO HER, DIDN'T YOU?
EXCUSE ME? WHO—
"TRACY AND TANYA"; GAIL'S OLD POSSE...
HOW ELSE COULD YOU HAVE KNOWN THAT?
OH FOR GOODNESS' SAKE...
MS. MALONE LISTED THEM AS HER "POSSE" IN HER YEARBOOK CAPTION...
AND ANDRE THOMAS AS HER BOY-FRIEND...
THIS IS FROM YOUR YEARBOOK, GUY!
HMPF.
I TOLD YOU WE'D DONE SOME RESEARCH BEFORE-HAND...
BUT OUR BUDGET DIDN'T ALLOW FOR ANYTHING AS OBSES-SIVE AS WHAT YOU'RE SUGGESTING.
FINE. I WON'T ARGUE WITH YOU.
STILL... MY MR. GREEN IMPRESSION...
HOW DO YOU KNOW THOSE THINGS?
=AHEM!= WHAT ARE YOU DOING?
WE HAVE A LOT OF GROUND TO COVER.
NOT TODAY...
I'VE GOT A BAD CASE OF THE PARANOIAS...
I NEED TO THINK THINGS OVER...
BUT—
SLAM
NOT A VERY COMPLIANT SUBJECT YOU CHOSE, IS HE?
SHHH! LET ME THINK...

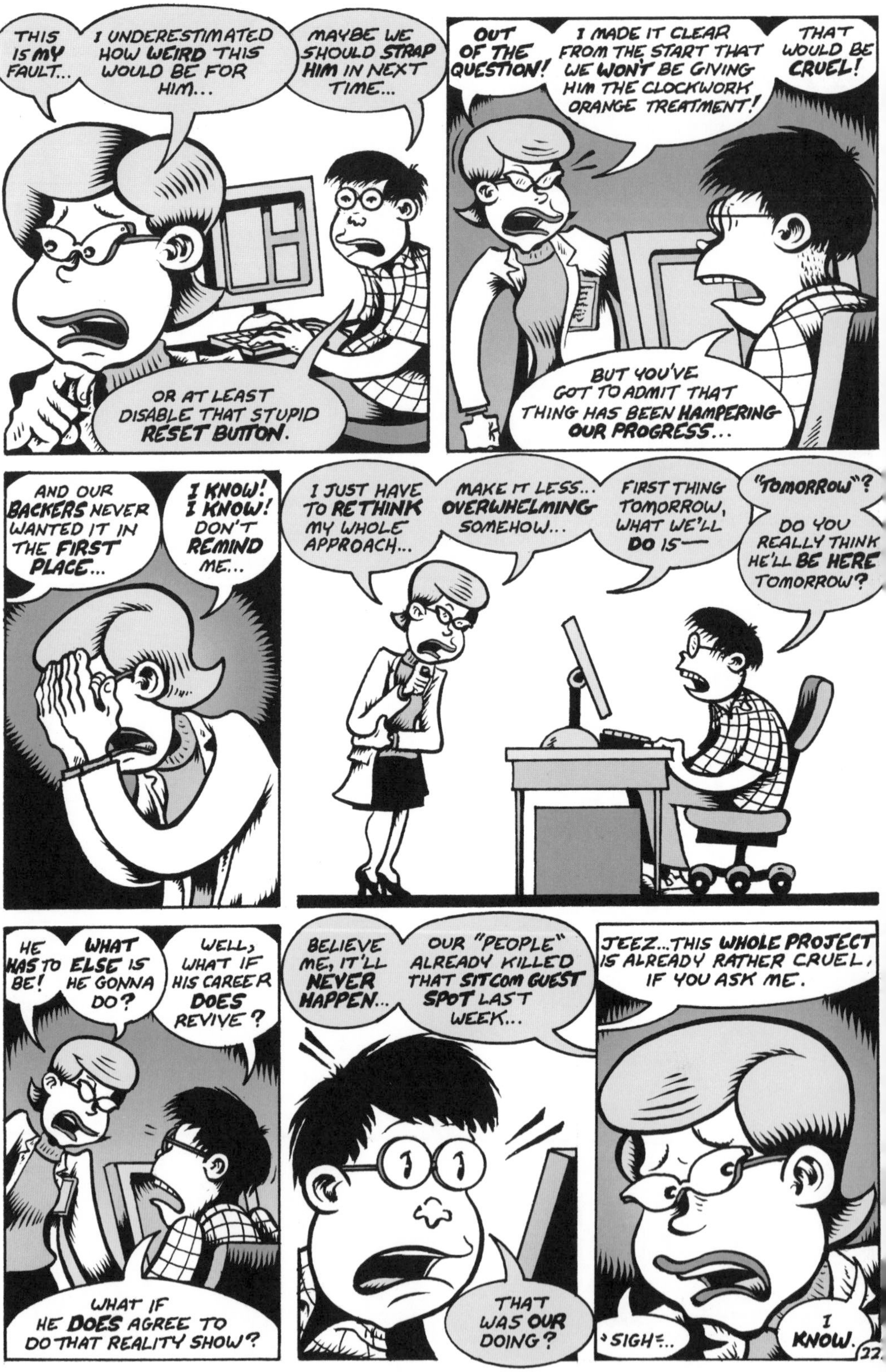
THIS IS MY FAULT...
I UNDERESTIMATED HOW WEIRD THIS WOULD BE FOR HIM...
MAYBE WE SHOULD STRAP HIM IN NEXT TIME...
OR AT LEAST DISABLE THAT STUPID RESET BUTTON.
OUT OF THE QUESTION!
I MADE IT CLEAR FROM THE START THAT WE WON'T BE GIVING HIM THE CLOCKWORK ORANGE TREATMENT!
THAT WOULD BE CRUEL!
BUT YOU'VE GOT TO ADMIT THAT THING HAS BEEN HAMPERING OUR PROGRESS...
AND OUR BACKERS NEVER WANTED IT IN THE FIRST PLACE...
I KNOW! I KNOW! DON'T REMIND ME...
I JUST HAVE TO RETHINK MY WHOLE APPROACH...
MAKE IT LESS... OVERWHELMING SOMEHOW...
FIRST THING TOMORROW, WHAT WE'LL DO IS—
"TOMORROW"? DO YOU REALLY THINK HE'LL BE HERE TOMORROW?
HE HAS TO BE!
WHAT ELSE IS HE GONNA DO?
WELL, WHAT IF HIS CAREER DOES REVIVE?
WHAT IF HE DOES AGREE TO DO THAT REALITY SHOW?
BELIEVE ME, IT'LL NEVER HAPPEN...
OUR "PEOPLE" ALREADY KILLED THAT SITCOM GUEST SPOT LAST WEEK...
THAT WAS OUR DOING?
JEEZ... THIS WHOLE PROJECT IS ALREADY RATHER CRUEL, IF YOU ASK ME.
SIGH...
I KNOW.

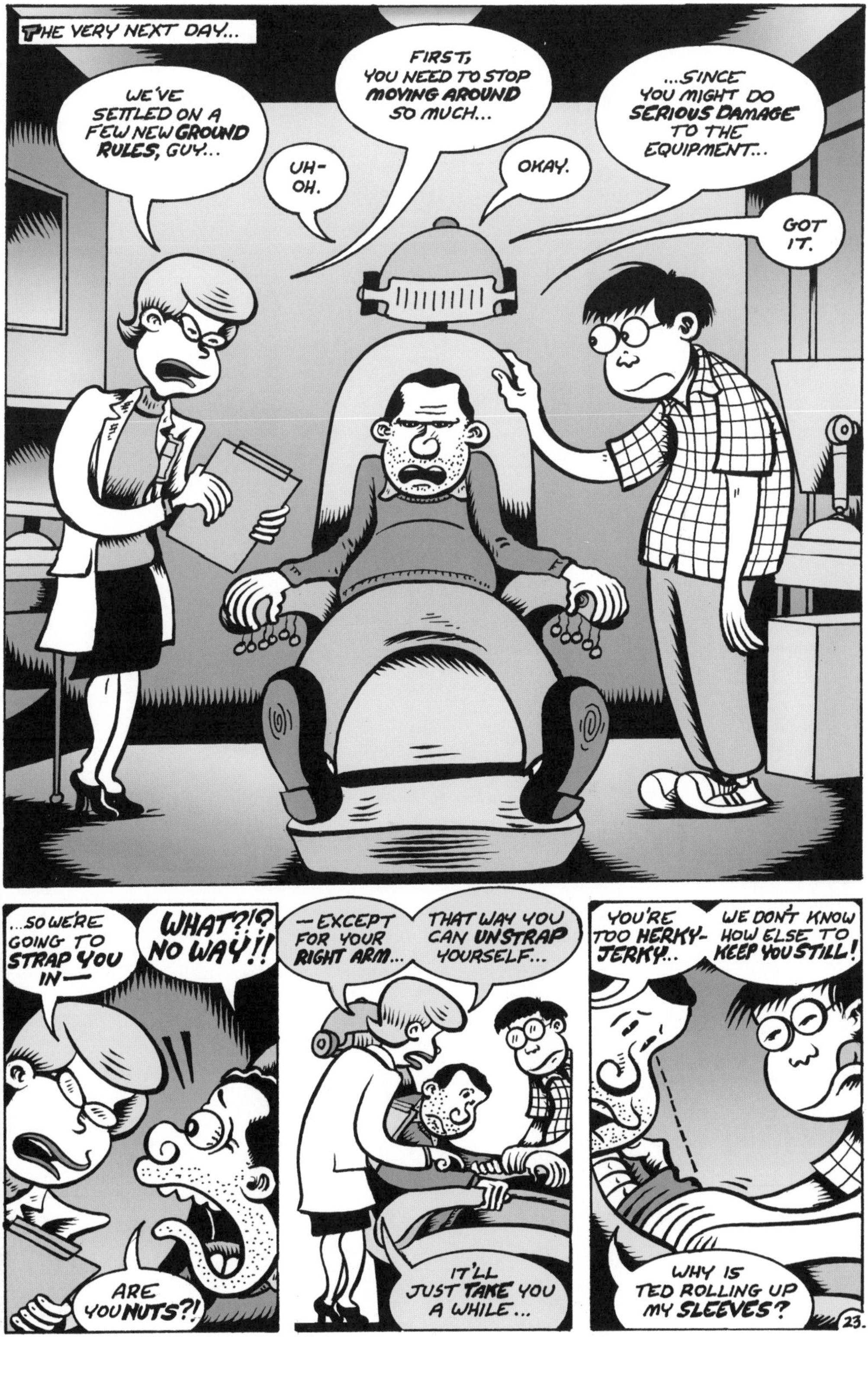
THE VERY NEXT DAY...
WE'VE SETTLED ON A FEW NEW GROUND RULES, GUY...
UH-OH.
FIRST, YOU NEED TO STOP MOVING AROUND SO MUCH...
OKAY.
...SINCE YOU MIGHT DO SERIOUS DAMAGE TO THE EQUIPMENT...
GOT IT.
...SO WE'RE GOING TO STRAP YOU IN—
WHAT?!? NO WAY!!
ARE YOU NUTS?!
—EXCEPT FOR YOUR RIGHT ARM...
THAT WAY YOU CAN UNSTRAP YOURSELF...
IT'LL JUST TAKE YOU A WHILE...
YOU'RE TOO HERKY-JERKY...
WE DON'T KNOW HOW ELSE TO KEEP YOU STILL!
WHY IS TED ROLLING UP MY SLEEVES?

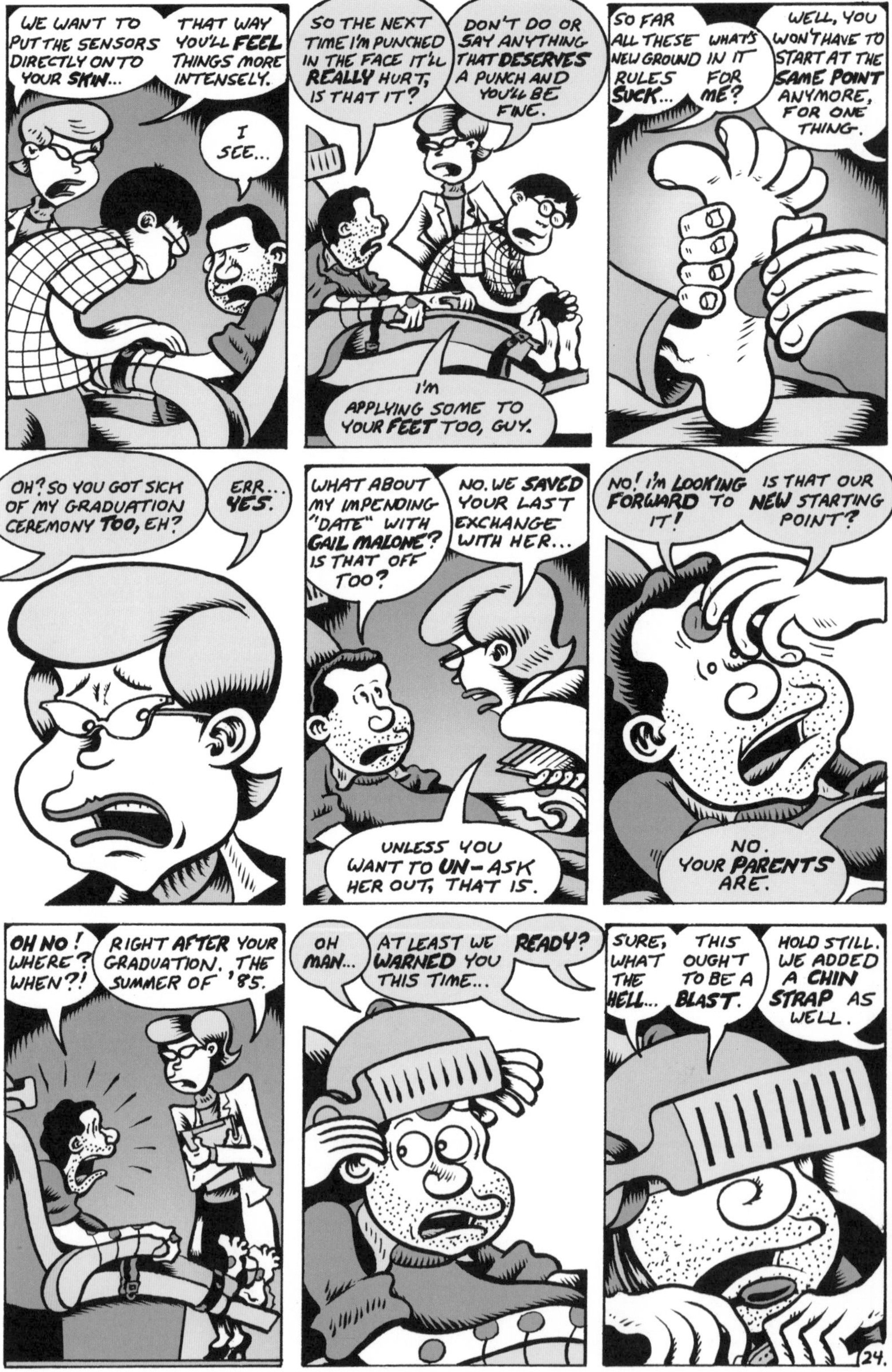
WE WANT TO PUT THE SENSORS DIRECTLY ONTO YOUR SKIN...
THAT WAY YOU'LL FEEL THINGS MORE INTENSELY.
I SEE...
SO THE NEXT TIME I'M PUNCHED IN THE FACE IT'LL REALLY HURT, IS THAT IT?
DON'T DO OR SAY ANYTHING THAT DESERVES A PUNCH AND YOU'LL BE FINE.
I'M APPLYING SOME TO YOUR FEET TOO, GUY.
SO FAR ALL THESE NEW GROUND RULES SUCK...
WHAT'S IN IT FOR ME?
WELL, YOU WON'T HAVE TO START AT THE SAME POINT ANYMORE, FOR ONE THING.
OH? SO YOU GOT SICK OF MY GRADUATION CEREMONY TOO, EH?
ERR... YES.
WHAT ABOUT MY IMPENDING "DATE" WITH GAIL MALONE? IS THAT OFF TOO?
NO. WE SAVED YOUR LAST EXCHANGE WITH HER...
UNLESS YOU WANT TO UN-ASK HER OUT, THAT IS.
NO! I'M LOOKING FORWARD TO IT!
IS THAT OUR NEW STARTING POINT?
NO. YOUR PARENTS ARE.
OH NO! WHERE? WHEN?!
RIGHT AFTER YOUR GRADUATION, THE SUMMER OF '85.
OH MAN...
AT LEAST WE WARNED YOU THIS TIME...
READY?
SURE, WHAT THE HELL...
THIS OUGHT TO BE A BLAST.
HOLD STILL. WE ADDED A CHIN STRAP AS WELL.

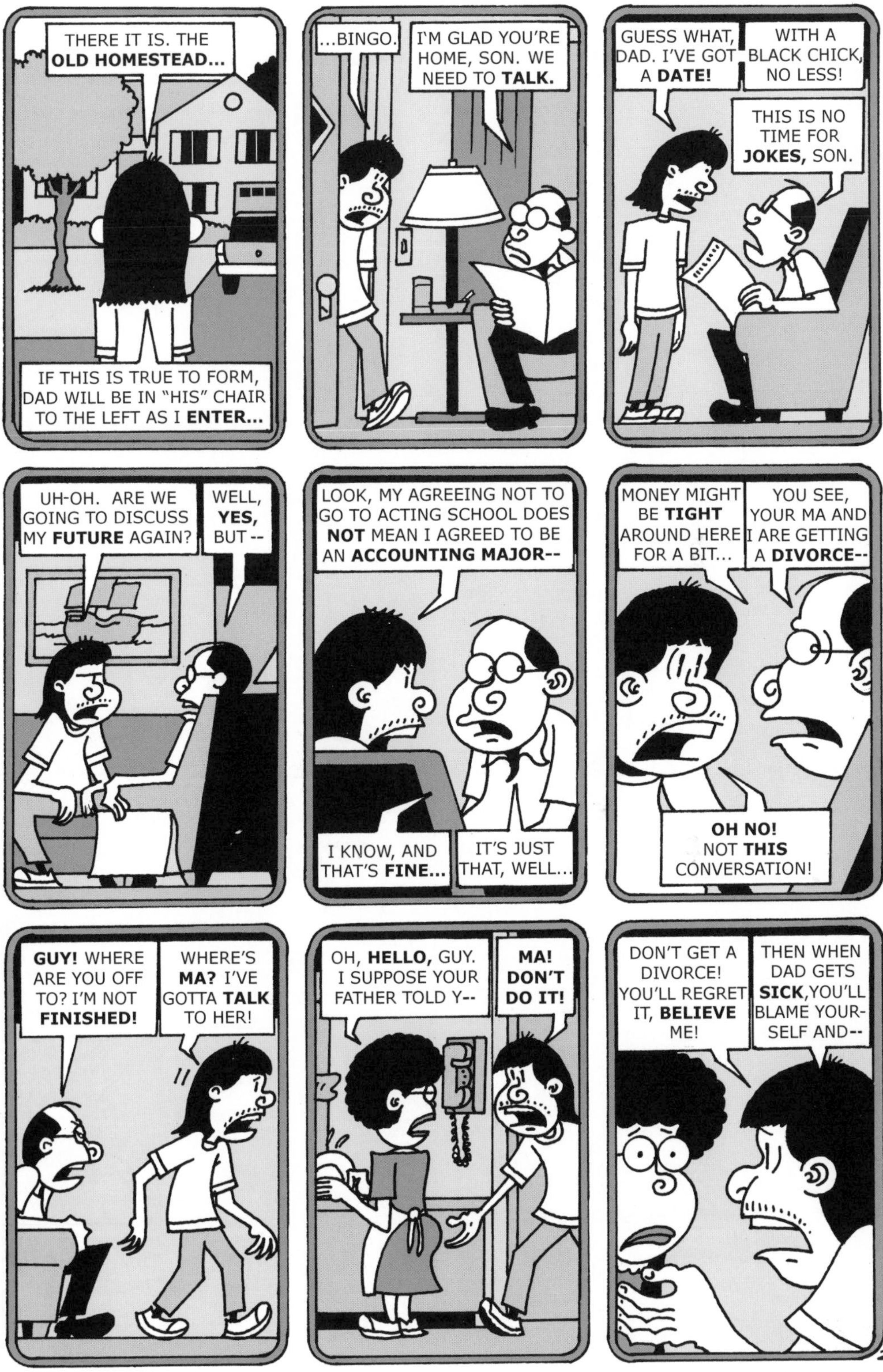
THERE IT IS. THE **OLD HOMESTEAD...**
IF THIS IS TRUE TO FORM, DAD WILL BE IN "HIS" CHAIR TO THE LEFT AS I **ENTER...**
...BINGO.
I'M GLAD YOU'RE HOME, SON. WE NEED TO **TALK.**
GUESS WHAT, DAD. I'VE GOT A **DATE!**
WITH A BLACK CHICK, NO LESS!
THIS IS NO TIME FOR **JOKES,** SON.
UH-OH. ARE WE GOING TO DISCUSS MY **FUTURE** AGAIN?
WELL, **YES,** BUT --
LOOK, MY AGREEING NOT TO GO TO ACTING SCHOOL DOES **NOT** MEAN I AGREED TO BE AN **ACCOUNTING MAJOR--**
I KNOW, AND THAT'S **FINE...**
IT'S JUST THAT, WELL...
MONEY MIGHT BE **TIGHT** AROUND HERE FOR A BIT...
YOU SEE, YOUR MA AND I ARE GETTING A **DIVORCE--**
OH NO! NOT **THIS** CONVERSATION!
GUY! WHERE ARE YOU OFF TO? I'M NOT **FINISHED!**
WHERE'S **MA?** I'VE GOTTA **TALK** TO HER!
OH, **HELLO,** GUY. I SUPPOSE YOUR FATHER TOLD Y--
MA! DON'T DO IT!
DON'T GET A DIVORCE! YOU'LL REGRET IT, **BELIEVE** ME!
THEN WHEN DAD GETS **SICK,**YOU'LL BLAME YOURSELF AND--

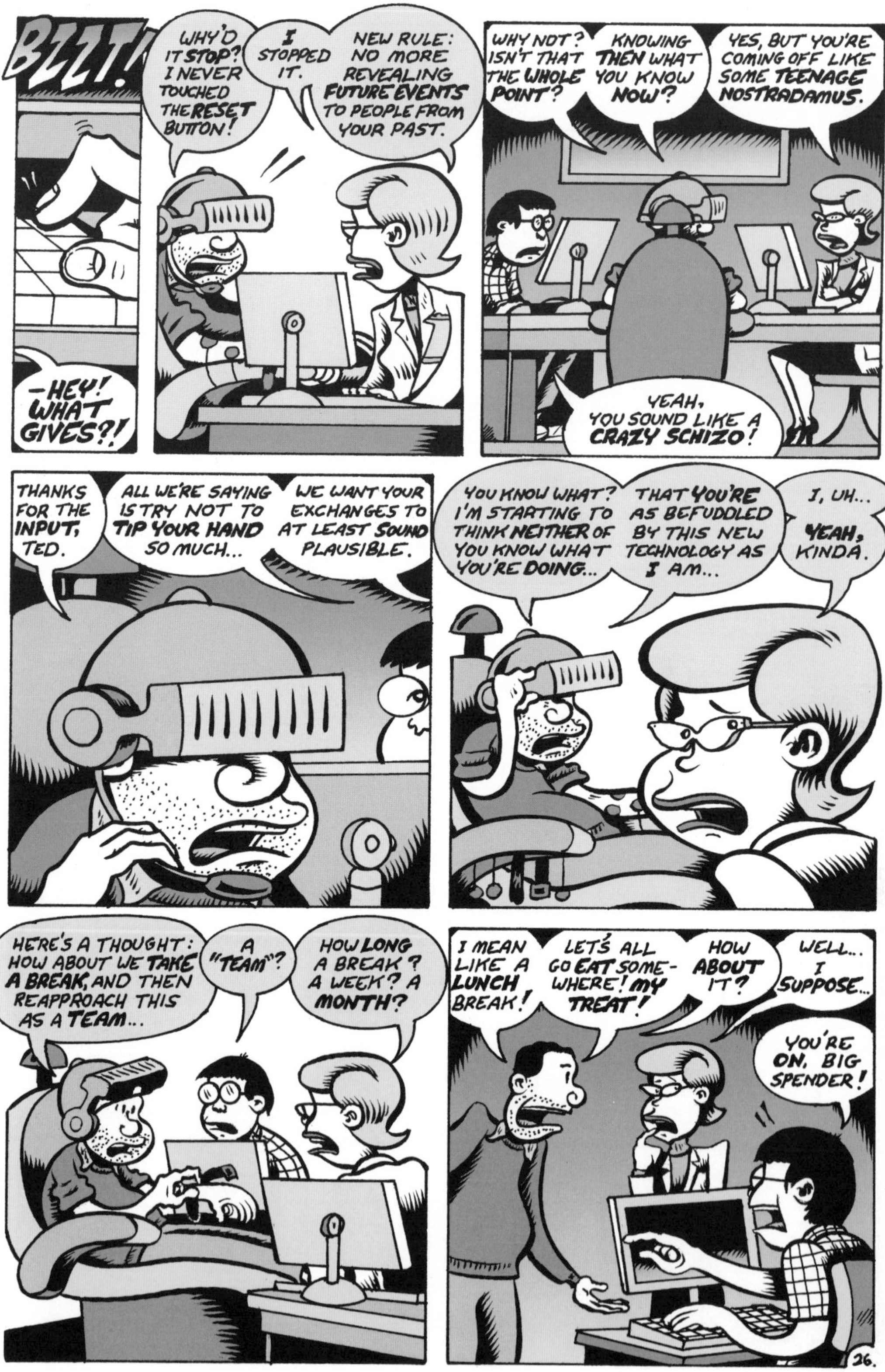
BZZT!
—HEY! WHAT GIVES?!
WHY'D IT STOP? I NEVER TOUCHED THE RESET BUTTON!
I STOPPED IT.
NEW RULE: NO MORE REVEALING FUTURE EVENTS TO PEOPLE FROM YOUR PAST.
WHY NOT? ISN'T THAT THE WHOLE POINT?
KNOWING THEN WHAT YOU KNOW NOW?
YES, BUT YOU'RE COMING OFF LIKE SOME TEENAGE NOSTRADAMUS.
YEAH, YOU SOUND LIKE A CRAZY SCHIZO!
THANKS FOR THE INPUT, TED.
ALL WE'RE SAYING IS TRY NOT TO TIP YOUR HAND SO MUCH...
WE WANT YOUR EXCHANGES TO AT LEAST SOUND PLAUSIBLE.
YOU KNOW WHAT? I'M STARTING TO THINK NEITHER OF YOU KNOW WHAT YOU'RE DOING...
THAT YOU'RE AS BEFUDDLED BY THIS NEW TECHNOLOGY AS I AM...
I, UH... YEAH, KINDA.
HERE'S A THOUGHT: HOW ABOUT WE TAKE A BREAK, AND THEN REAPPROACH THIS AS A TEAM...
A "TEAM"?
HOW LONG A BREAK? A WEEK? A MONTH?
I MEAN LIKE A LUNCH BREAK!
LET'S ALL GO EAT SOMEWHERE! MY TREAT!
HOW ABOUT IT?
WELL... I SUPPOSE...
YOU'RE ON, BIG SPENDER!

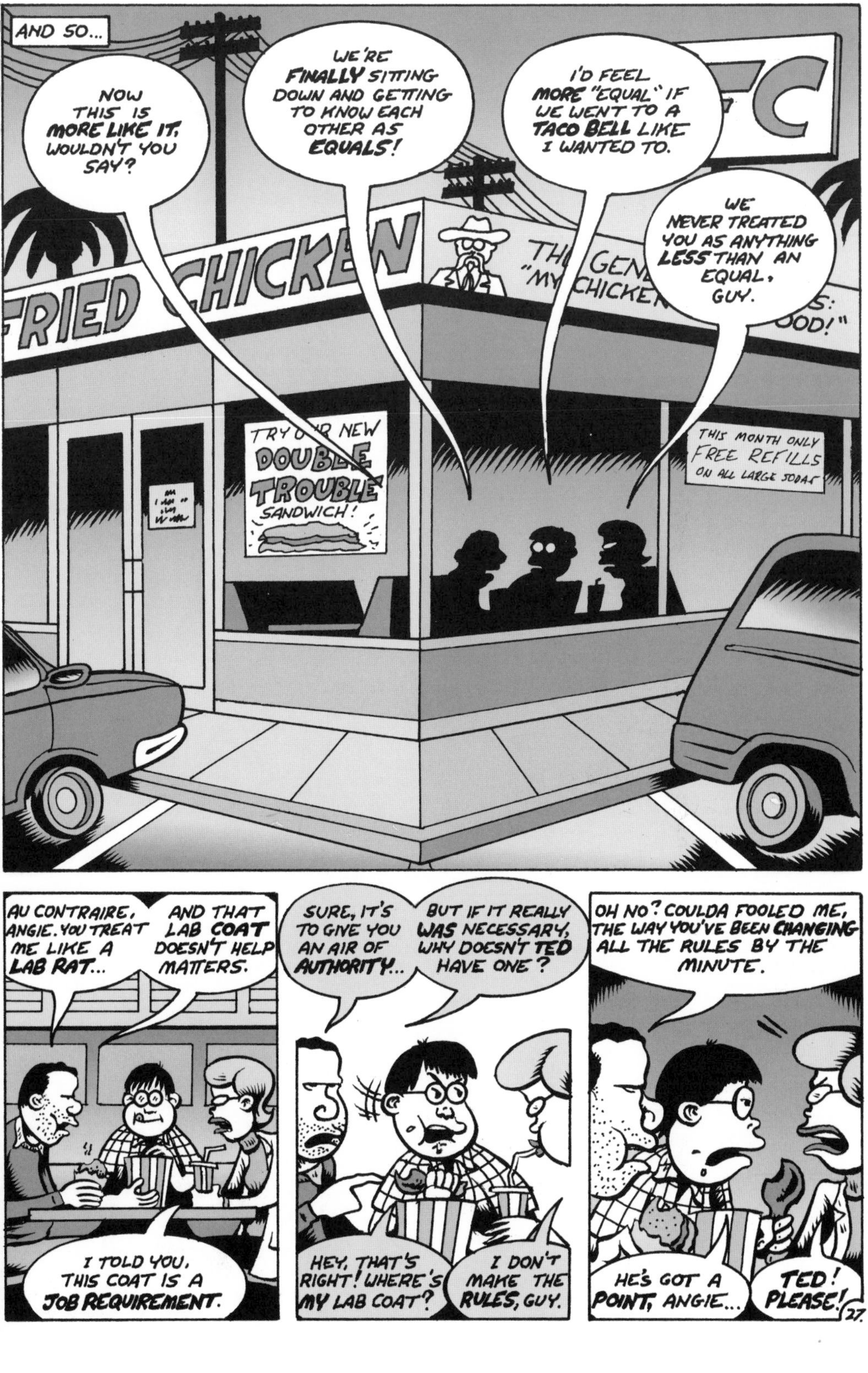
AND SO...
NOW THIS IS MORE LIKE IT, WOULDN'T YOU SAY?
WE'RE FINALLY SITTING DOWN AND GETTING TO KNOW EACH OTHER AS EQUALS!
I'D FEEL MORE "EQUAL" IF WE WENT TO A TACO BELL LIKE I WANTED TO.
WE NEVER TREATED YOU AS ANYTHING LESS THAN AN EQUAL, GUY.
FRIED CHICKEN
DOUBLE TROUBLE SANDWICH!
THIS MONTH ONLY FREE REFILLS ON ALL LARGE SODAS
AU CONTRAIRE, ANGIE. YOU TREAT ME LIKE A LAB RAT...
AND THAT LAB COAT DOESN'T HELP MATTERS.
I TOLD YOU, THIS COAT IS A JOB REQUIREMENT.
SURE, IT'S TO GIVE YOU AN AIR OF AUTHORITY...
BUT IF IT REALLY WAS NECESSARY, WHY DOESN'T TED HAVE ONE?
HEY, THAT'S RIGHT! WHERE'S MY LAB COAT?
I DON'T MAKE THE RULES, GUY.
OH NO? COULDA FOOLED ME, THE WAY YOU'VE BEEN CHANGING ALL THE RULES BY THE MINUTE.
HE'S GOT A POINT, ANGIE...
TED! PLEASE!

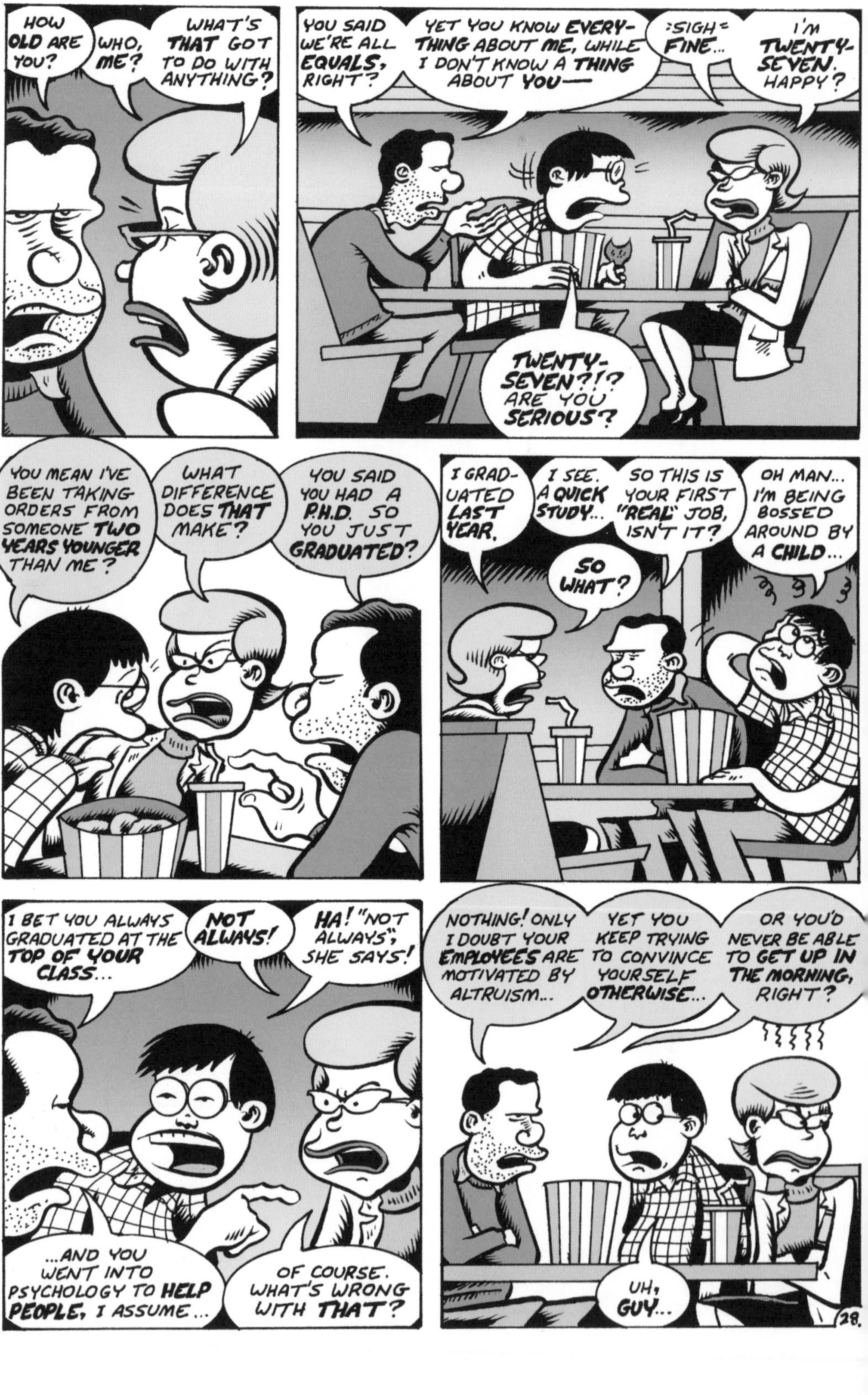

HOW OLD ARE YOU?
WHO, ME?
WHAT'S THAT GOT TO DO WITH ANYTHING?
YOU SAID WE'RE ALL EQUALS, RIGHT?
YET YOU KNOW EVERYTHING ABOUT ME, WHILE I DON'T KNOW A THING ABOUT YOU—
=SIGH= FINE...
I'M TWENTY-SEVEN. HAPPY?
TWENTY-SEVEN?!? ARE YOU SERIOUS?
YOU MEAN I'VE BEEN TAKING ORDERS FROM SOMEONE TWO YEARS YOUNGER THAN ME?
WHAT DIFFERENCE DOES THAT MAKE?
YOU SAID YOU HAD A P.H.D. SO YOU JUST GRADUATED?
I GRADUATED LAST YEAR.
I SEE. A QUICK STUDY...
SO THIS IS YOUR FIRST "REAL" JOB, ISN'T IT?
SO WHAT?
OH MAN... I'M BEING BOSSED AROUND BY A CHILD...
I BET YOU ALWAYS GRADUATED AT THE TOP OF YOUR CLASS...
NOT ALWAYS!
HA! "NOT ALWAYS", SHE SAYS!
...AND YOU WENT INTO PSYCHOLOGY TO HELP PEOPLE, I ASSUME...
OF COURSE. WHAT'S WRONG WITH THAT?
NOTHING! ONLY I DOUBT YOUR EMPLOYEES ARE MOTIVATED BY ALTRUISM...
YET YOU KEEP TRYING TO CONVINCE YOURSELF OTHERWISE...
OR YOU'D NEVER BE ABLE TO GET UP IN THE MORNING, RIGHT?
UH, GUY...

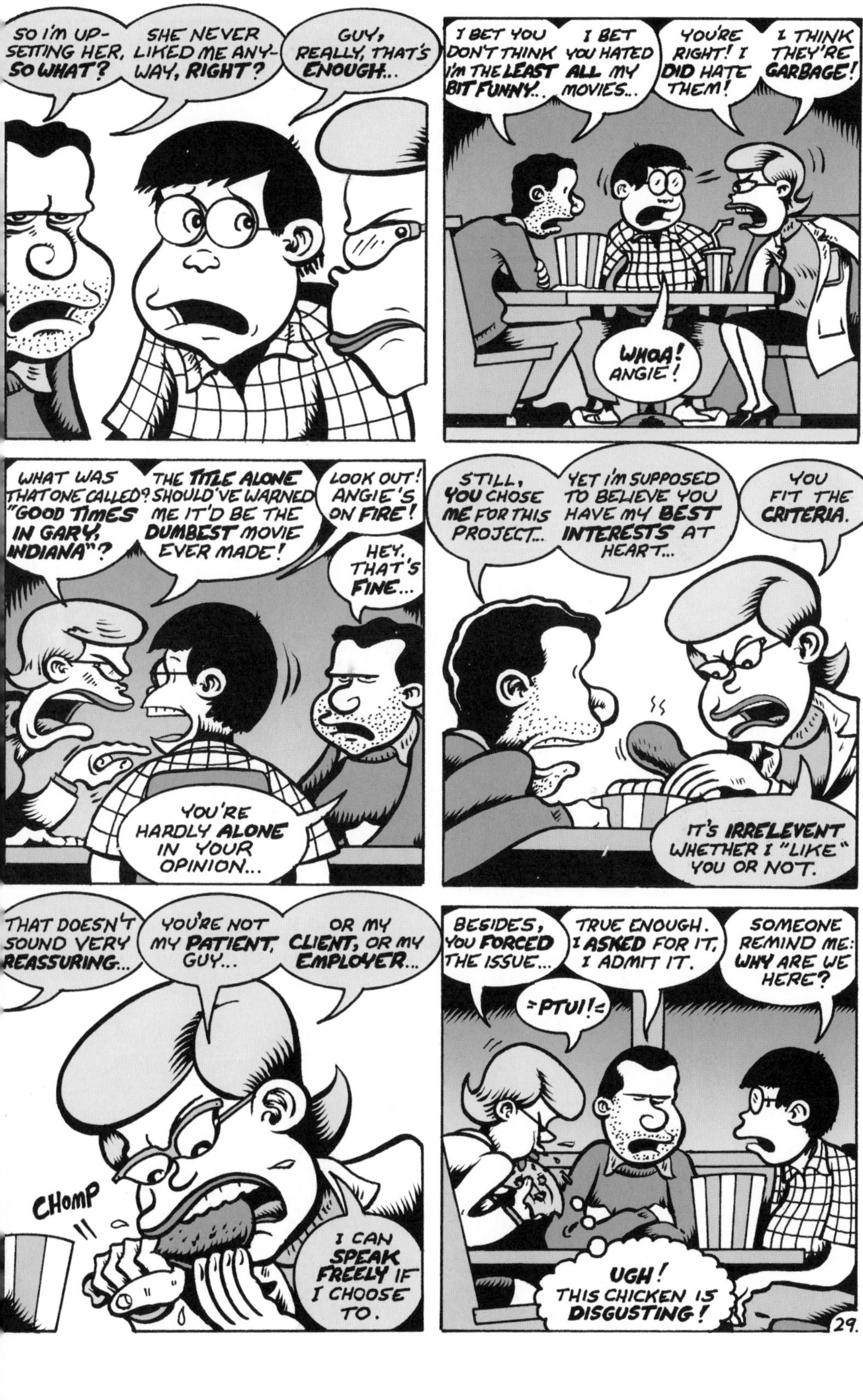
SO I'M UP-SETTING HER, SO WHAT?
SHE NEVER LIKED ME ANY-WAY, RIGHT?
GUY, REALLY, THAT'S ENOUGH...
I BET YOU DON'T THINK I'M THE LEAST BIT FUNNY...
I BET YOU HATED ALL MY MOVIES...
YOU'RE RIGHT! I DID HATE THEM!
I THINK THEY'RE GARBAGE!
WHOA! ANGIE!
WHAT WAS THAT ONE CALLED? "GOOD TIMES IN GARY, INDIANA"?
THE TITLE ALONE SHOULD'VE WARNED ME IT'D BE THE DUMBEST MOVIE EVER MADE!
LOOK OUT! ANGIE'S ON FIRE!
HEY. THAT'S FINE...
YOU'RE HARDLY ALONE IN YOUR OPINION...
STILL, YOU CHOSE ME FOR THIS PROJECT...
YET I'M SUPPOSED TO BELIEVE YOU HAVE MY BEST INTERESTS AT HEART...
YOU FIT THE CRITERIA.
IT'S IRRELEVENT WHETHER I "LIKE" YOU OR NOT.
THAT DOESN'T SOUND VERY REASSURING...
YOU'RE NOT MY PATIENT, GUY...
OR MY CLIENT, OR MY EMPLOYER...
CHOMP
I CAN SPEAK FREELY IF I CHOOSE TO.
BESIDES, YOU FORCED THE ISSUE...
TRUE ENOUGH. I ASKED FOR IT, I ADMIT IT.
SOMEONE REMIND ME: WHY ARE WE HERE?
=PTUI!=
UGH! THIS CHICKEN IS DISGUSTING!

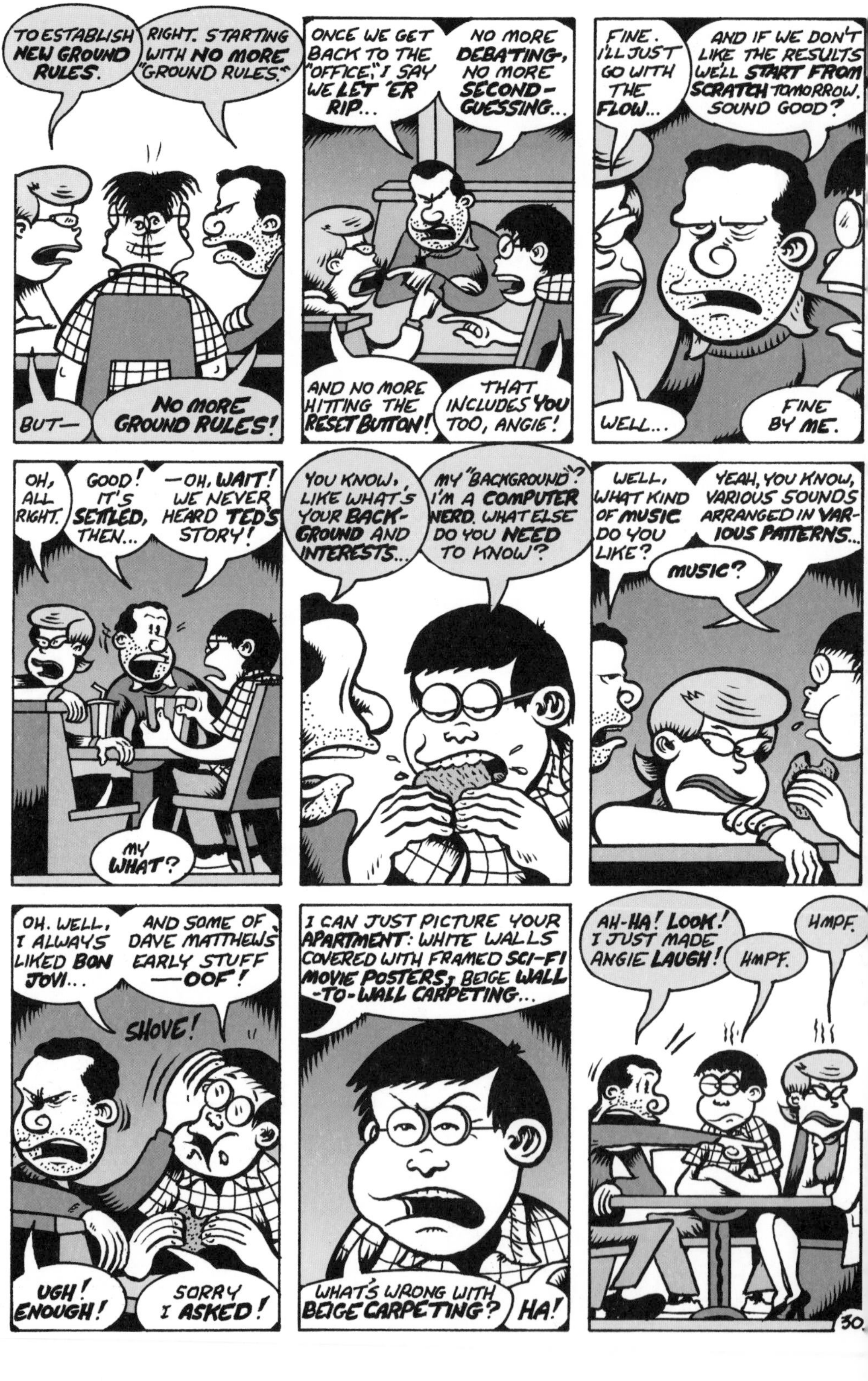
TO ESTABLISH NEW GROUND RULES.
RIGHT. STARTING WITH NO MORE "GROUND RULES."
BUT—
NO MORE GROUND RULES!
ONCE WE GET BACK TO THE "OFFICE," I SAY WE LET 'ER RIP...
NO MORE DEBATING, NO MORE SECOND-GUESSING...
AND NO MORE HITTING THE RESET BUTTON!
THAT INCLUDES YOU TOO, ANGIE!
FINE. I'LL JUST GO WITH THE FLOW...
AND IF WE DON'T LIKE THE RESULTS WE'LL START FROM SCRATCH TOMORROW. SOUND GOOD?
WELL...
FINE BY ME.
OH, ALL RIGHT.
GOOD! IT'S SETTLED, THEN...
—OH, WAIT! WE NEVER HEARD TED'S STORY!
MY WHAT?
YOU KNOW, LIKE WHAT'S YOUR BACKGROUND AND INTERESTS...
MY "BACKGROUND"? I'M A COMPUTER NERD. WHAT ELSE DO YOU NEED TO KNOW?
WELL, WHAT KIND OF MUSIC DO YOU LIKE?
YEAH, YOU KNOW, VARIOUS SOUNDS ARRANGED IN VARIOUS PATTERNS...
MUSIC?
OH. WELL, I ALWAYS LIKED BON JOVI...
AND SOME OF DAVE MATTHEWS' EARLY STUFF —OOF!
SHOVE!
UGH! ENOUGH!
SORRY I ASKED!
I CAN JUST PICTURE YOUR APARTMENT: WHITE WALLS COVERED WITH FRAMED SCI-FI MOVIE POSTERS, BEIGE WALL-TO-WALL CARPETING...
WHAT'S WRONG WITH BEIGE CARPETING?
HA!
AH-HA! LOOK! I JUST MADE ANGIE LAUGH!
HMPF.
HMPF.

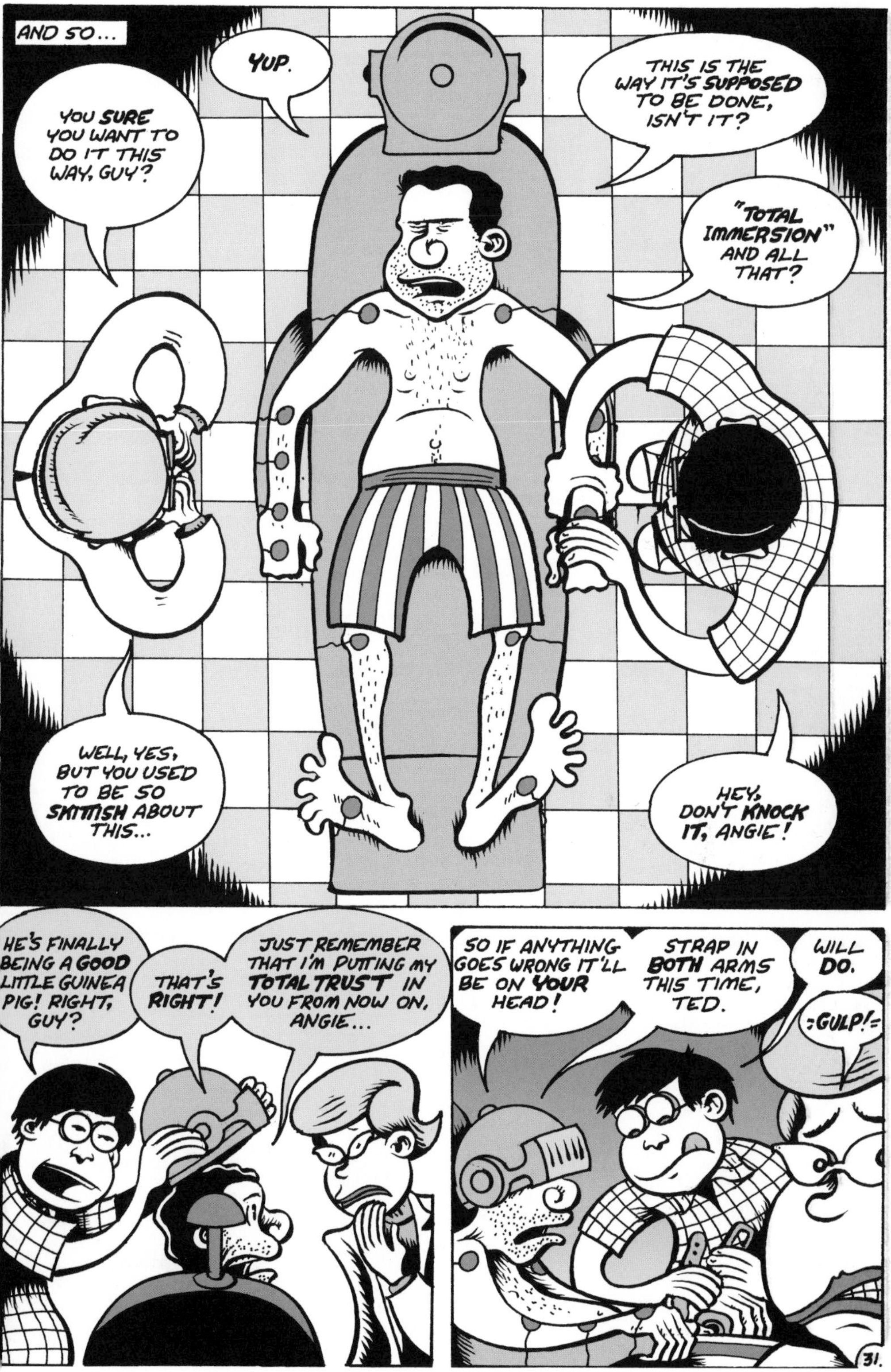
AND SO...
YOU SURE YOU WANT TO DO IT THIS WAY, GUY?
YUP.
THIS IS THE WAY IT'S SUPPOSED TO BE DONE, ISN'T IT?
"TOTAL IMMERSION" AND ALL THAT?
WELL, YES, BUT YOU USED TO BE SO SKITTISH ABOUT THIS...
HEY, DON'T KNOCK IT, ANGIE!
HE'S FINALLY BEING A GOOD LITTLE GUINEA PIG! RIGHT, GUY?
THAT'S RIGHT!
JUST REMEMBER THAT I'M PUTTING MY TOTAL TRUST IN YOU FROM NOW ON, ANGIE...
SO IF ANYTHING GOES WRONG IT'LL BE ON YOUR HEAD!
STRAP IN BOTH ARMS THIS TIME, TED.
WILL DO.
=GULP!=

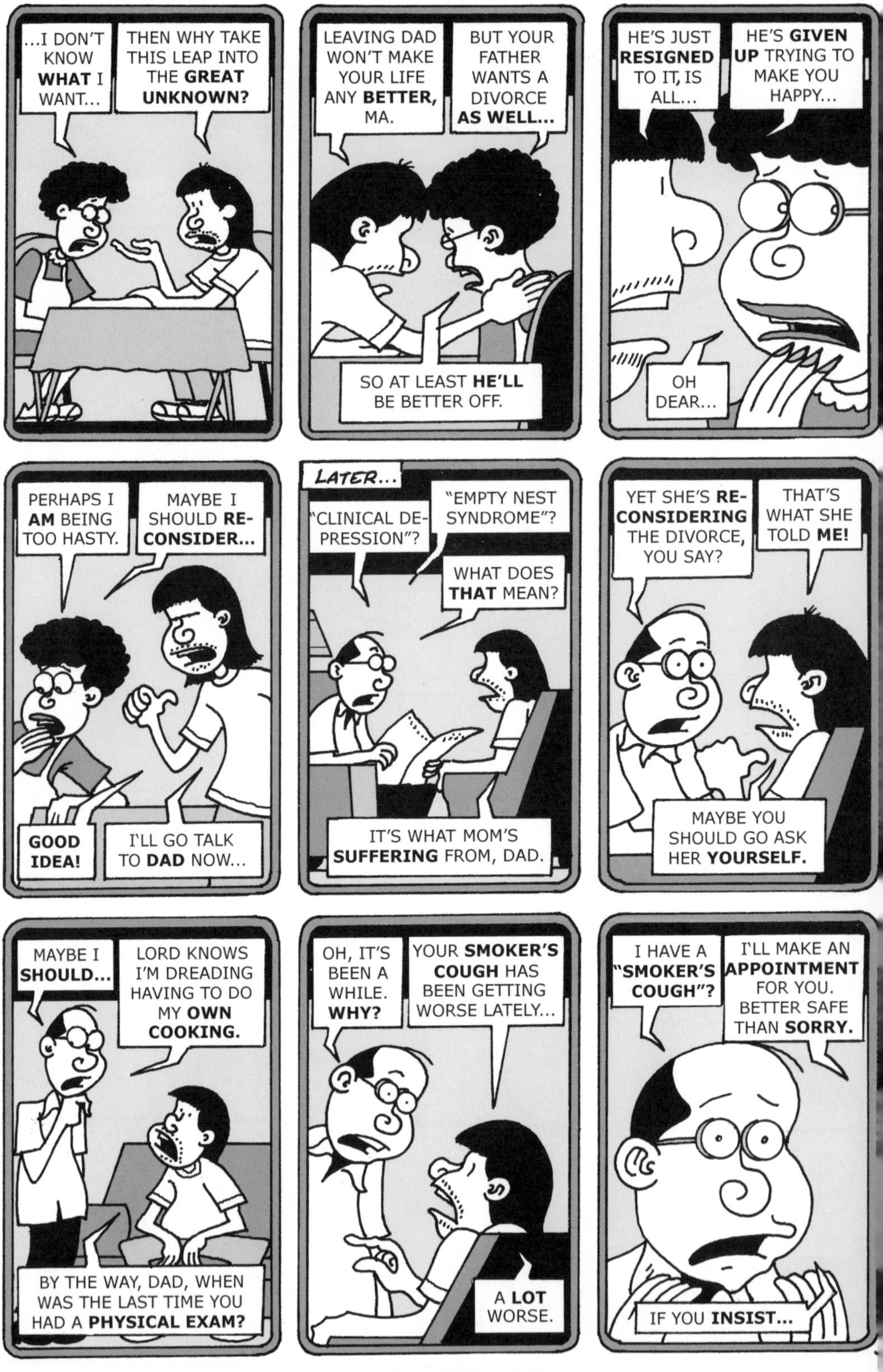
...I DON'T KNOW **WHAT** I WANT...
THEN WHY TAKE THIS LEAP INTO THE **GREAT UNKNOWN?**
LEAVING DAD WON'T MAKE YOUR LIFE ANY **BETTER,** MA.
BUT YOUR FATHER WANTS A DIVORCE **AS WELL...**
SO AT LEAST **HE'LL** BE BETTER OFF.
HE'S JUST **RESIGNED** TO IT, IS ALL...
HE'S **GIVEN UP** TRYING TO MAKE YOU HAPPY...
OH DEAR...
PERHAPS I **AM** BEING TOO HASTY.
MAYBE I SHOULD **RE-CONSIDER...**
GOOD IDEA!
I'LL GO TALK TO **DAD** NOW...
LATER...
"CLINICAL DE-PRESSION"?
"EMPTY NEST SYNDROME"?
WHAT DOES **THAT** MEAN?
IT'S WHAT MOM'S **SUFFERING** FROM, DAD.
YET SHE'S **RE-CONSIDERING** THE DIVORCE, YOU SAY?
THAT'S WHAT SHE TOLD **ME!**
MAYBE YOU SHOULD GO ASK HER **YOURSELF.**
MAYBE I **SHOULD...**
LORD KNOWS I'M DREADING HAVING TO DO MY **OWN COOKING.**
BY THE WAY, DAD, WHEN WAS THE LAST TIME YOU HAD A **PHYSICAL EXAM?**
OH, IT'S BEEN A WHILE. **WHY?**
YOUR **SMOKER'S COUGH** HAS BEEN GETTING WORSE LATELY...
A **LOT** WORSE.
I HAVE A **"SMOKER'S COUGH"?**
I'LL MAKE AN **APPOINTMENT** FOR YOU. BETTER SAFE THAN **SORRY.**
IF YOU **INSIST...**

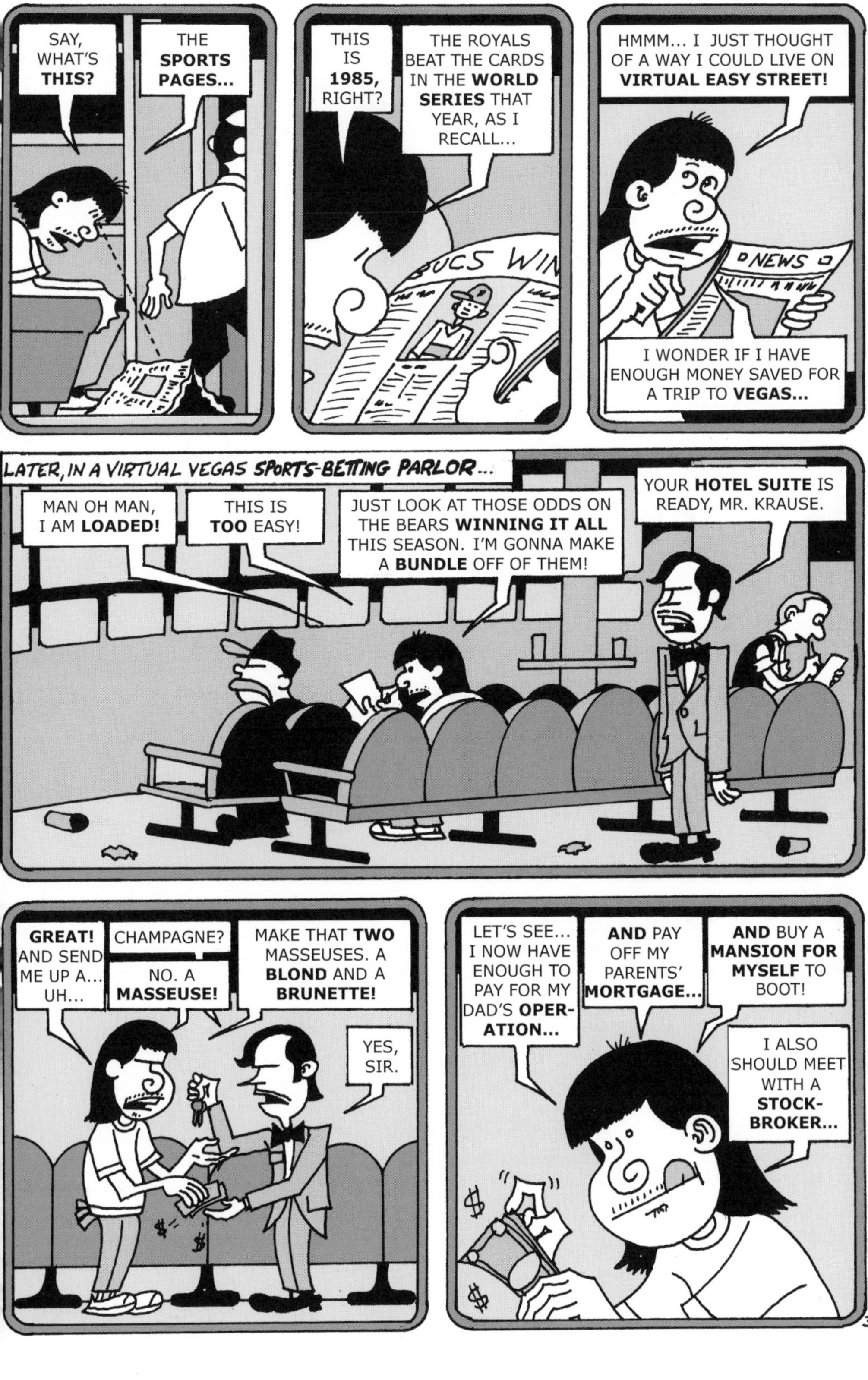

SAY, WHAT'S **THIS?**
THE **SPORTS PAGES...**
THIS IS **1985,** RIGHT?
THE ROYALS BEAT THE CARDS IN THE **WORLD SERIES** THAT YEAR, AS I RECALL...
BUCS WIN
HMMM... I JUST THOUGHT OF A WAY I COULD LIVE ON **VIRTUAL EASY STREET!**
NEWS
I WONDER IF I HAVE ENOUGH MONEY SAVED FOR A TRIP TO **VEGAS...**
LATER, IN A VIRTUAL VEGAS SPORTS-BETTING PARLOR...
MAN OH MAN, I AM **LOADED!**
THIS IS **TOO** EASY!
JUST LOOK AT THOSE ODDS ON THE BEARS **WINNING IT ALL** THIS SEASON. I'M GONNA MAKE A **BUNDLE** OFF OF THEM!
YOUR **HOTEL SUITE** IS READY, MR. KRAUSE.
GREAT! AND SEND ME UP A... UH...
CHAMPAGNE?
NO. A **MASSEUSE!**
MAKE THAT **TWO** MASSEUSES. A **BLOND** AND A **BRUNETTE!**
YES, SIR.
LET'S SEE... I NOW HAVE ENOUGH TO PAY FOR MY DAD'S **OPERATION...**
AND PAY OFF MY PARENTS' **MORTGAGE...**
AND BUY A **MANSION FOR MYSELF** TO BOOT!
I ALSO SHOULD MEET WITH A **STOCKBROKER...**

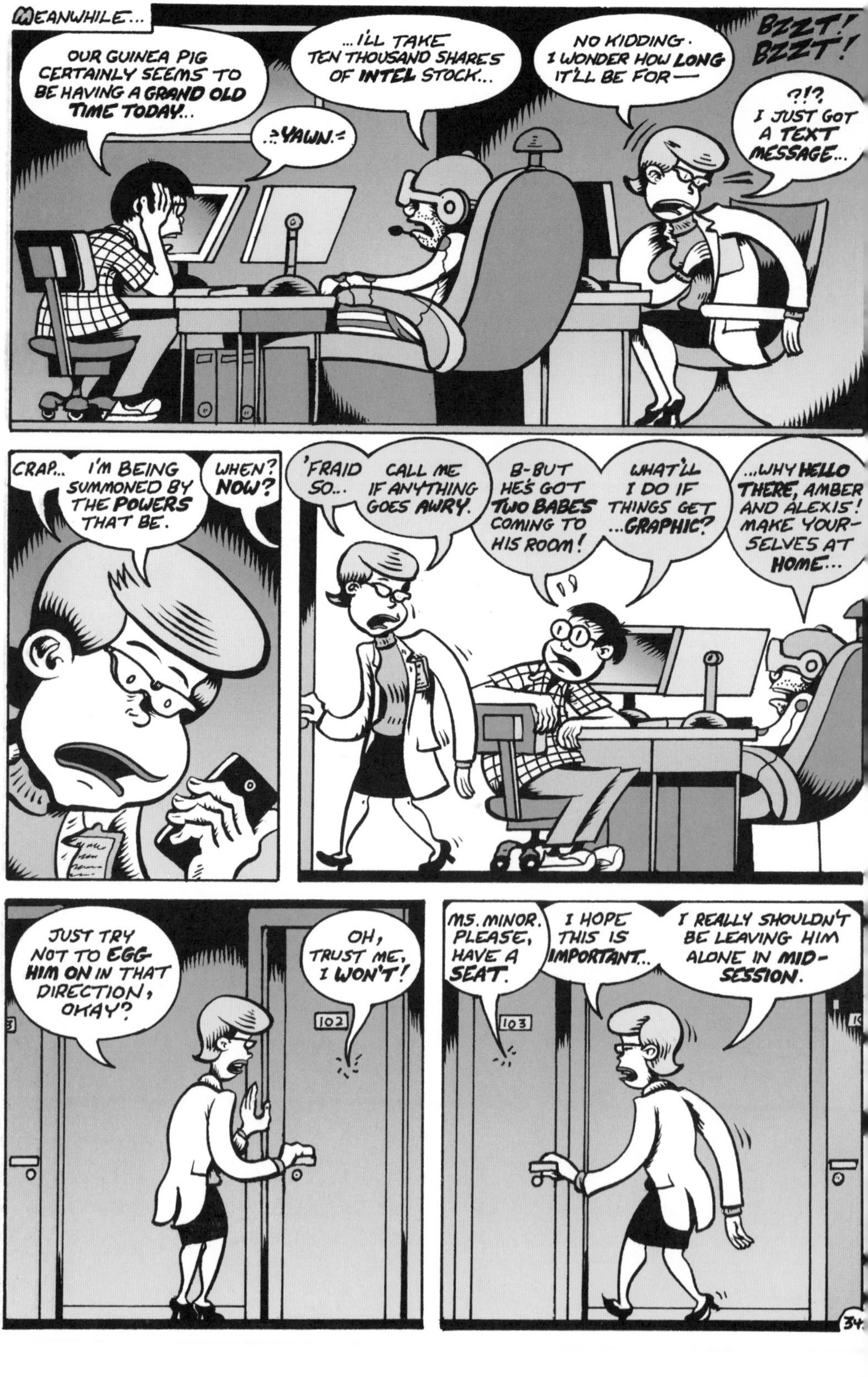

MEANWHILE...
OUR GUINEA PIG CERTAINLY SEEMS TO BE HAVING A GRAND OLD TIME TODAY...
...YAWN...
...I'LL TAKE TEN THOUSAND SHARES OF INTEL STOCK...
NO KIDDING. I WONDER HOW LONG IT'LL BE FOR—
BZZT! BZZT!
?!? I JUST GOT A TEXT MESSAGE...
CRAP... I'M BEING SUMMONED BY THE POWERS THAT BE.
WHEN? NOW?
'FRAID SO... CALL ME IF ANYTHING GOES AWRY.
B-BUT HE'S GOT TWO BABES COMING TO HIS ROOM!
WHAT'LL I DO IF THINGS GET ...GRAPHIC?
...WHY HELLO THERE, AMBER AND ALEXIS! MAKE YOURSELVES AT HOME...
JUST TRY NOT TO EGG HIM ON IN THAT DIRECTION, OKAY?
OH, TRUST ME, I WON'T!
102
MS. MINOR. PLEASE, HAVE A SEAT.
103
I HOPE THIS IS IMPORTANT...
I REALLY SHOULDN'T BE LEAVING HIM ALONE IN MID-SESSION.

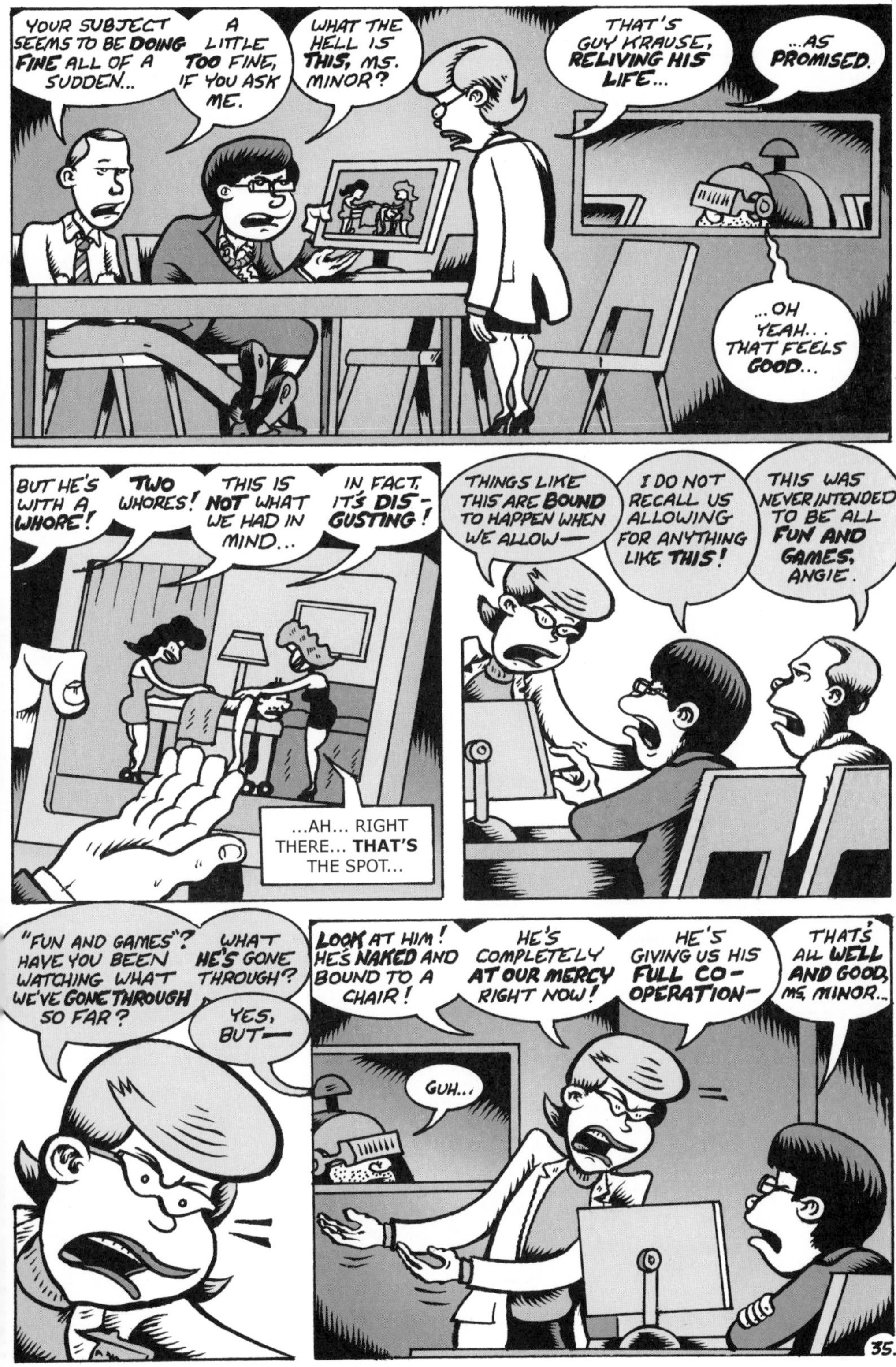
YOUR SUBJECT SEEMS TO BE DOING FINE ALL OF A SUDDEN...
A LITTLE TOO FINE, IF YOU ASK ME.
WHAT THE HELL IS THIS, MS. MINOR?
THAT'S GUY KRAUSE, RELIVING HIS LIFE...
...AS PROMISED.
...OH YEAH... THAT FEELS GOOD...
BUT HE'S WITH A WHORE!
TWO WHORES!
THIS IS NOT WHAT WE HAD IN MIND...
IN FACT, IT'S DIS-GUSTING!
...AH... RIGHT THERE... THAT'S THE SPOT...
THINGS LIKE THIS ARE BOUND TO HAPPEN WHEN WE ALLOW—
I DO NOT RECALL US ALLOWING FOR ANYTHING LIKE THIS!
THIS WAS NEVER INTENDED TO BE ALL FUN AND GAMES, ANGIE.
"FUN AND GAMES"? HAVE YOU BEEN WATCHING WHAT WE'VE GONE THROUGH SO FAR?
WHAT HE'S GONE THROUGH?
YES, BUT—
LOOK AT HIM! HE'S NAKED AND BOUND TO A CHAIR!
HE'S COMPLETELY AT OUR MERCY RIGHT NOW!
HE'S GIVING US HIS FULL CO-OPERATION—
GUH...
THAT'S ALL WELL AND GOOD, MS. MINOR...

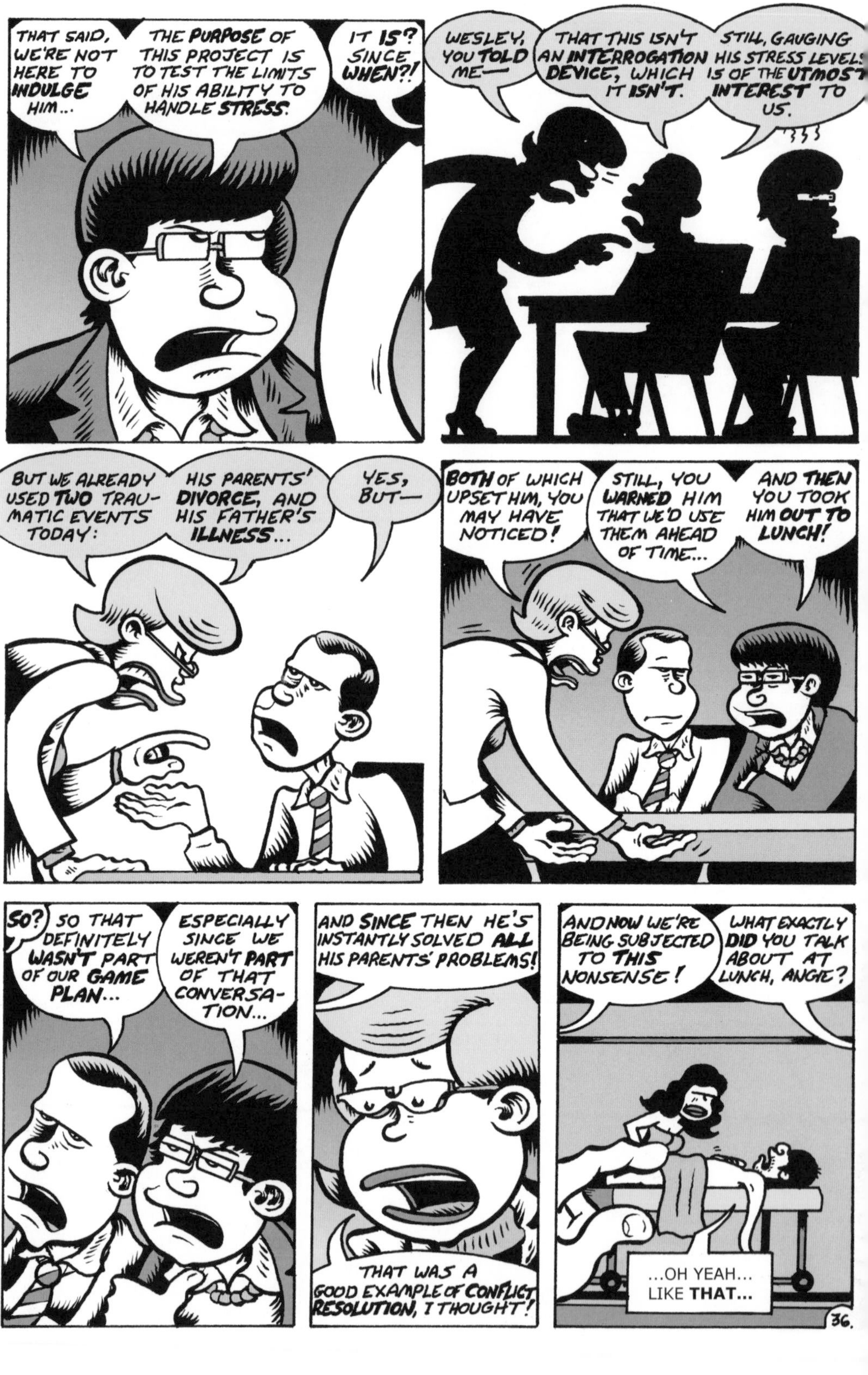
THAT SAID, WE'RE NOT HERE TO INDULGE HIM...
THE PURPOSE OF THIS PROJECT IS TO TEST THE LIMITS OF HIS ABILITY TO HANDLE STRESS.
IT IS? SINCE WHEN?!
WESLEY, YOU TOLD ME—
THAT THIS ISN'T AN INTERROGATION DEVICE, WHICH IT ISN'T.
STILL, GAUGING HIS STRESS LEVELS IS OF THE UTMOST INTEREST TO US.
BUT WE ALREADY USED TWO TRAUMATIC EVENTS TODAY:
HIS PARENTS' DIVORCE, AND HIS FATHER'S ILLNESS...
YES, BUT—
BOTH OF WHICH UPSET HIM, YOU MAY HAVE NOTICED!
STILL, YOU WARNED HIM THAT WE'D USE THEM AHEAD OF TIME...
AND THEN YOU TOOK HIM OUT TO LUNCH!
SO?
SO THAT DEFINITELY WASN'T PART OF OUR GAME PLAN...
ESPECIALLY SINCE WE WEREN'T PART OF THAT CONVERSATION...
AND SINCE THEN HE'S INSTANTLY SOLVED ALL HIS PARENTS' PROBLEMS!
THAT WAS A GOOD EXAMPLE OF CONFLICT RESOLUTION, I THOUGHT!
AND NOW WE'RE BEING SUBJECTED TO THIS NONSENSE!
WHAT EXACTLY DID YOU TALK ABOUT AT LUNCH, ANGIE?
...OH YEAH... LIKE THAT...

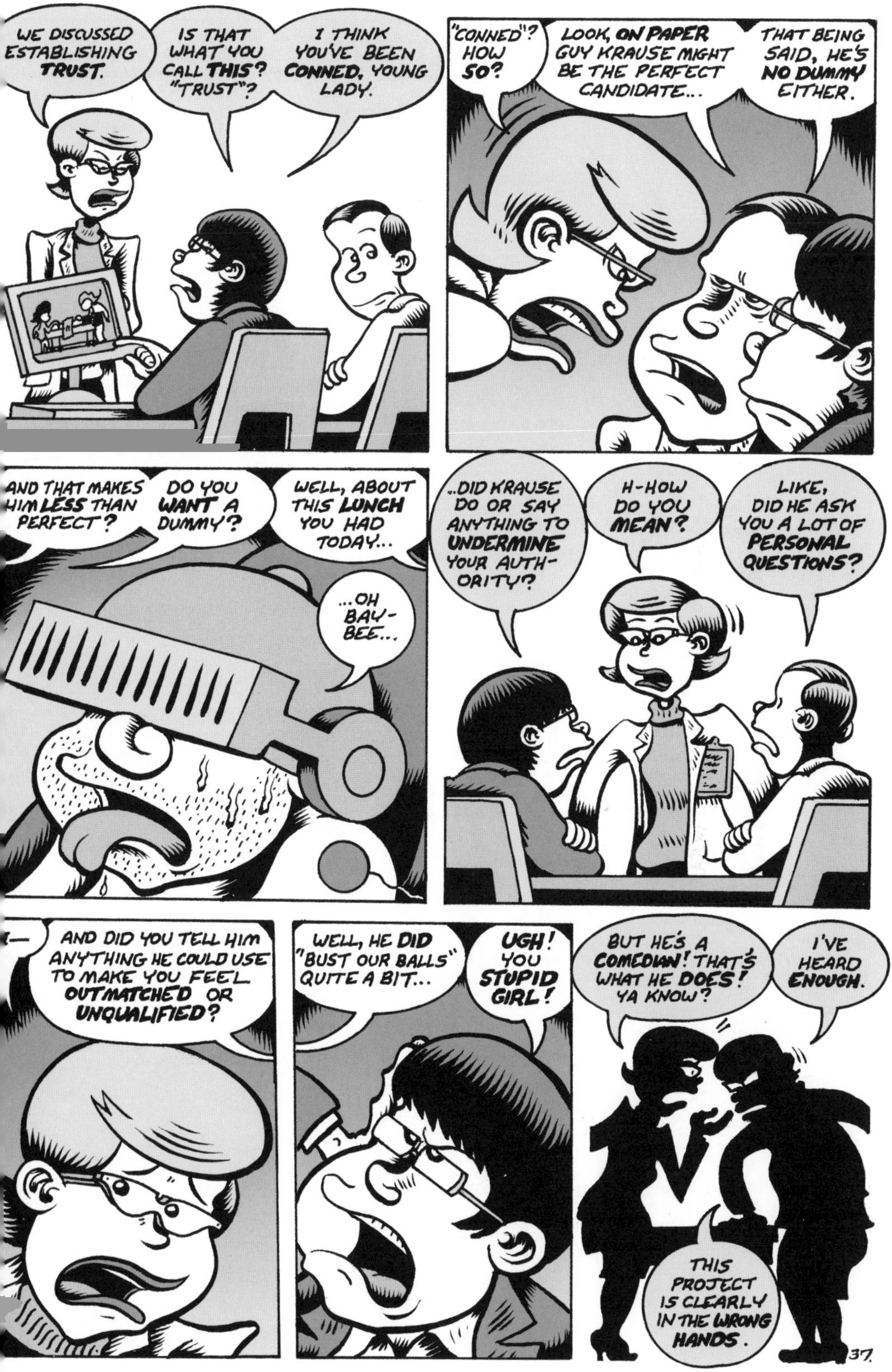
WE DISCUSSED ESTABLISHING **TRUST**.
IS THAT WHAT YOU CALL **THIS**? "TRUST"?
I THINK YOU'VE BEEN **CONNED**, YOUNG LADY.
"CONNED"? HOW **SO**?
LOOK, **ON PAPER** GUY KRAUSE MIGHT BE THE PERFECT CANDIDATE...
THAT BEING SAID, HE'S **NO DUMMY** EITHER.
AND THAT MAKES HIM **LESS** THAN PERFECT?
DO YOU **WANT** A DUMMY?
WELL, ABOUT THIS **LUNCH** YOU HAD TODAY...
...OH BAY-BEE...
...DID KRAUSE DO OR SAY ANYTHING TO **UNDERMINE** YOUR AUTH-ORITY?
H-HOW DO YOU **MEAN**?
LIKE, DID HE ASK YOU A LOT OF **PERSONAL QUESTIONS**?
AND DID YOU TELL HIM ANYTHING HE COULD USE TO MAKE YOU FEEL **OUTMATCHED** OR **UNQUALIFIED**?
WELL, HE **DID** "BUST OUR BALLS" QUITE A BIT...
UGH! YOU **STUPID GIRL**!
BUT HE'S A **COMEDIAN**! THAT'S WHAT HE **DOES**! YA KNOW?
I'VE HEARD **ENOUGH**.
THIS PROJECT IS CLEARLY IN THE **WRONG HANDS**.

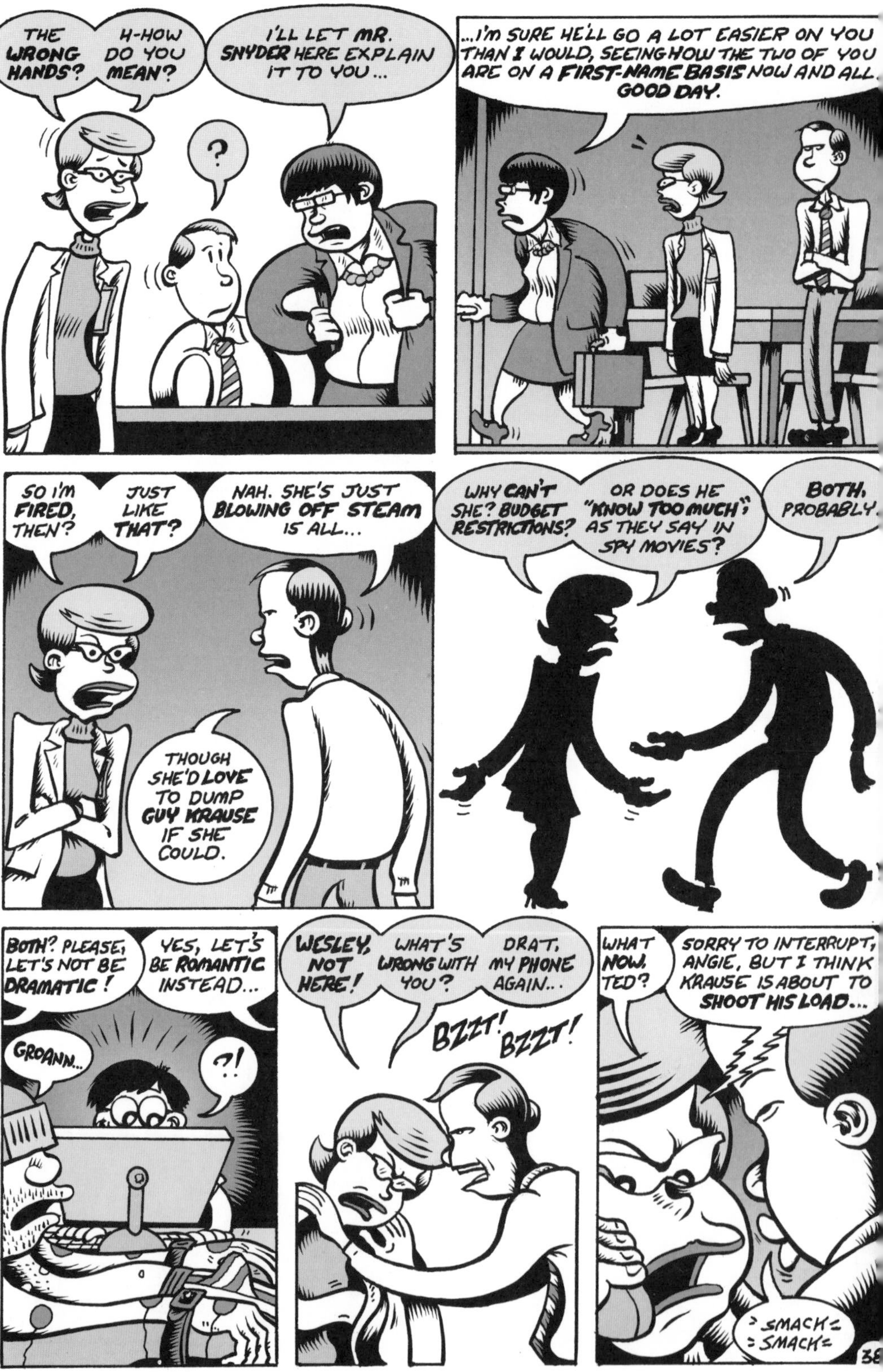
THE WRONG HANDS?
H-HOW DO YOU MEAN?
?
I'LL LET MR. SNYDER HERE EXPLAIN IT TO YOU...
...I'M SURE HE'LL GO A LOT EASIER ON YOU THAN I WOULD, SEEING HOW THE TWO OF YOU ARE ON A FIRST-NAME BASIS NOW AND ALL. GOOD DAY.
SO I'M FIRED, THEN?
JUST LIKE THAT?
NAH. SHE'S JUST BLOWING OFF STEAM IS ALL...
THOUGH SHE'D LOVE TO DUMP GUY KRAUSE IF SHE COULD.
WHY CAN'T SHE? BUDGET RESTRICTIONS?
OR DOES HE "KNOW TOO MUCH", AS THEY SAY IN SPY MOVIES?
BOTH, PROBABLY.
BOTH? PLEASE, LET'S NOT BE DRAMATIC!
YES, LET'S BE ROMANTIC INSTEAD...
GROANN...
?!
WESLEY, NOT HERE!
WHAT'S WRONG WITH YOU?
DRAT, MY PHONE AGAIN...
BZZT! BZZT!
WHAT NOW, TED?
SORRY TO INTERRUPT, ANGIE, BUT I THINK KRAUSE IS ABOUT TO SHOOT HIS LOAD...
SMACK
SMACK

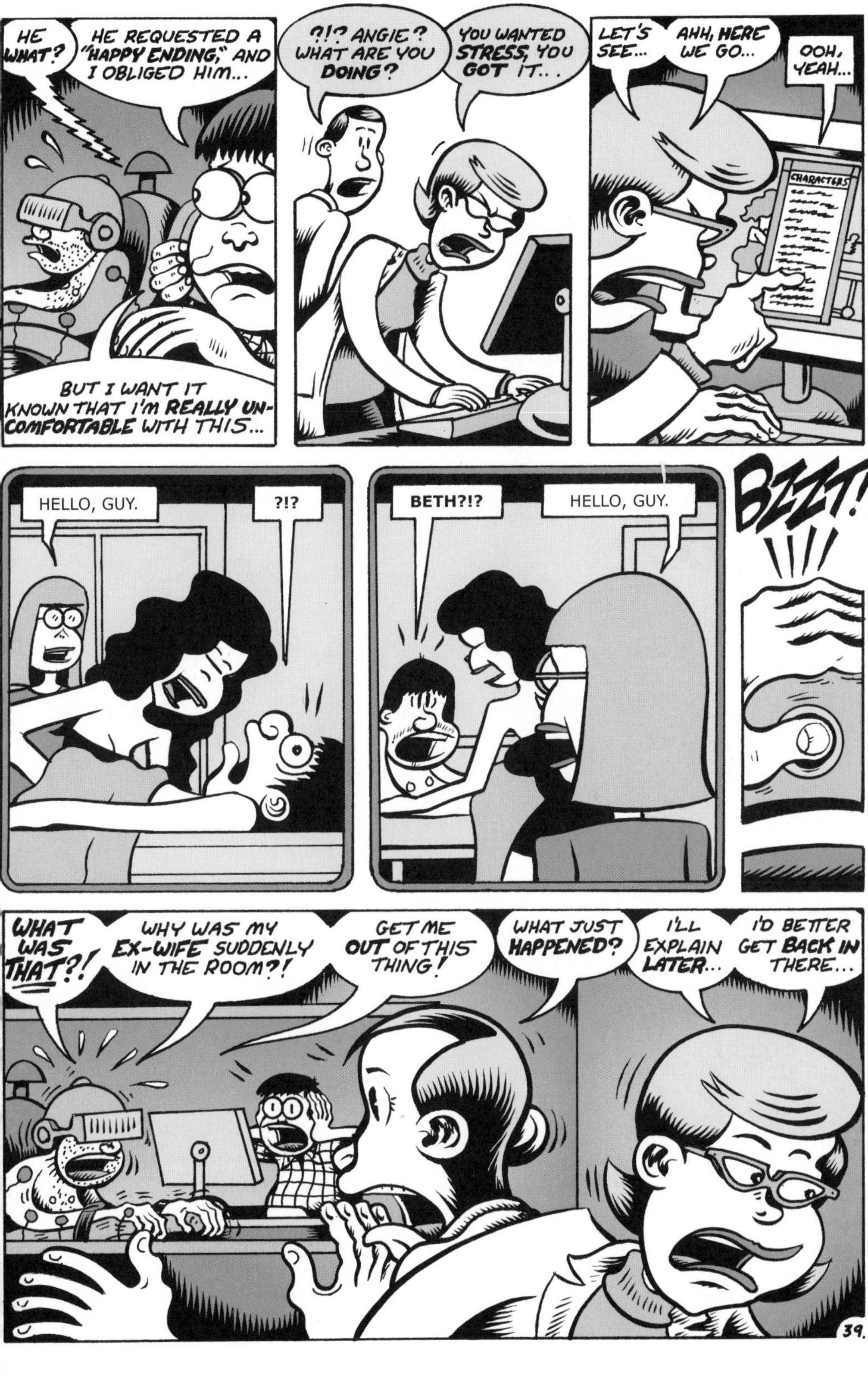
HE WHAT?
HE REQUESTED A "HAPPY ENDING," AND I OBLIGED HIM...
BUT I WANT IT KNOWN THAT I'M REALLY UN-COMFORTABLE WITH THIS...
?!? ANGIE? WHAT ARE YOU DOING?
YOU WANTED STRESS, YOU GOT IT...
LET'S SEE...
AHH, HERE WE GO...
OOH, YEAH...
CHARACTERS
HELLO, GUY.
?!?
BETH?!?
HELLO, GUY.
BZZZT!
WHAT WAS THAT?!
WHY WAS MY EX-WIFE SUDDENLY IN THE ROOM?!
GET ME OUT OF THIS THING!
WHAT JUST HAPPENED?
I'LL EXPLAIN LATER...
I'D BETTER GET BACK IN THERE...
39.

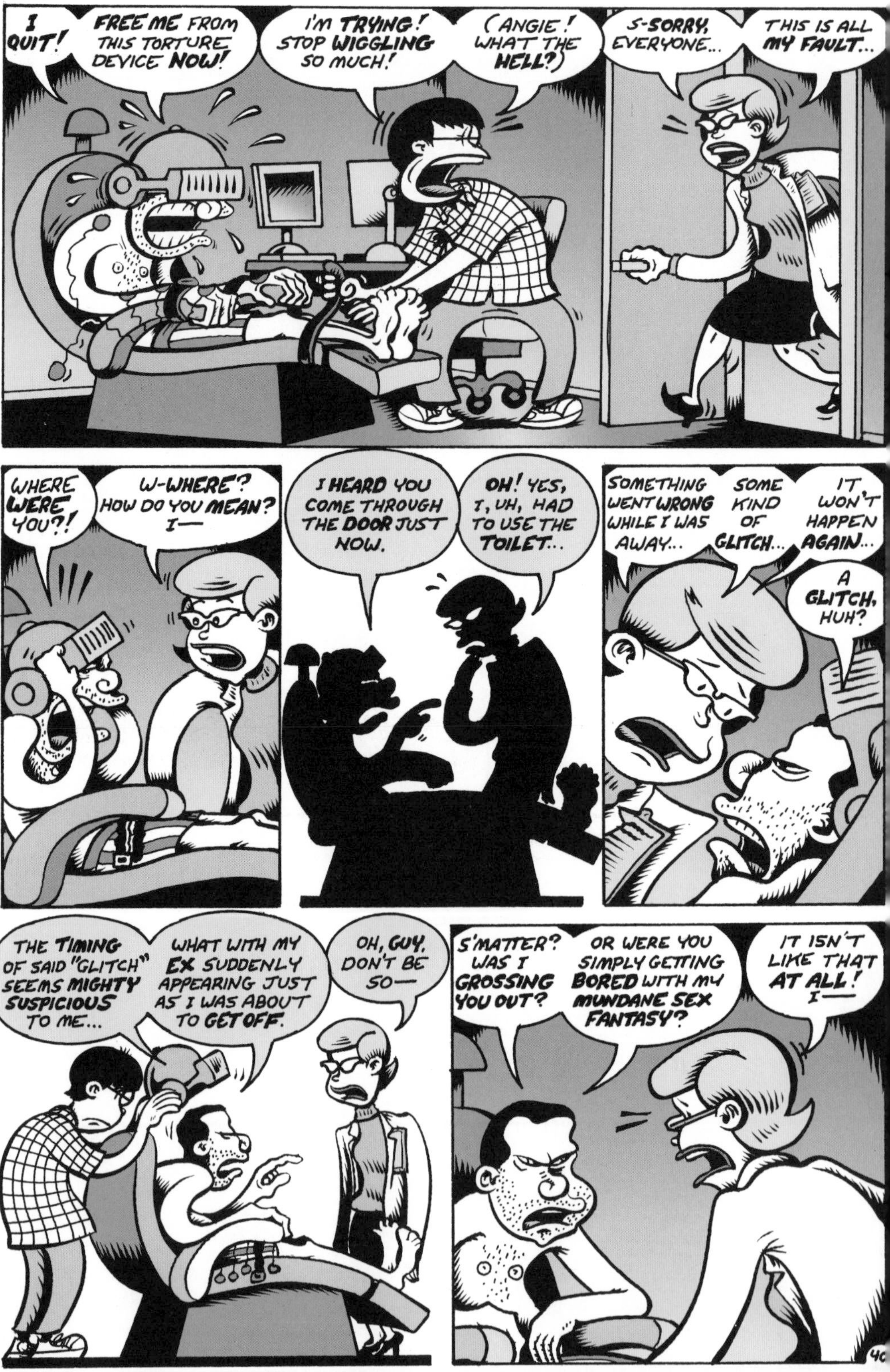
I QUIT!
FREE ME FROM THIS TORTURE DEVICE NOW!
I'M TRYING! STOP WIGGLING SO MUCH!
(ANGIE! WHAT THE HELL?)
S-SORRY, EVERYONE...
THIS IS ALL MY FAULT...
WHERE WERE YOU?!
W-WHERE? HOW DO YOU MEAN? I—
I HEARD YOU COME THROUGH THE DOOR JUST NOW.
OH! YES, I, UH, HAD TO USE THE TOILET...
SOMETHING WENT WRONG WHILE I WAS AWAY...
SOME KIND OF GLITCH...
IT WON'T HAPPEN AGAIN...
A GLITCH, HUH?
THE TIMING OF SAID "GLITCH" SEEMS MIGHTY SUSPICIOUS TO ME...
WHAT WITH MY EX SUDDENLY APPEARING JUST AS I WAS ABOUT TO GET OFF.
OH, GUY, DON'T BE SO—
S'MATTER? WAS I GROSSING YOU OUT?
OR WERE YOU SIMPLY GETTING BORED WITH MY MUNDANE SEX FANTASY?
IT ISN'T LIKE THAT AT ALL! I—

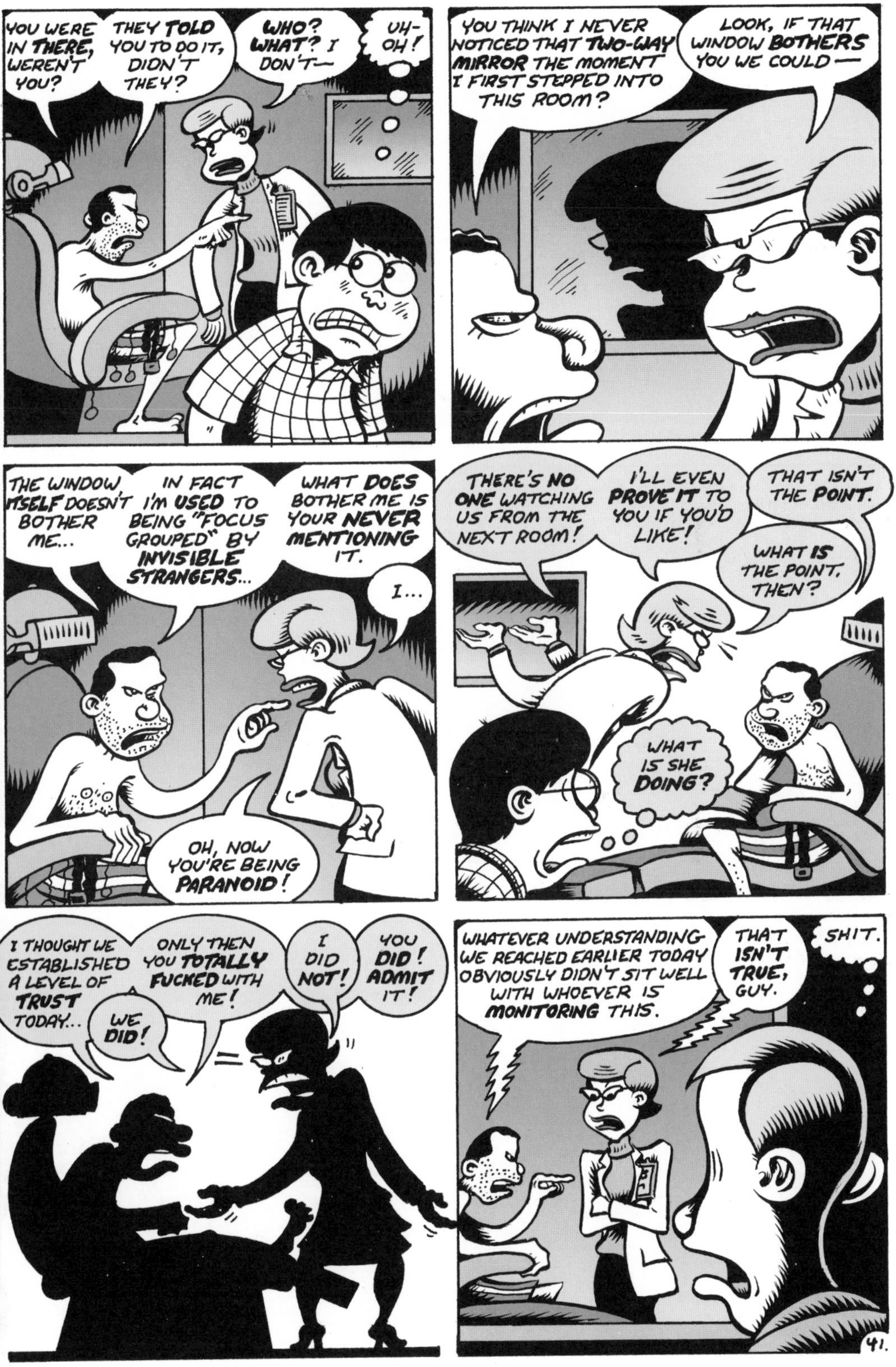
YOU WERE IN THERE, WEREN'T YOU?
THEY TOLD YOU TO DO IT, DIDN'T THEY?
WHO? WHAT? I DON'T—
UH-OH!
YOU THINK I NEVER NOTICED THAT TWO-WAY MIRROR THE MOMENT I FIRST STEPPED INTO THIS ROOM?
LOOK, IF THAT WINDOW BOTHERS YOU WE COULD—
THE WINDOW ITSELF DOESN'T BOTHER ME...
IN FACT I'M USED TO BEING "FOCUS GROUPED" BY INVISIBLE STRANGERS...
WHAT DOES BOTHER ME IS YOUR NEVER MENTIONING IT.
I...
OH, NOW YOU'RE BEING PARANOID!
THERE'S NO ONE WATCHING US FROM THE NEXT ROOM!
I'LL EVEN PROVE IT TO YOU IF YOU'D LIKE!
THAT ISN'T THE POINT.
WHAT IS THE POINT, THEN?
WHAT IS SHE DOING?
I THOUGHT WE ESTABLISHED A LEVEL OF TRUST TODAY...
WE DID!
ONLY THEN YOU TOTALLY FUCKED WITH ME!
I DID NOT!
YOU DID! ADMIT IT!
WHATEVER UNDERSTANDING WE REACHED EARLIER TODAY OBVIOUSLY DIDN'T SIT WELL WITH WHOEVER IS MONITORING THIS.
THAT ISN'T TRUE, GUY.
SHIT.

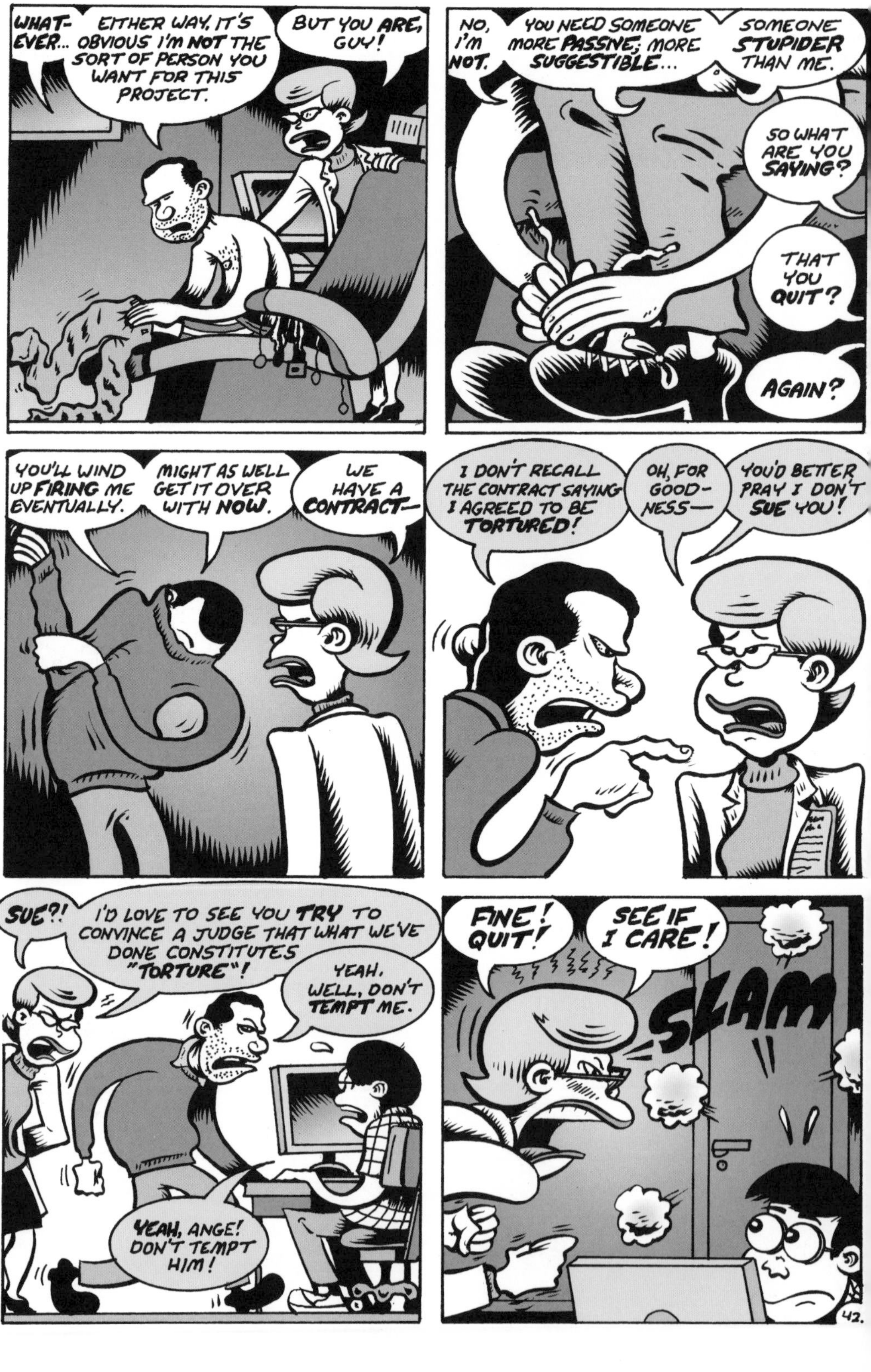
WHAT-EVER...
EITHER WAY, IT'S OBVIOUS I'M NOT THE SORT OF PERSON YOU WANT FOR THIS PROJECT.
BUT YOU ARE, GUY!
NO, I'M NOT.
YOU NEED SOMEONE MORE PASSIVE; MORE SUGGESTIBLE...
SOMEONE STUPIDER THAN ME.
SO WHAT ARE YOU SAYING?
THAT YOU QUIT?
AGAIN?
YOU'LL WIND UP FIRING ME EVENTUALLY.
MIGHT AS WELL GET IT OVER WITH NOW.
WE HAVE A CONTRACT—
I DON'T RECALL THE CONTRACT SAYING I AGREED TO BE TORTURED!
OH, FOR GOOD-NESS—
YOU'D BETTER PRAY I DON'T SUE YOU!
SUE?!
I'D LOVE TO SEE YOU TRY TO CONVINCE A JUDGE THAT WHAT WE'VE DONE CONSTITUTES "TORTURE"!
YEAH, WELL, DON'T TEMPT ME.
YEAH, ANGE! DON'T TEMPT HIM!
FINE! QUIT!
SEE IF I CARE!
SLAM

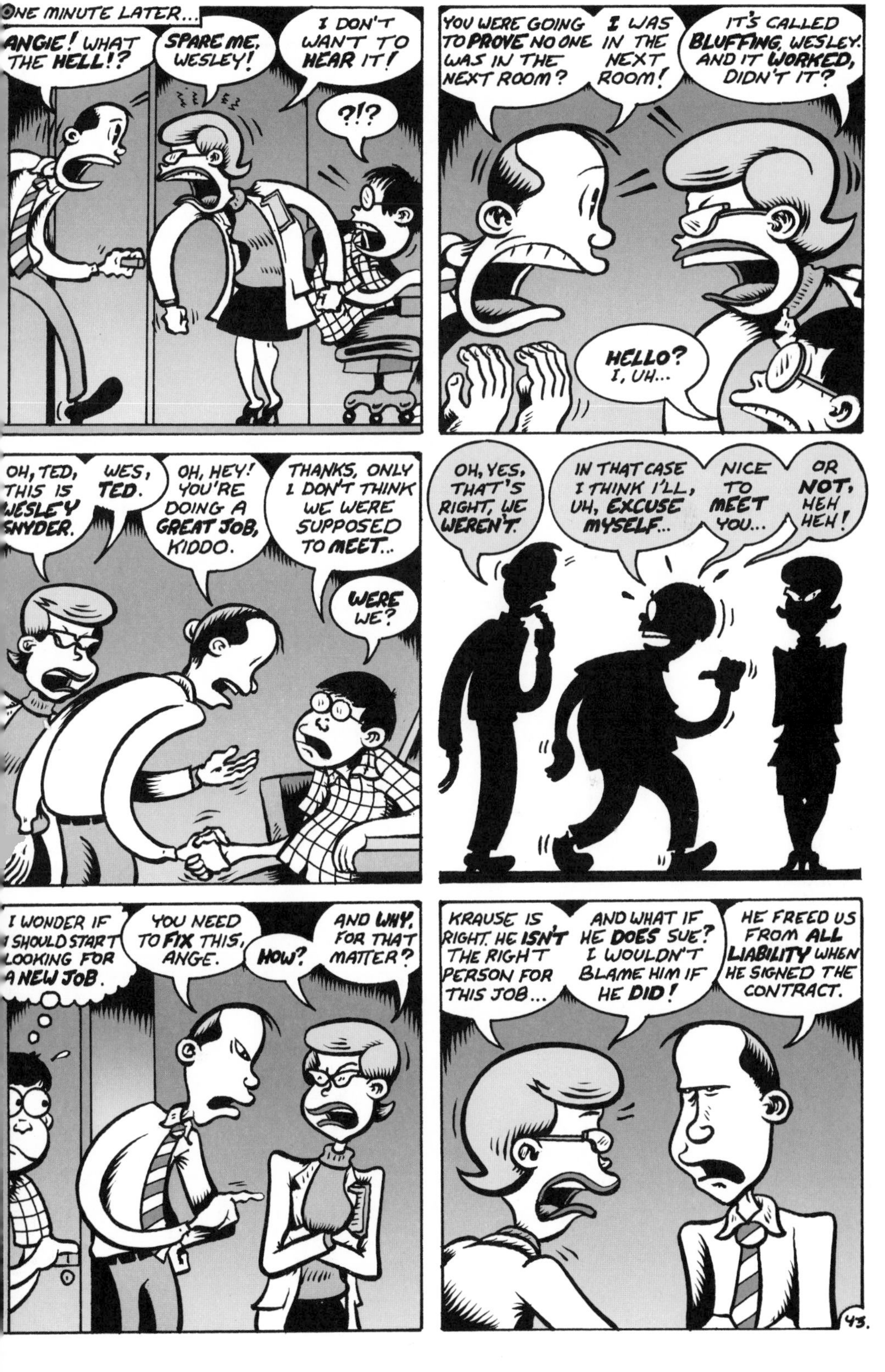
ONE MINUTE LATER...
ANGIE! WHAT THE HELL!?
SPARE ME, WESLEY!
I DON'T WANT TO HEAR IT!
?!?
YOU WERE GOING TO PROVE NO ONE WAS IN THE NEXT ROOM?
I WAS IN THE NEXT ROOM!
IT'S CALLED BLUFFING, WESLEY. AND IT WORKED, DIDN'T IT?
HELLO? I, UH...
OH, TED, THIS IS WESLEY SNYDER.
WES, TED.
OH, HEY! YOU'RE DOING A GREAT JOB, KIDDO.
THANKS, ONLY I DON'T THINK WE WERE SUPPOSED TO MEET...
WERE WE?
OH, YES, THAT'S RIGHT, WE WEREN'T.
IN THAT CASE I THINK I'LL, UH, EXCUSE MYSELF...
NICE TO MEET YOU...
OR NOT, HEH HEH!
I WONDER IF I SHOULD START LOOKING FOR A NEW JOB.
YOU NEED TO FIX THIS, ANGE.
HOW?
AND WHY, FOR THAT MATTER?
KRAUSE IS RIGHT. HE ISN'T THE RIGHT PERSON FOR THIS JOB...
AND WHAT IF HE DOES SUE? I WOULDN'T BLAME HIM IF HE DID!
HE FREED US FROM ALL LIABILITY WHEN HE SIGNED THE CONTRACT.

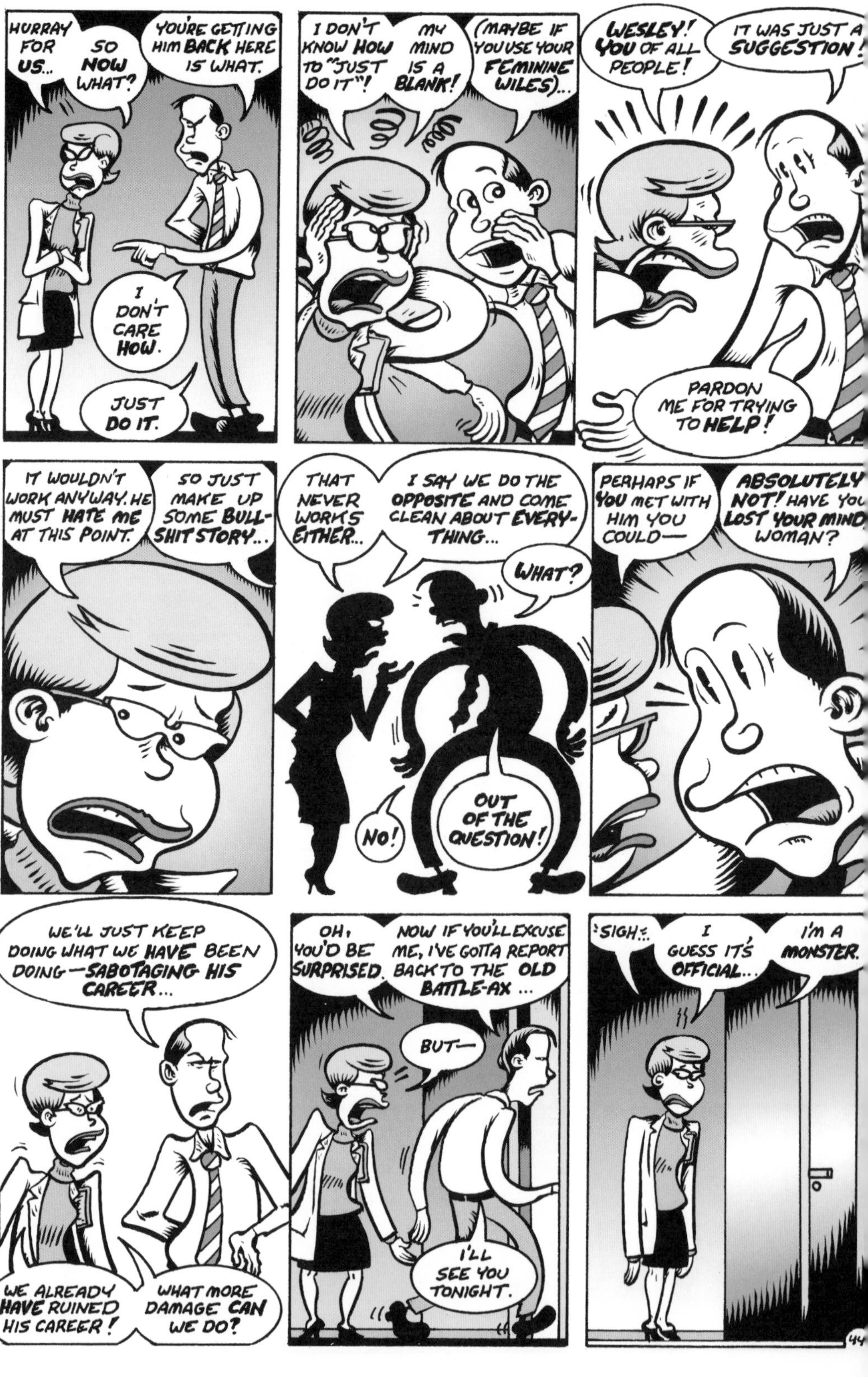
HURRAY FOR US...
SO NOW WHAT?
YOU'RE GETTING HIM BACK HERE IS WHAT.
I DON'T CARE HOW.
JUST DO IT.
I DON'T KNOW HOW TO "JUST DO IT"!
MY MIND IS A BLANK!
(MAYBE IF YOU USE YOUR FEMININE WILES)...
WESLEY! YOU OF ALL PEOPLE!
IT WAS JUST A SUGGESTION!
PARDON ME FOR TRYING TO HELP!
IT WOULDN'T WORK ANYWAY. HE MUST HATE ME AT THIS POINT.
SO JUST MAKE UP SOME BULL-SHIT STORY...
THAT NEVER WORKS EITHER...
I SAY WE DO THE OPPOSITE AND COME CLEAN ABOUT EVERY-THING...
WHAT?
NO!
OUT OF THE QUESTION!
PERHAPS IF YOU MET WITH HIM YOU COULD—
ABSOLUTELY NOT! HAVE YOU LOST YOUR MIND, WOMAN?
WE'LL JUST KEEP DOING WHAT WE HAVE BEEN DOING—SABOTAGING HIS CAREER...
WE ALREADY HAVE RUINED HIS CAREER!
WHAT MORE DAMAGE CAN WE DO?
OH, YOU'D BE SURPRISED.
NOW IF YOU'LL EXCUSE ME, I'VE GOTTA REPORT BACK TO THE OLD BATTLE-AX ...
BUT—
I'LL SEE YOU TONIGHT.
:SIGH:
I GUESS IT'S OFFICIAL...
I'M A MONSTER.
44

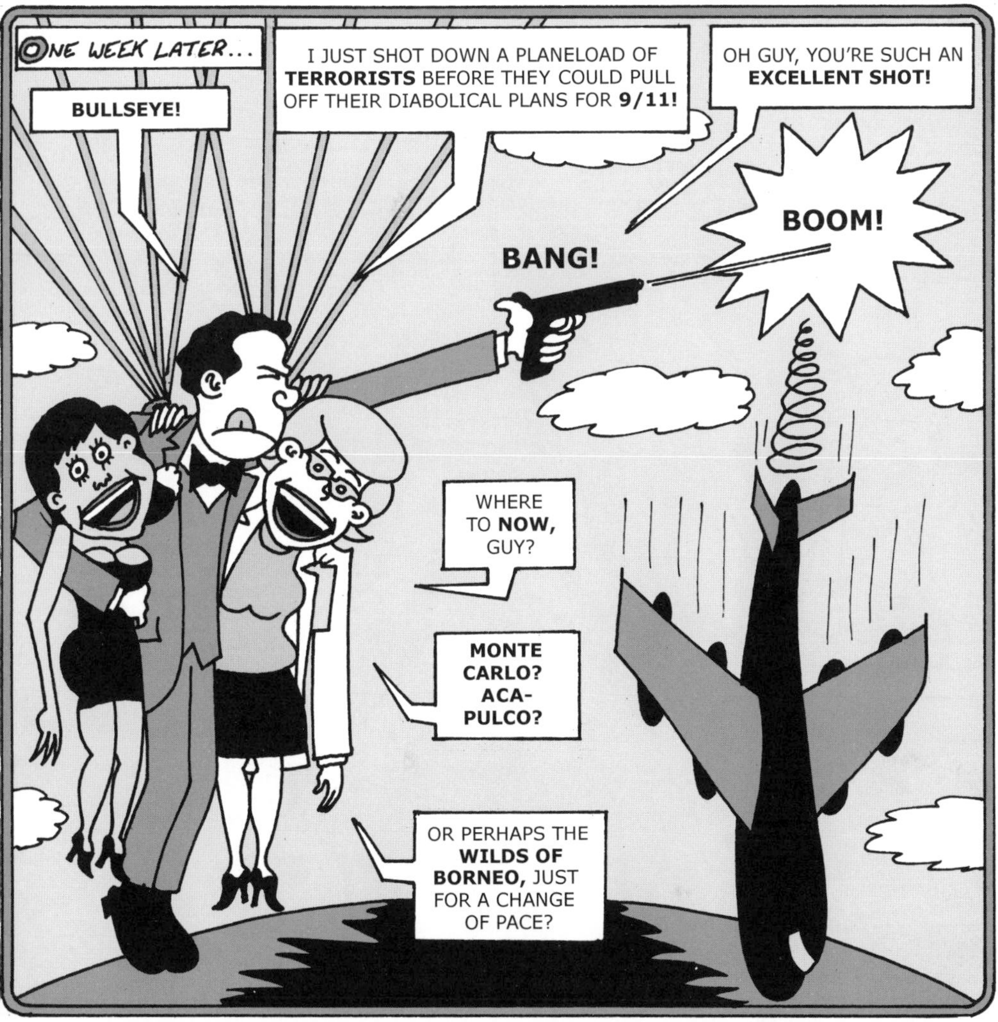
ONE WEEK LATER...
BULLSEYE!
I JUST SHOT DOWN A PLANELOAD OF **TERRORISTS** BEFORE THEY COULD PULL OFF THEIR DIABOLICAL PLANS FOR **9/11!**
OH GUY, YOU'RE SUCH AN **EXCELLENT SHOT!**
BOOM!
BANG!
WHERE TO **NOW,** GUY?
MONTE CARLO? ACA-PULCO?
OR PERHAPS THE **WILDS OF BORNEO,** JUST FOR A CHANGE OF PACE?

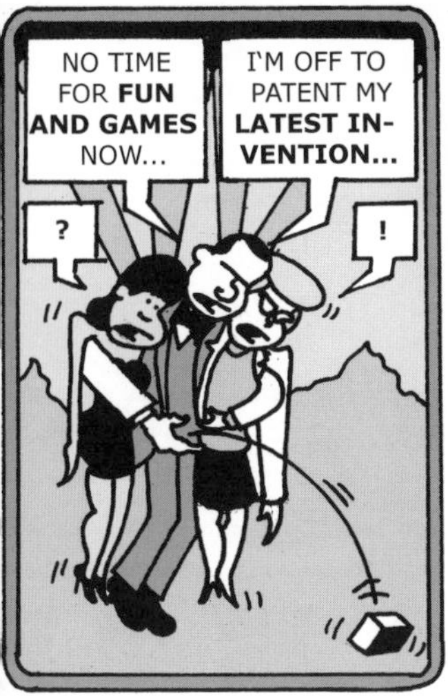
NO TIME FOR **FUN AND GAMES** NOW...
I'M OFF TO PATENT MY **LATEST IN-VENTION...**
?
!

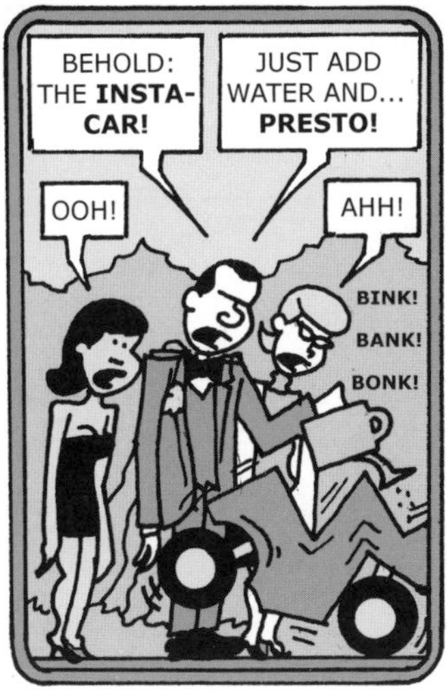
BEHOLD: THE **INSTA-CAR!**
JUST ADD WATER AND... **PRESTO!**
OOH!
AHH!
BINK!
BANK!
BONK!

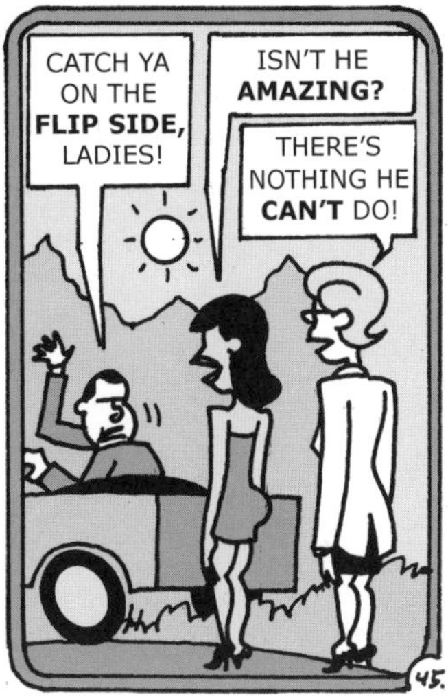
CATCH YA ON THE **FLIP SIDE,** LADIES!
ISN'T HE **AMAZING?**
THERE'S NOTHING HE **CAN'T** DO!

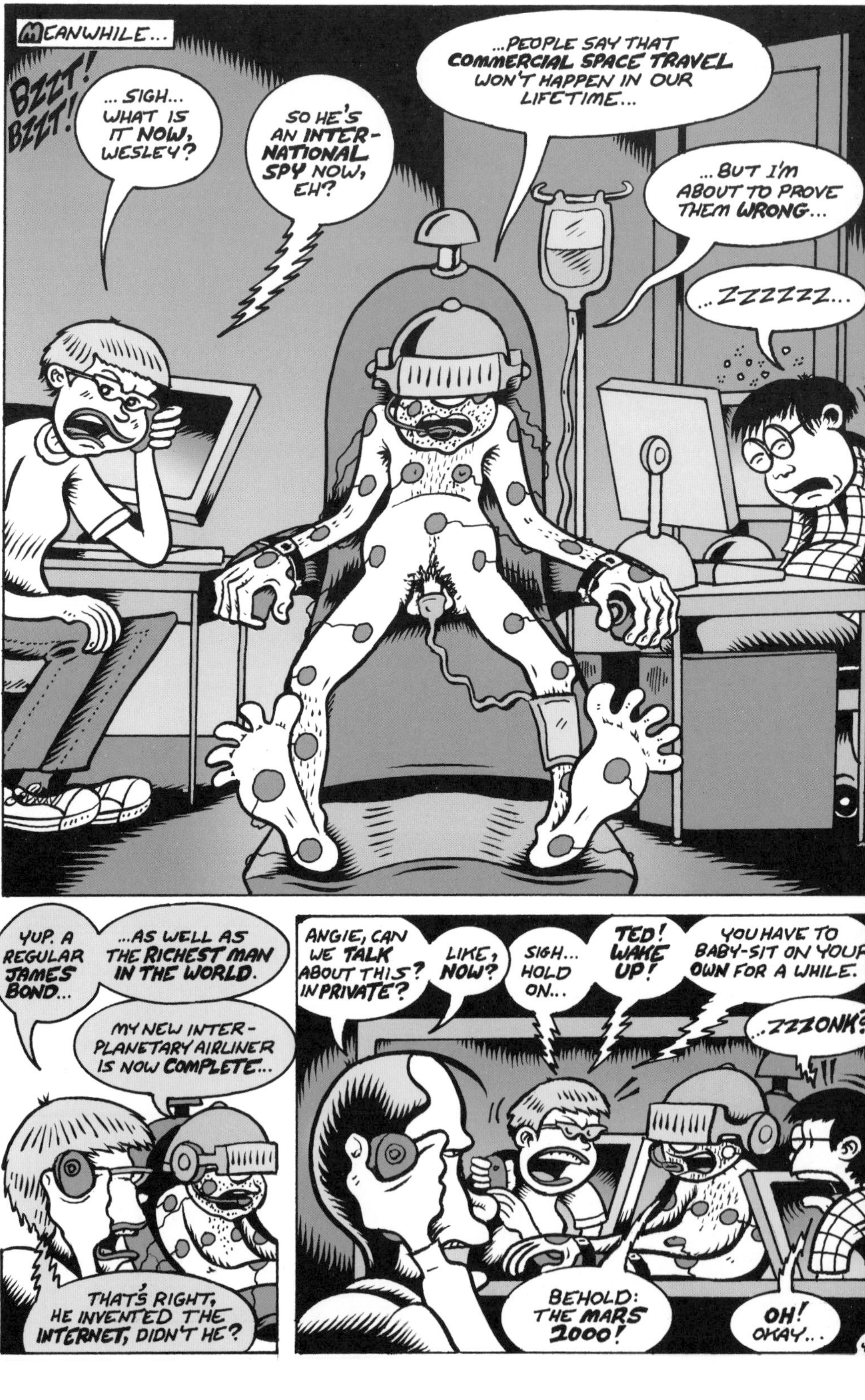
MEANWHILE...
BZZT! BZZT!
... SIGH... WHAT IS IT NOW, WESLEY?
SO HE'S AN INTER-NATIONAL SPY NOW, EH?
...PEOPLE SAY THAT COMMERCIAL SPACE TRAVEL WON'T HAPPEN IN OUR LIFETIME...
...BUT I'M ABOUT TO PROVE THEM WRONG...
...ZZZZZZ...
YUP. A REGULAR JAMES BOND...
...AS WELL AS THE RICHEST MAN IN THE WORLD.
MY NEW INTER-PLANETARY AIRLINER IS NOW COMPLETE...
THAT'S RIGHT, HE INVENTED THE INTERNET, DIDN'T HE?
ANGIE, CAN WE TALK ABOUT THIS? IN PRIVATE?
LIKE, NOW?
SIGH... HOLD ON...
TED! WAKE UP!
YOU HAVE TO BABY-SIT ON YOUR OWN FOR A WHILE.
..ZZZONK?
BEHOLD: THE MARS 2000!
OH! OKAY...

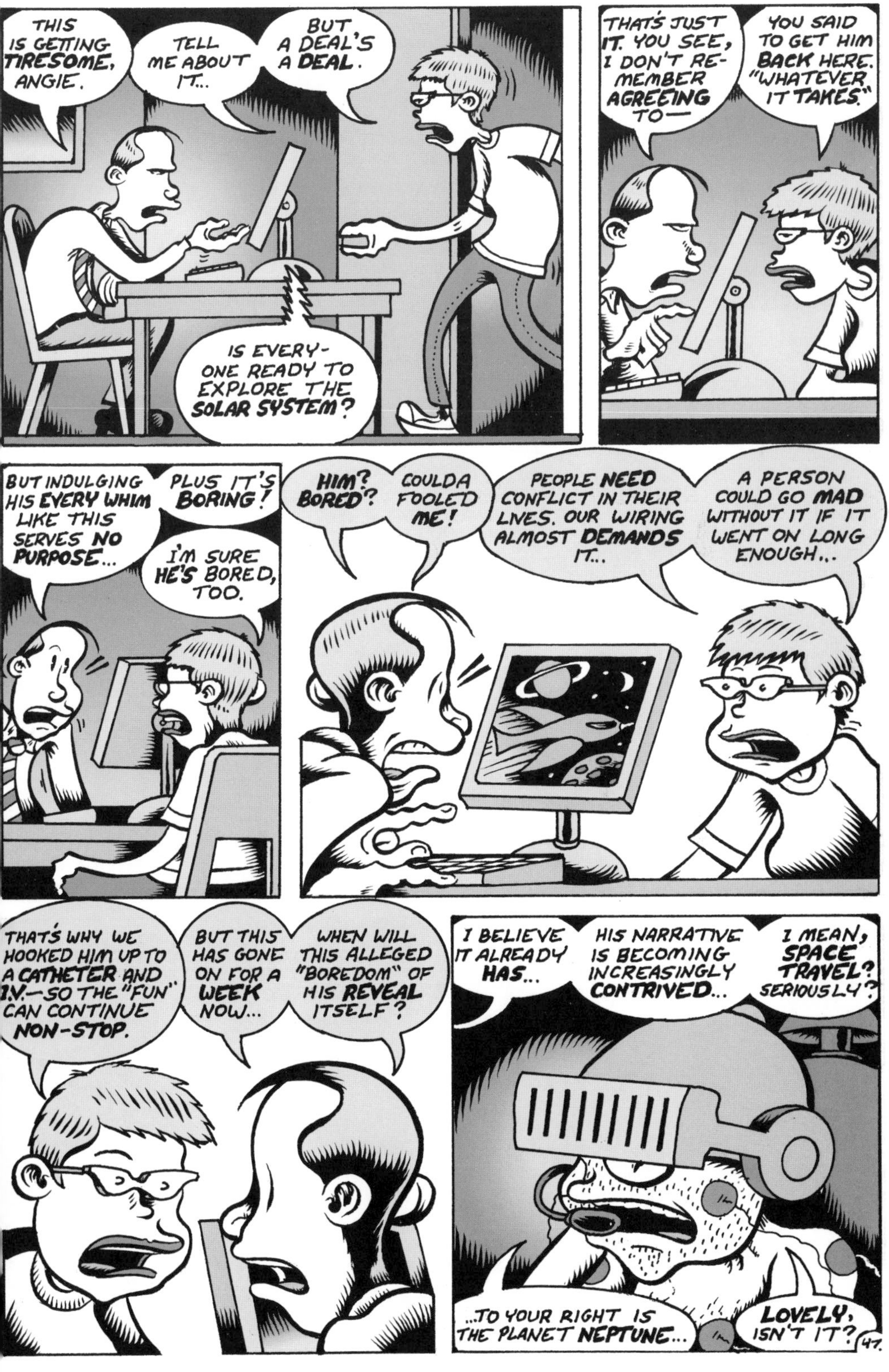
THIS IS GETTING TIRESOME, ANGIE.
TELL ME ABOUT IT...
BUT A DEAL'S A DEAL.
IS EVERYONE READY TO EXPLORE THE SOLAR SYSTEM?
THAT'S JUST IT. YOU SEE, I DON'T REMEMBER AGREEING TO—
YOU SAID TO GET HIM BACK HERE. "WHATEVER IT TAKES."
BUT INDULGING HIS EVERY WHIM LIKE THIS SERVES NO PURPOSE...
PLUS IT'S BORING!
I'M SURE HE'S BORED, TOO.
HIM? BORED?
COULDA FOOLED ME!
PEOPLE NEED CONFLICT IN THEIR LIVES. OUR WIRING ALMOST DEMANDS IT...
A PERSON COULD GO MAD WITHOUT IT IF IT WENT ON LONG ENOUGH...
THAT'S WHY WE HOOKED HIM UP TO A CATHETER AND I.V.—SO THE "FUN" CAN CONTINUE NON-STOP.
BUT THIS HAS GONE ON FOR A WEEK NOW...
WHEN WILL THIS ALLEGED "BOREDOM" OF HIS REVEAL ITSELF?
I BELIEVE IT ALREADY HAS...
HIS NARRATIVE IS BECOMING INCREASINGLY CONTRIVED...
I MEAN, SPACE TRAVEL? SERIOUSLY?
...TO YOUR RIGHT IS THE PLANET NEPTUNE...
LOVELY, ISN'T IT?

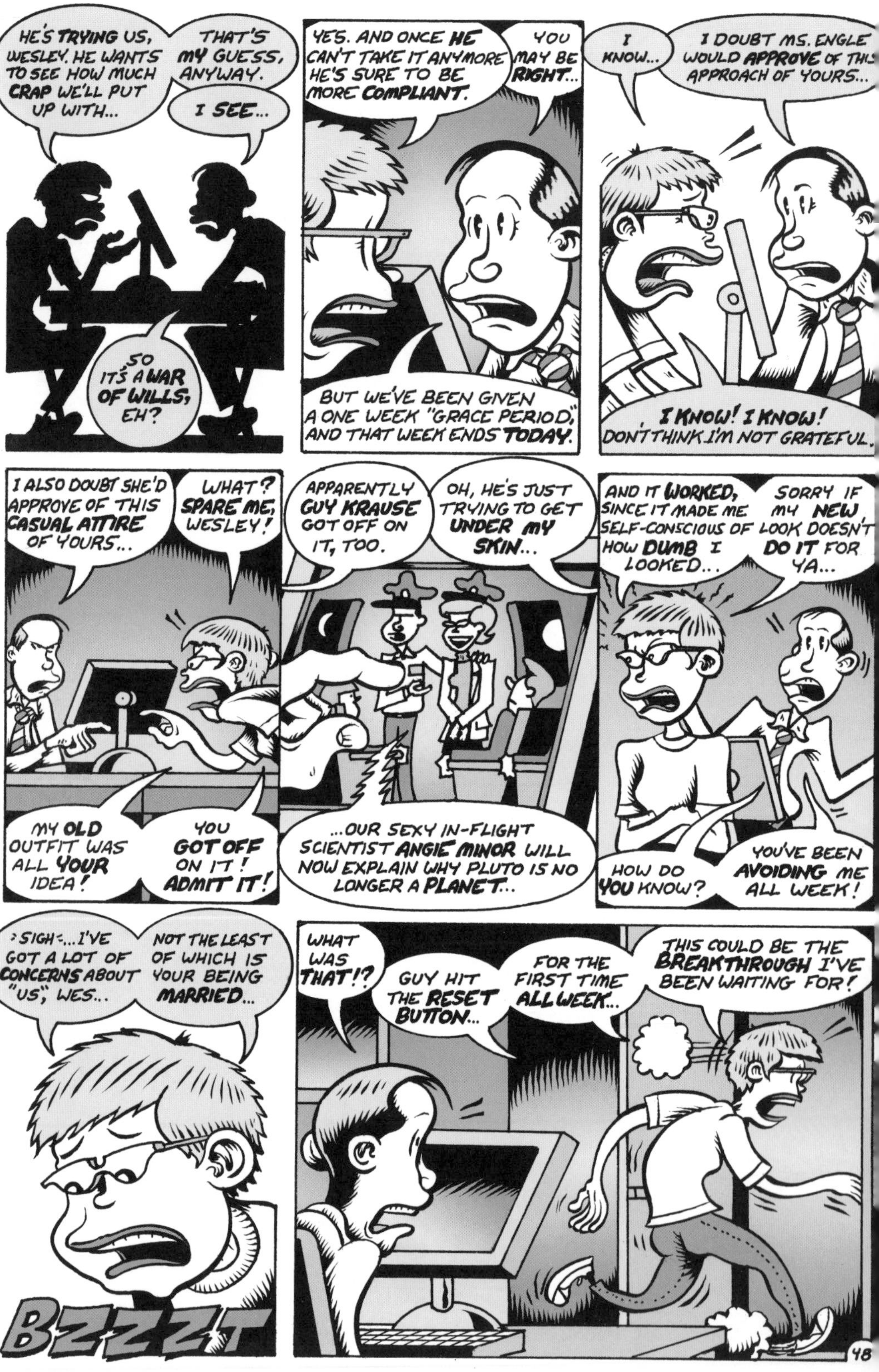
HE'S TRYING US, WESLEY. HE WANTS TO SEE HOW MUCH CRAP WE'LL PUT UP WITH...
THAT'S MY GUESS, ANYWAY.
I SEE...
SO IT'S A WAR OF WILLS, EH?
YES. AND ONCE HE CAN'T TAKE IT ANYMORE HE'S SURE TO BE MORE COMPLIANT.
YOU MAY BE RIGHT...
BUT WE'VE BEEN GIVEN A ONE WEEK "GRACE PERIOD," AND THAT WEEK ENDS TODAY.
I KNOW...
I DOUBT MS. ENGLE WOULD APPROVE OF THIS APPROACH OF YOURS...
I KNOW! I KNOW! DON'T THINK I'M NOT GRATEFUL.
I ALSO DOUBT SHE'D APPROVE OF THIS CASUAL ATTIRE OF YOURS...
WHAT? SPARE ME, WESLEY!
MY OLD OUTFIT WAS ALL YOUR IDEA!
YOU GOT OFF ON IT! ADMIT IT!
APPARENTLY GUY KRAUSE GOT OFF ON IT, TOO.
OH, HE'S JUST TRYING TO GET UNDER MY SKIN...
...OUR SEXY IN-FLIGHT SCIENTIST ANGIE MINOR WILL NOW EXPLAIN WHY PLUTO IS NO LONGER A PLANET...
AND IT WORKED, SINCE IT MADE ME SELF-CONSCIOUS OF HOW DUMB I LOOKED...
SORRY IF MY NEW LOOK DOESN'T DO IT FOR YA...
HOW DO YOU KNOW?
YOU'VE BEEN AVOIDING ME ALL WEEK!
-SIGH-...I'VE GOT A LOT OF CONCERNS ABOUT "US," WES...
NOT THE LEAST OF WHICH IS YOUR BEING MARRIED...
BZZZT
WHAT WAS THAT!?
GUY HIT THE RESET BUTTON...
FOR THE FIRST TIME ALL WEEK...
THIS COULD BE THE BREAKTHROUGH I'VE BEEN WAITING FOR!

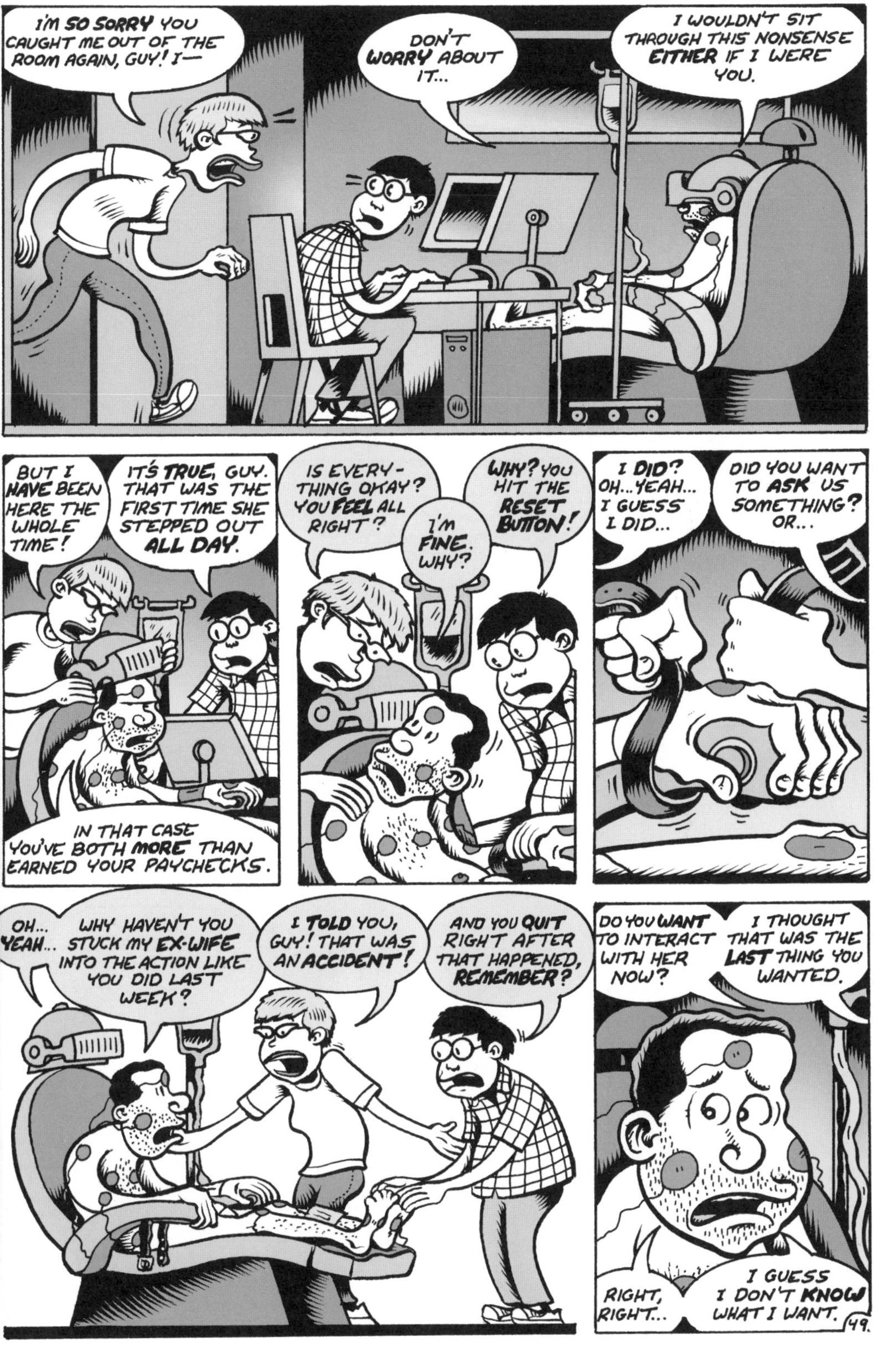
I'M SO SORRY YOU CAUGHT ME OUT OF THE ROOM AGAIN, GUY! I—
DON'T WORRY ABOUT IT...
I WOULDN'T SIT THROUGH THIS NONSENSE EITHER IF I WERE YOU.
BUT I HAVE BEEN HERE THE WHOLE TIME!
IT'S TRUE, GUY. THAT WAS THE FIRST TIME SHE STEPPED OUT ALL DAY.
IN THAT CASE YOU'VE BOTH MORE THAN EARNED YOUR PAYCHECKS.
IS EVERY-THING OKAY? YOU FEEL ALL RIGHT?
I'M FINE. WHY?
WHY? YOU HIT THE RESET BUTTON!
I DID? OH...YEAH... I GUESS I DID...
DID YOU WANT TO ASK US SOMETHING? OR...
OH... YEAH...
WHY HAVEN'T YOU STUCK MY EX-WIFE INTO THE ACTION LIKE YOU DID LAST WEEK?
I TOLD YOU, GUY! THAT WAS AN ACCIDENT!
AND YOU QUIT RIGHT AFTER THAT HAPPENED, REMEMBER?
DO YOU WANT TO INTERACT WITH HER NOW?
I THOUGHT THAT WAS THE LAST THING YOU WANTED.
RIGHT, RIGHT...
I GUESS I DON'T KNOW WHAT I WANT.

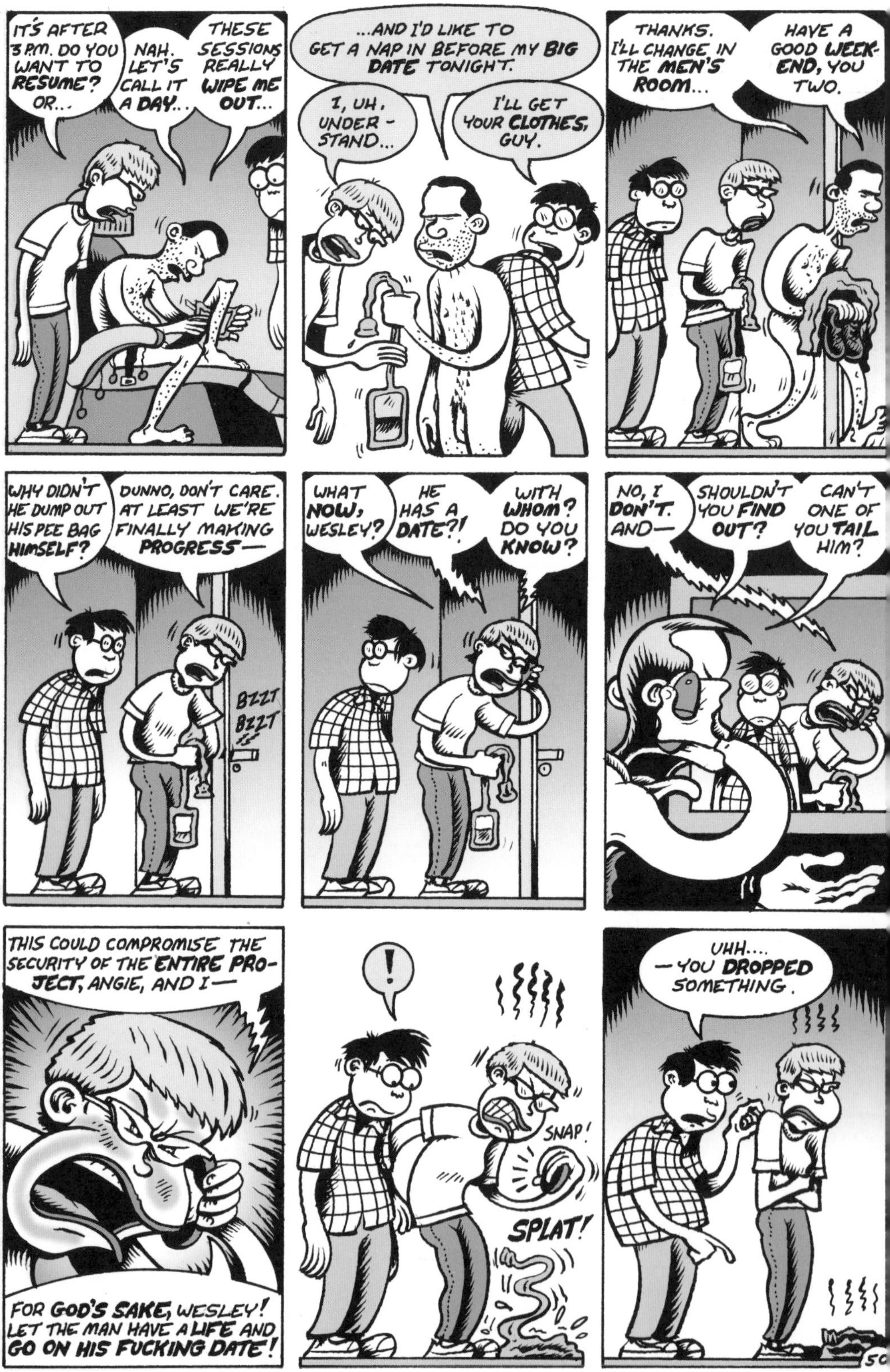
IT'S AFTER 3 P.M. DO YOU WANT TO RESUME? OR...
NAH. LET'S CALL IT A DAY...
THESE SESSIONS REALLY WIPE ME OUT...
...AND I'D LIKE TO GET A NAP IN BEFORE MY BIG DATE TONIGHT.
I, UH, UNDER-STAND...
I'LL GET YOUR CLOTHES, GUY.
THANKS. I'LL CHANGE IN THE MEN'S ROOM...
HAVE A GOOD WEEK-END, YOU TWO.
WHY DIDN'T HE DUMP OUT HIS PEE BAG HIMSELF?
DUNNO, DON'T CARE. AT LEAST WE'RE FINALLY MAKING PROGRESS—
BZZT BZZT
WHAT NOW, WESLEY?
HE HAS A DATE?!
WITH WHOM? DO YOU KNOW?
NO, I DON'T. AND—
SHOULDN'T YOU FIND OUT?
CAN'T ONE OF YOU TAIL HIM?
THIS COULD COMPROMISE THE SECURITY OF THE ENTIRE PRO-JECT, ANGIE, AND I—
FOR GOD'S SAKE, WESLEY! LET THE MAN HAVE A LIFE AND GO ON HIS FUCKING DATE!
!
SNAP!
SPLAT!
UHH.... —YOU DROPPED SOMETHING.

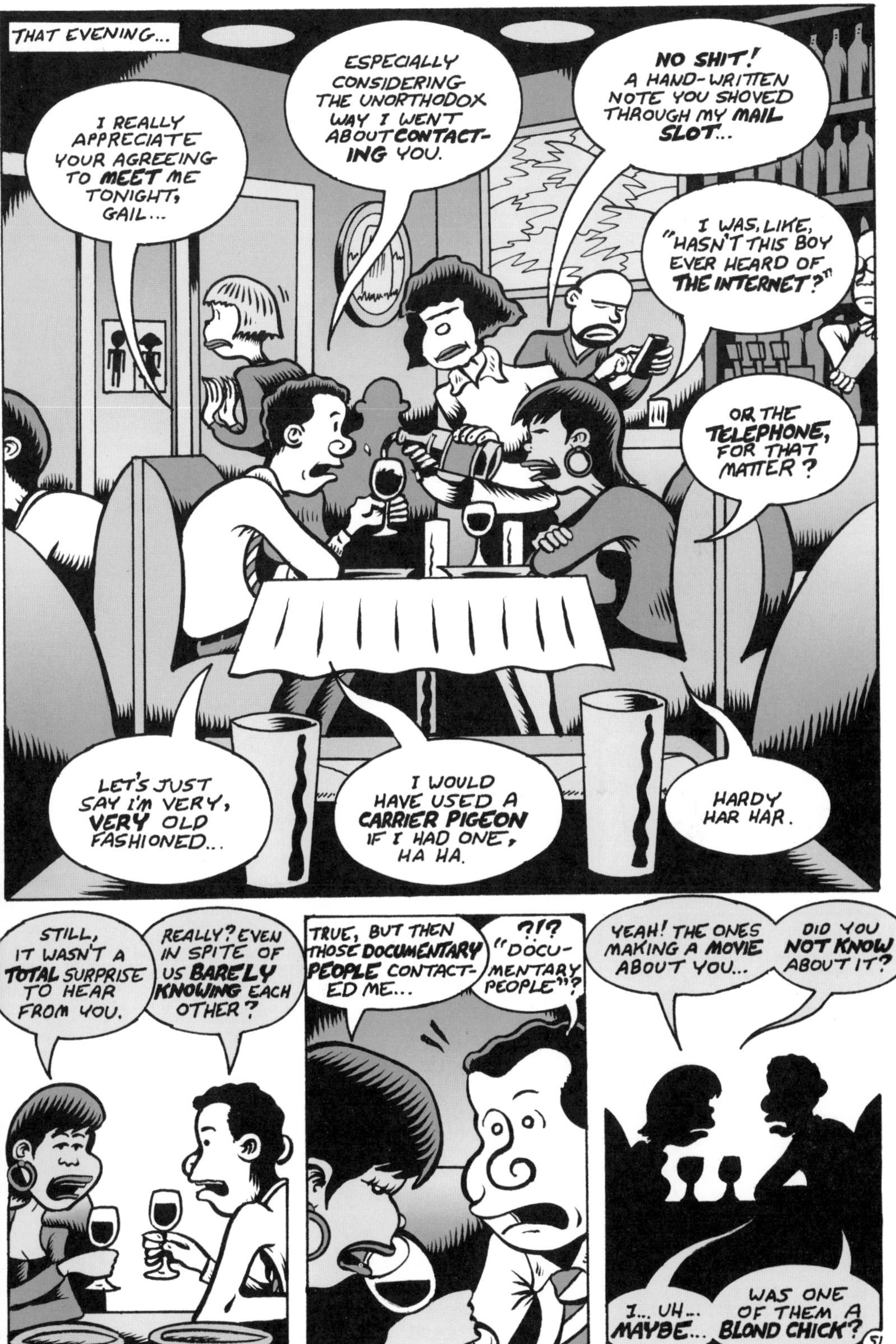

THAT EVENING...
I REALLY APPRECIATE YOUR AGREEING TO **MEET** ME TONIGHT, GAIL...
ESPECIALLY CONSIDERING THE UNORTHODOX WAY I WENT ABOUT **CONTACTING** YOU.
NO SHIT! A HAND-WRITTEN NOTE YOU SHOVED THROUGH MY **MAIL SLOT**...
I WAS, LIKE, "HASN'T THIS BOY EVER HEARD OF **THE INTERNET**?"
OR THE **TELEPHONE,** FOR THAT MATTER?
LET'S JUST SAY I'M VERY, **VERY** OLD FASHIONED...
I WOULD HAVE USED A **CARRIER PIGEON** IF I HAD ONE, HA HA.
HARDY HAR HAR.
STILL, IT WASN'T A **TOTAL** SURPRISE TO HEAR FROM YOU.
REALLY? EVEN IN SPITE OF US **BARELY KNOWING** EACH OTHER?
TRUE, BUT THEN THOSE **DOCUMENTARY PEOPLE** CONTACTED ME...
?!? "DOCUMENTARY PEOPLE"?
YEAH! THE ONES MAKING A **MOVIE** ABOUT YOU...
DID YOU **NOT KNOW** ABOUT IT?
I... UH... **MAYBE**...
WAS ONE OF THEM A **BLOND CHICK**?

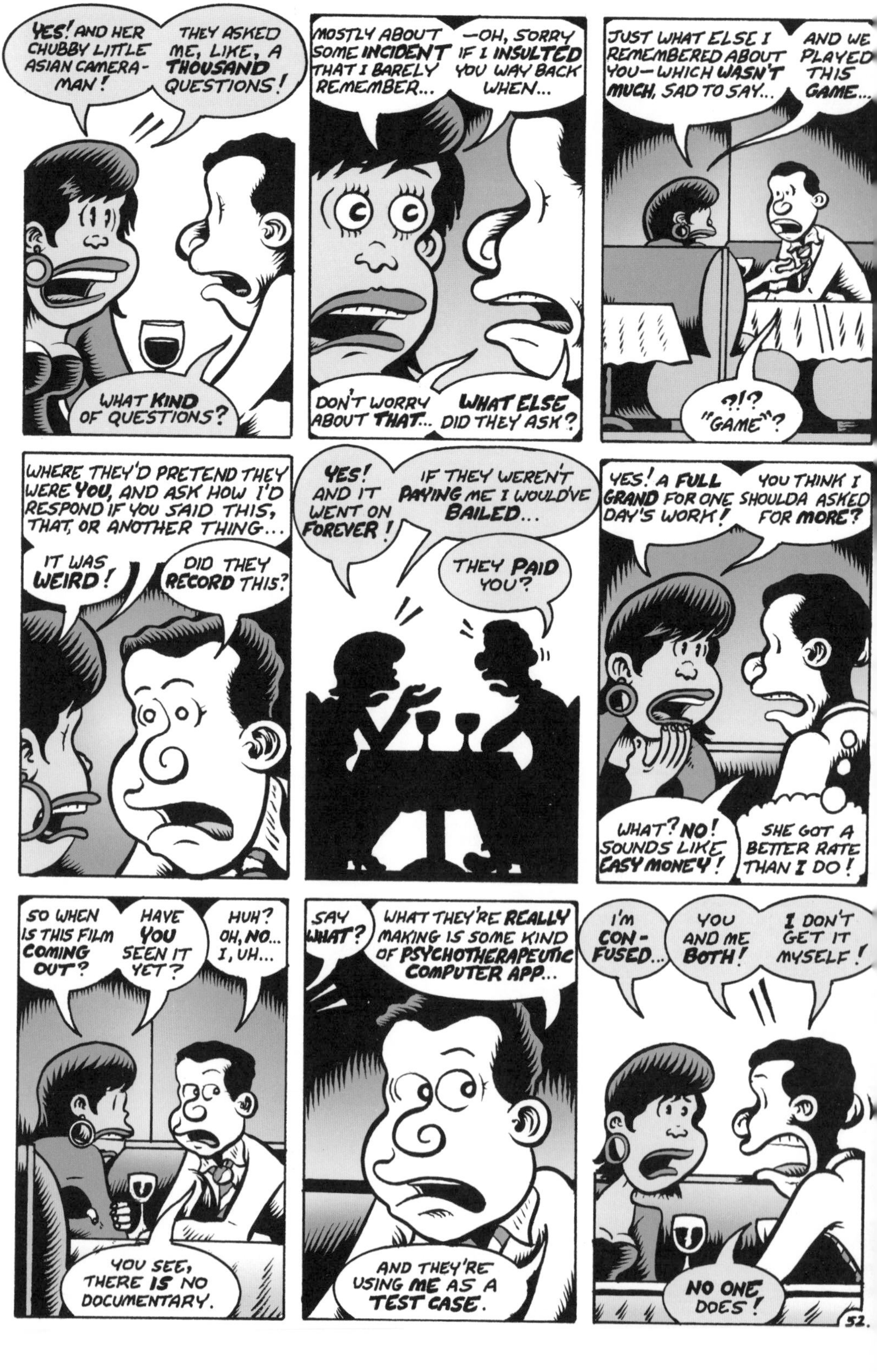
YES! AND HER CHUBBY LITTLE ASIAN CAMERA-MAN!
THEY ASKED ME, LIKE, A THOUSAND QUESTIONS!
WHAT KIND OF QUESTIONS?
MOSTLY ABOUT SOME INCIDENT THAT I BARELY REMEMBER...
—OH, SORRY IF I INSULTED YOU WAY BACK WHEN...
DON'T WORRY ABOUT THAT...
WHAT ELSE DID THEY ASK?
JUST WHAT ELSE I REMEMBERED ABOUT YOU—WHICH WASN'T MUCH, SAD TO SAY...
AND WE PLAYED THIS GAME...
?!? "GAME"?
WHERE THEY'D PRETEND THEY WERE YOU, AND ASK HOW I'D RESPOND IF YOU SAID THIS, THAT, OR ANOTHER THING...
IT WAS WEIRD!
DID THEY RECORD THIS?
YES! AND IT WENT ON FOREVER!
IF THEY WEREN'T PAYING ME I WOULD'VE BAILED...
THEY PAID YOU?
YES! A FULL GRAND FOR ONE DAY'S WORK!
YOU THINK I SHOULDA ASKED FOR MORE?
WHAT? NO! SOUNDS LIKE EASY MONEY!
SHE GOT A BETTER RATE THAN I DO!
SO WHEN IS THIS FILM COMING OUT?
HAVE YOU SEEN IT YET?
HUH? OH, NO... I, UH...
YOU SEE, THERE IS NO DOCUMENTARY.
SAY WHAT?
WHAT THEY'RE REALLY MAKING IS SOME KIND OF PSYCHOTHERAPEUTIC COMPUTER APP...
AND THEY'RE USING ME AS A TEST CASE.
I'M CON-FUSED...
YOU AND ME BOTH!
I DON'T GET IT MYSELF!
NO ONE DOES!

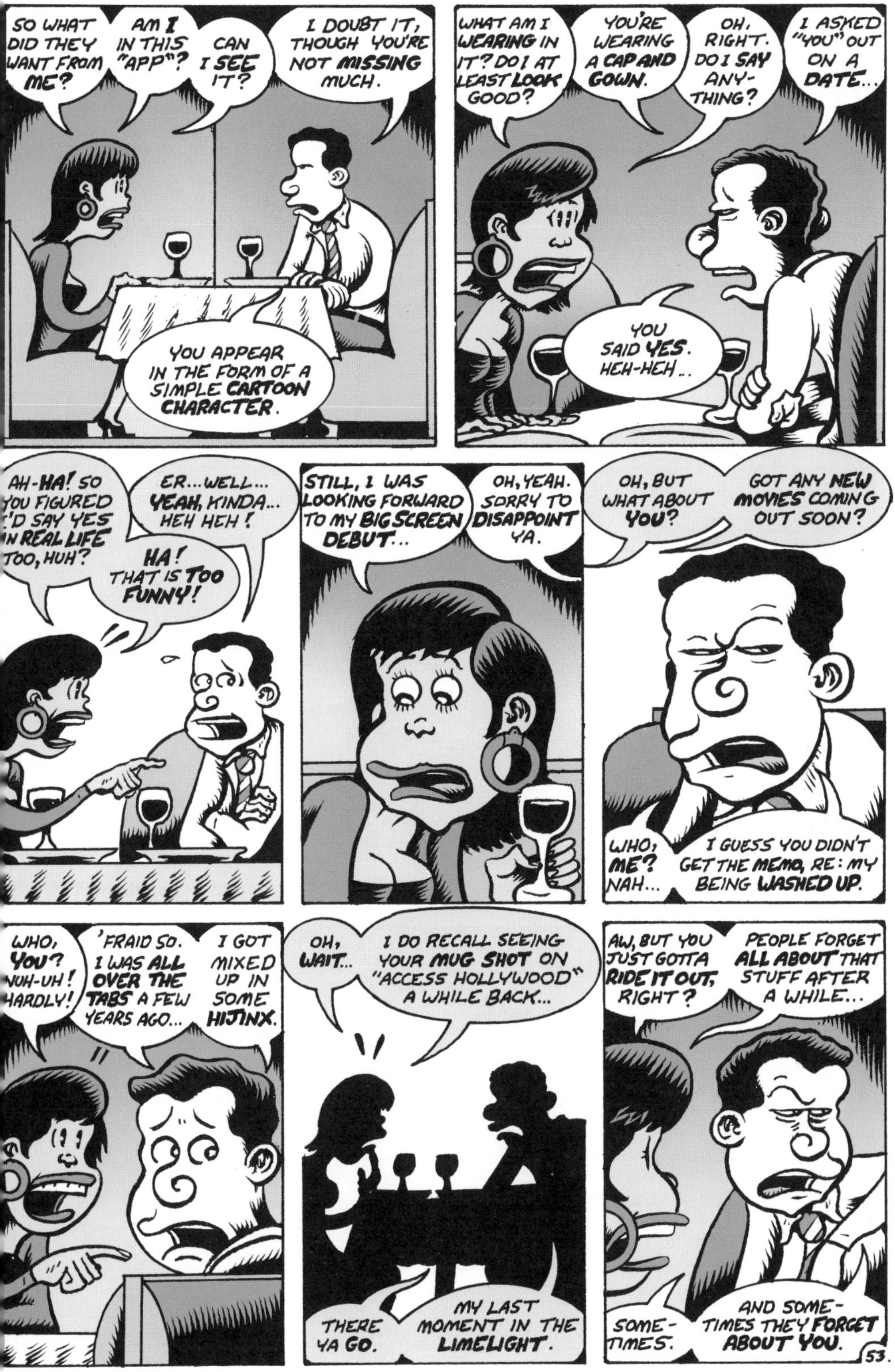
SO WHAT DID THEY WANT FROM ME?
AM I IN THIS "APP"?
CAN I SEE IT?
I DOUBT IT, THOUGH YOU'RE NOT MISSING MUCH.
YOU APPEAR IN THE FORM OF A SIMPLE CARTOON CHARACTER.
WHAT AM I WEARING IN IT? DO I AT LEAST LOOK GOOD?
YOU'RE WEARING A CAP AND GOWN.
OH, RIGHT. DO I SAY ANY-THING?
I ASKED "YOU" OUT ON A DATE...
YOU SAID YES. HEH-HEH...
AH-HA! SO YOU FIGURED I'D SAY YES IN REAL LIFE TOO, HUH?
ER...WELL... YEAH, KINDA... HEH HEH!
HA! THAT IS TOO FUNNY!
STILL, I WAS LOOKING FORWARD TO MY BIG SCREEN DEBUT...
OH, YEAH. SORRY TO DISAPPOINT YA.
OH, BUT WHAT ABOUT YOU?
GOT ANY NEW MOVIES COMING OUT SOON?
WHO, ME? NAH...
I GUESS YOU DIDN'T GET THE MEMO, RE: MY BEING WASHED UP.
WHO, YOU? NUH-UH! HARDLY!
'FRAID SO. I WAS ALL OVER THE TABS A FEW YEARS AGO...
I GOT MIXED UP IN SOME HIJINX.
OH, WAIT...
I DO RECALL SEEING YOUR MUG SHOT ON "ACCESS HOLLYWOOD" A WHILE BACK...
THERE YA GO.
MY LAST MOMENT IN THE LIMELIGHT.
AW, BUT YOU JUST GOTTA RIDE IT OUT, RIGHT?
PEOPLE FORGET ALL ABOUT THAT STUFF AFTER A WHILE...
SOME-TIMES.
AND SOME-TIMES THEY FORGET ABOUT YOU.

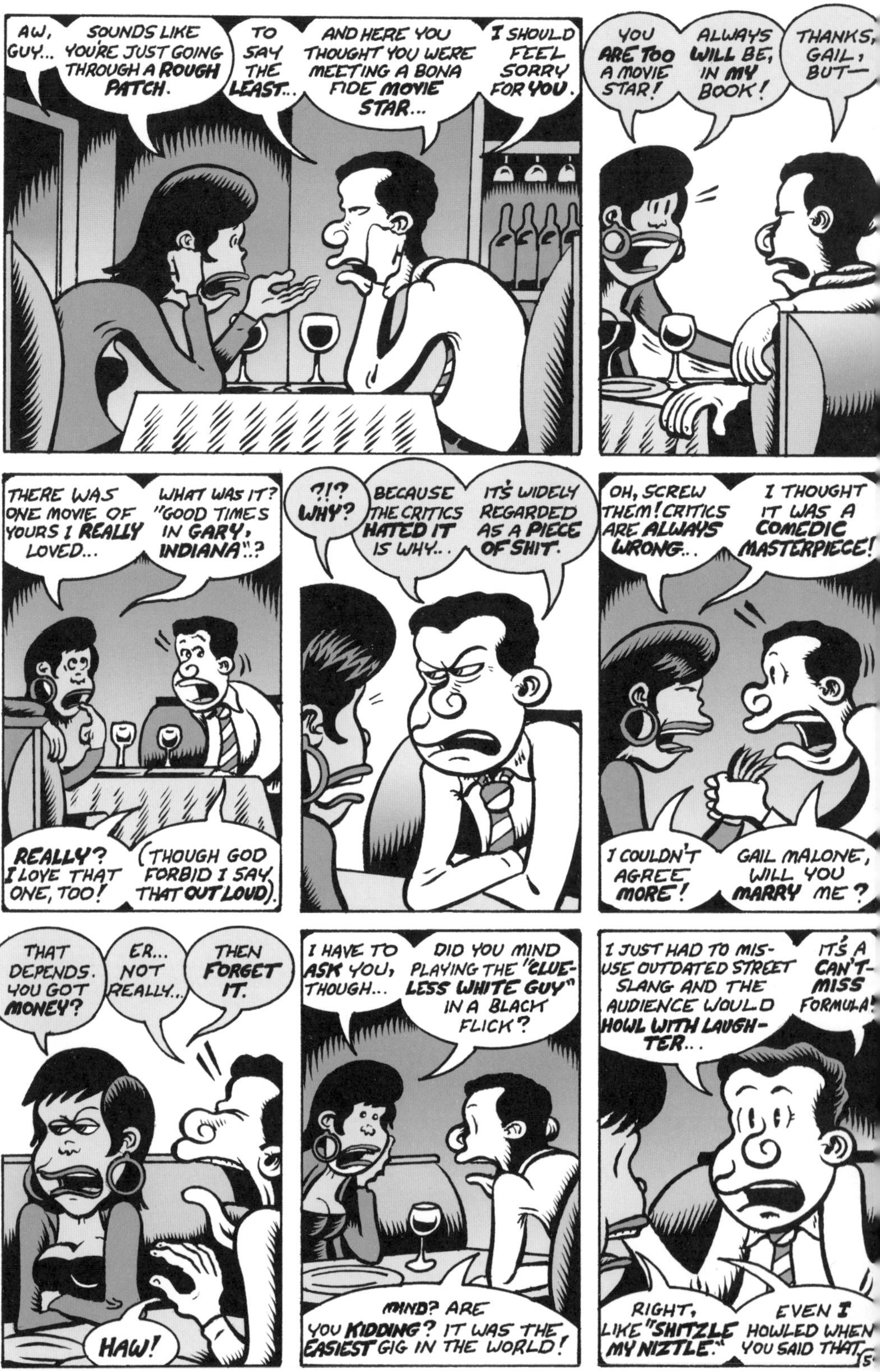
AW, GUY...
SOUNDS LIKE YOU'RE JUST GOING THROUGH A ROUGH PATCH.
TO SAY THE LEAST...
AND HERE YOU THOUGHT YOU WERE MEETING A BONA FIDE MOVIE STAR...
I SHOULD FEEL SORRY FOR YOU.
YOU ARE TOO A MOVIE STAR!
ALWAYS WILL BE, IN MY BOOK!
THANKS, GAIL, BUT—
THERE WAS ONE MOVIE OF YOURS I REALLY LOVED...
WHAT WAS IT? "GOOD TIMES IN GARY, INDIANA"..?
REALLY? I LOVE THAT ONE, TOO!
(THOUGH GOD FORBID I SAY THAT OUT LOUD).
?!? WHY?
BECAUSE THE CRITICS HATED IT IS WHY...
IT'S WIDELY REGARDED AS A PIECE OF SHIT.
OH, SCREW THEM! CRITICS ARE ALWAYS WRONG...
I THOUGHT IT WAS A COMEDIC MASTERPIECE!
I COULDN'T AGREE MORE!
GAIL MALONE, WILL YOU MARRY ME?
THAT DEPENDS. YOU GOT MONEY?
ER... NOT REALLY...
THEN FORGET IT.
HAW!
I HAVE TO ASK YOU, THOUGH...
DID YOU MIND PLAYING THE "CLUELESS WHITE GUY" IN A BLACK FLICK?
MIND? ARE YOU KIDDING? IT WAS THE EASIEST GIG IN THE WORLD!
I JUST HAD TO MISUSE OUTDATED STREET SLANG AND THE AUDIENCE WOULD HOWL WITH LAUGHTER...
IT'S A CAN'T-MISS FORMULA!
RIGHT, LIKE "SHITZLE MY NIZTLE."
EVEN I HOWLED WHEN YOU SAID THAT.
5

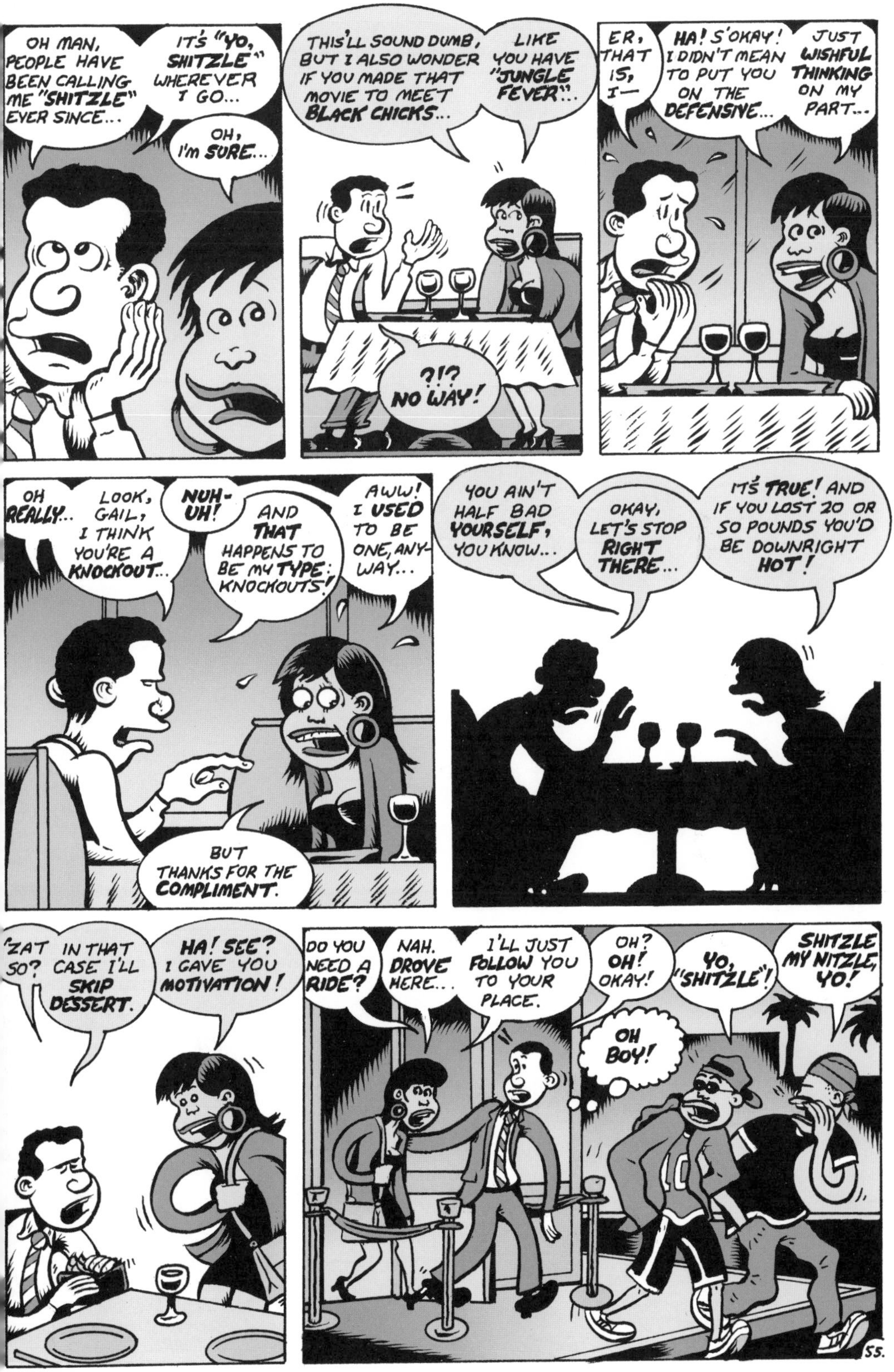

OH MAN, PEOPLE HAVE BEEN CALLING ME "SHITZLE" EVER SINCE...
IT'S "YO, SHITZLE" WHEREVER I GO...
OH, I'M SURE...
THIS'LL SOUND DUMB, BUT I ALSO WONDER IF YOU MADE THAT MOVIE TO MEET BLACK CHICKS...
LIKE YOU HAVE "JUNGLE FEVER"...
?!? NO WAY!
ER, THAT IS, I—
HA! S'OKAY! I DIDN'T MEAN TO PUT YOU ON THE DEFENSIVE...
JUST WISHFUL THINKING ON MY PART...
OH REALLY...
LOOK, GAIL, I THINK YOU'RE A KNOCKOUT...
NUH-UH!
AND THAT HAPPENS TO BE MY TYPE: KNOCKOUTS!
AWW! I USED TO BE ONE, ANYWAY...
BUT THANKS FOR THE COMPLIMENT.
YOU AIN'T HALF BAD YOURSELF, YOU KNOW...
OKAY, LET'S STOP RIGHT THERE...
IT'S TRUE! AND IF YOU LOST 20 OR SO POUNDS YOU'D BE DOWNRIGHT HOT!
'ZAT SO?
IN THAT CASE I'LL SKIP DESSERT.
HA! SEE? I GAVE YOU MOTIVATION!
DO YOU NEED A RIDE?
NAH. DROVE HERE...
I'LL JUST FOLLOW YOU TO YOUR PLACE.
OH? OH! OKAY!
OH BOY!
YO, "SHITZLE"!
SHITZLE MY NITZLE, YO!

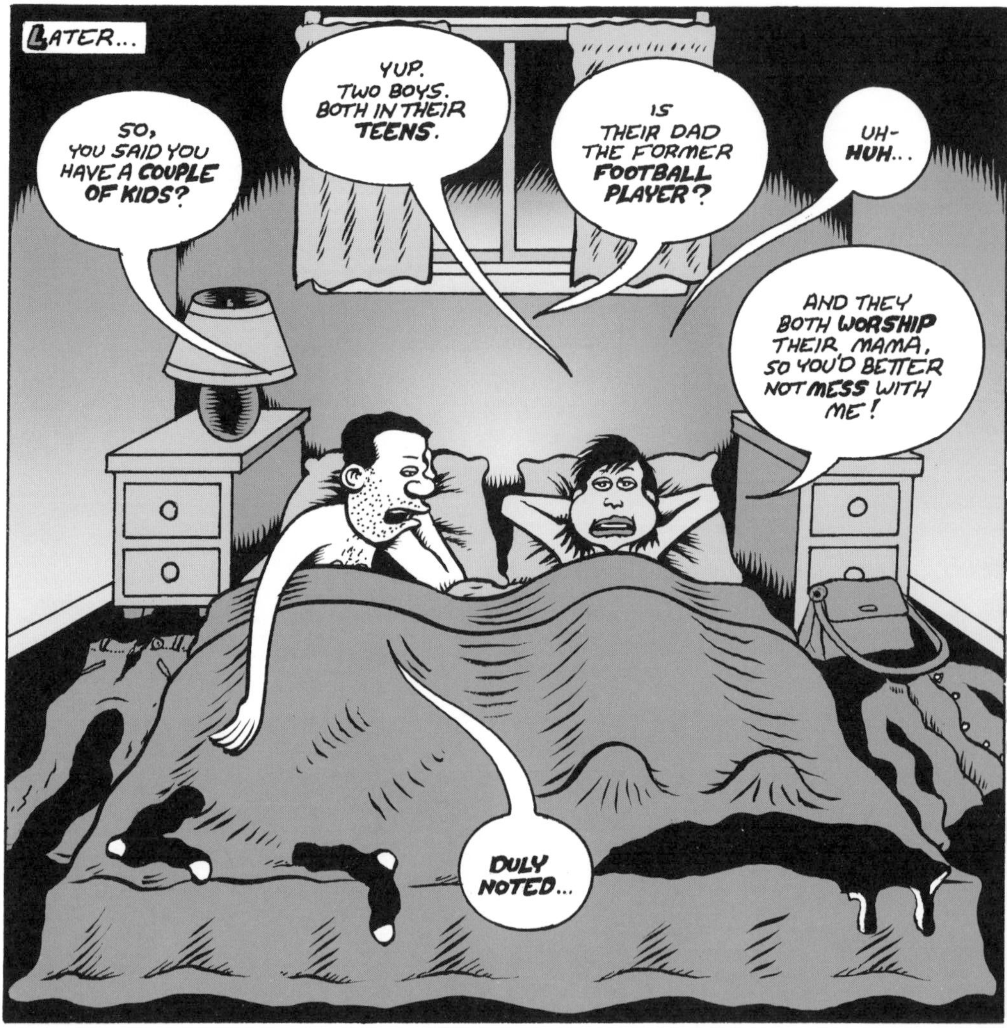
LATER...
SO, YOU SAID YOU HAVE A COUPLE OF KIDS?
YUP. TWO BOYS. BOTH IN THEIR TEENS.
IS THEIR DAD THE FORMER FOOTBALL PLAYER?
UH-HUH...
AND THEY BOTH WORSHIP THEIR MAMA, SO YOU'D BETTER NOT MESS WITH ME!
DULY NOTED...

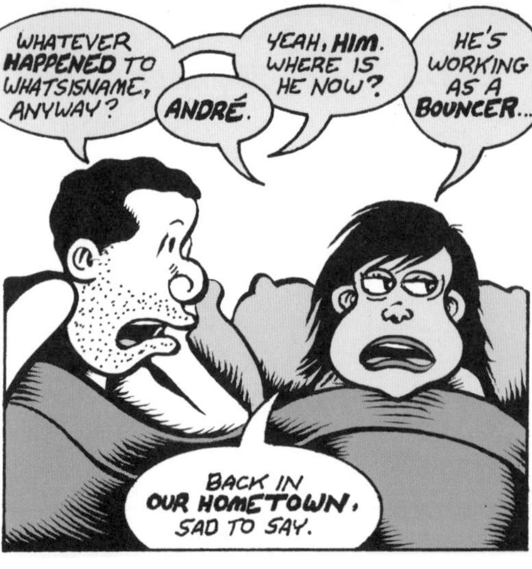
WHATEVER HAPPENED TO WHATSISNAME, ANYWAY?
ANDRÉ.
YEAH, HIM. WHERE IS HE NOW?
HE'S WORKING AS A BOUNCER...
BACK IN OUR HOMETOWN, SAD TO SAY.

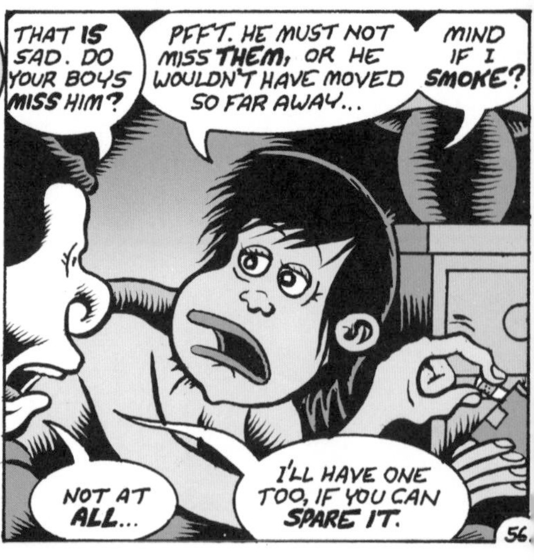
THAT IS SAD. DO YOUR BOYS MISS HIM?
PFFT. HE MUST NOT MISS THEM, OR HE WOULDN'T HAVE MOVED SO FAR AWAY...
MIND IF I SMOKE?
NOT AT ALL...
I'LL HAVE ONE TOO, IF YOU CAN SPARE IT.

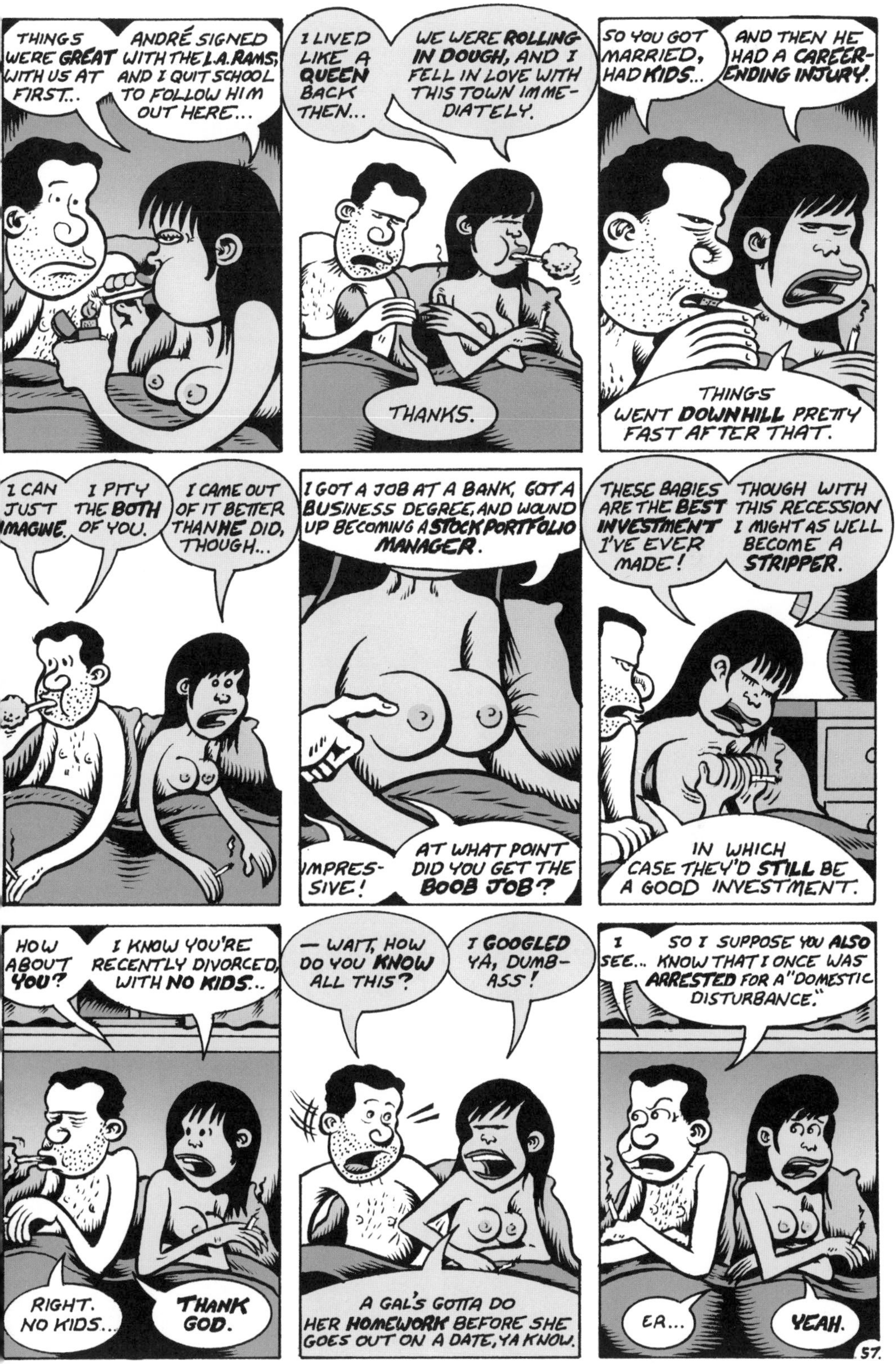
THINGS WERE GREAT WITH US AT FIRST...
ANDRÉ SIGNED WITH THE L.A. RAMS, AND I QUIT SCHOOL TO FOLLOW HIM OUT HERE...
I LIVED LIKE A QUEEN BACK THEN...
WE WERE ROLLING IN DOUGH, AND I FELL IN LOVE WITH THIS TOWN IMMEDIATELY.
THANKS.
SO YOU GOT MARRIED, HAD KIDS...
AND THEN HE HAD A CAREER-ENDING INJURY.
THINGS WENT DOWNHILL PRETTY FAST AFTER THAT.
I CAN JUST IMAGINE.
I PITY THE BOTH OF YOU.
I CAME OUT OF IT BETTER THAN HE DID, THOUGH...
I GOT A JOB AT A BANK, GOT A BUSINESS DEGREE, AND WOUND UP BECOMING A STOCK PORTFOLIO MANAGER.
IMPRES-SIVE!
AT WHAT POINT DID YOU GET THE BOOB JOB?
THESE BABIES ARE THE BEST INVESTMENT I'VE EVER MADE!
THOUGH WITH THIS RECESSION I MIGHT AS WELL BECOME A STRIPPER.
IN WHICH CASE THEY'D STILL BE A GOOD INVESTMENT.
HOW ABOUT YOU?
I KNOW YOU'RE RECENTLY DIVORCED, WITH NO KIDS...
RIGHT. NO KIDS...
THANK GOD.
— WAIT, HOW DO YOU KNOW ALL THIS?
I GOOGLED YA, DUMB-ASS!
A GAL'S GOTTA DO HER HOMEWORK BEFORE SHE GOES OUT ON A DATE, YA KNOW.
I SEE...
SO I SUPPOSE YOU ALSO KNOW THAT I ONCE WAS ARRESTED FOR A "DOMESTIC DISTURBANCE."
ER...
YEAH.

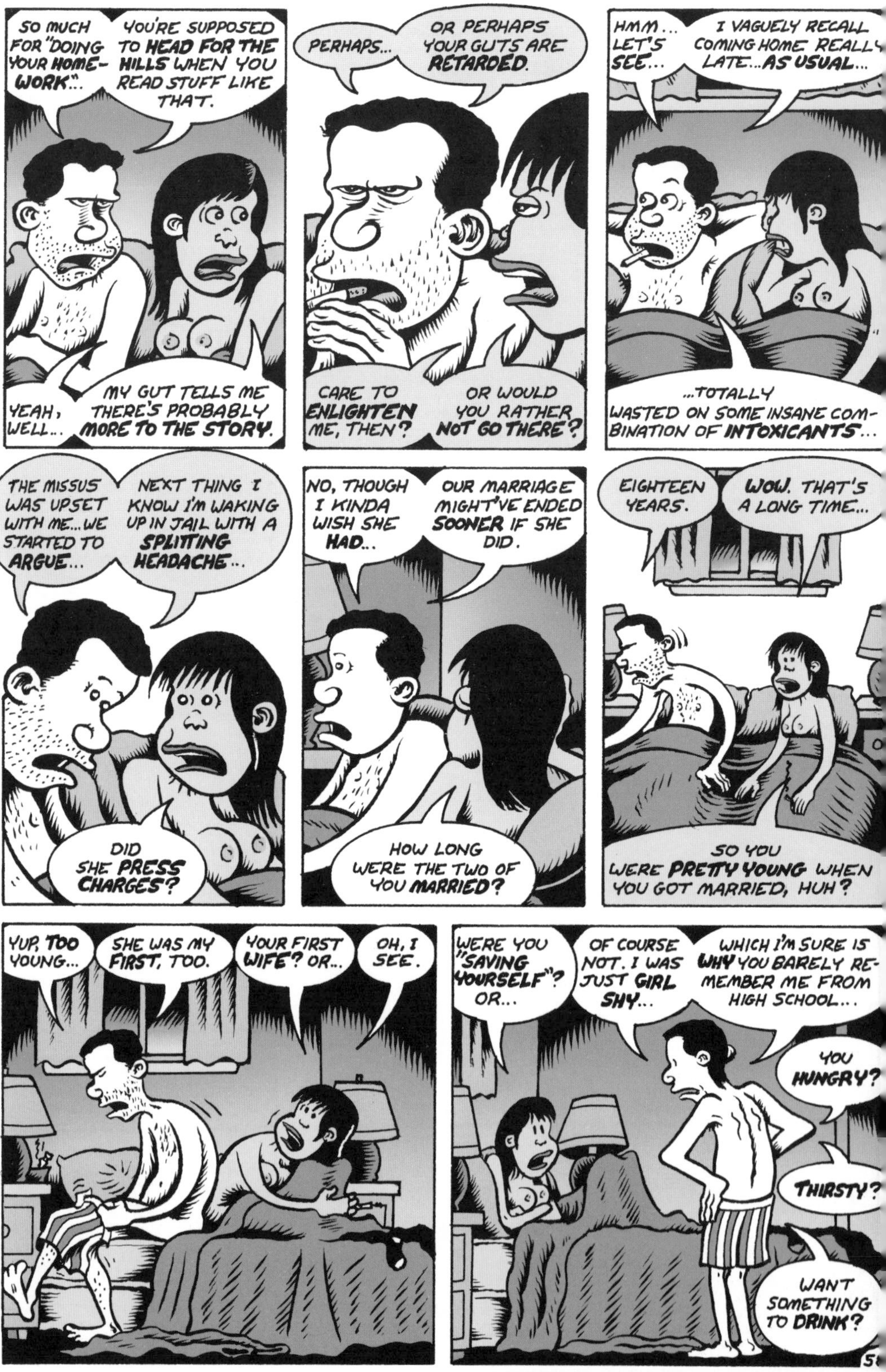
SO MUCH FOR "DOING YOUR HOME-WORK"...
YOU'RE SUPPOSED TO HEAD FOR THE HILLS WHEN YOU READ STUFF LIKE THAT.
YEAH, WELL...
MY GUT TELLS ME THERE'S PROBABLY MORE TO THE STORY.
PERHAPS...
OR PERHAPS YOUR GUTS ARE RETARDED.
CARE TO ENLIGHTEN ME, THEN?
OR WOULD YOU RATHER NOT GO THERE?
HMM... LET'S SEE...
I VAGUELY RECALL COMING HOME REALLY LATE... AS USUAL...
...TOTALLY WASTED ON SOME INSANE COM-BINATION OF INTOXICANTS...
THE MISSUS WAS UPSET WITH ME... WE STARTED TO ARGUE...
NEXT THING I KNOW I'M WAKING UP IN JAIL WITH A SPLITTING HEADACHE...
DID SHE PRESS CHARGES?
NO, THOUGH I KINDA WISH SHE HAD...
OUR MARRIAGE MIGHT'VE ENDED SOONER IF SHE DID.
HOW LONG WERE THE TWO OF YOU MARRIED?
EIGHTEEN YEARS.
WOW. THAT'S A LONG TIME...
SO YOU WERE PRETTY YOUNG WHEN YOU GOT MARRIED, HUH?
YUP, TOO YOUNG...
SHE WAS MY FIRST, TOO.
YOUR FIRST WIFE? OR...
OH, I SEE.
WERE YOU "SAVING YOURSELF"? OR...
OF COURSE NOT. I WAS JUST GIRL SHY...
WHICH I'M SURE IS WHY YOU BARELY RE-MEMBER ME FROM HIGH SCHOOL...
YOU HUNGRY?
THIRSTY?
WANT SOMETHING TO DRINK?

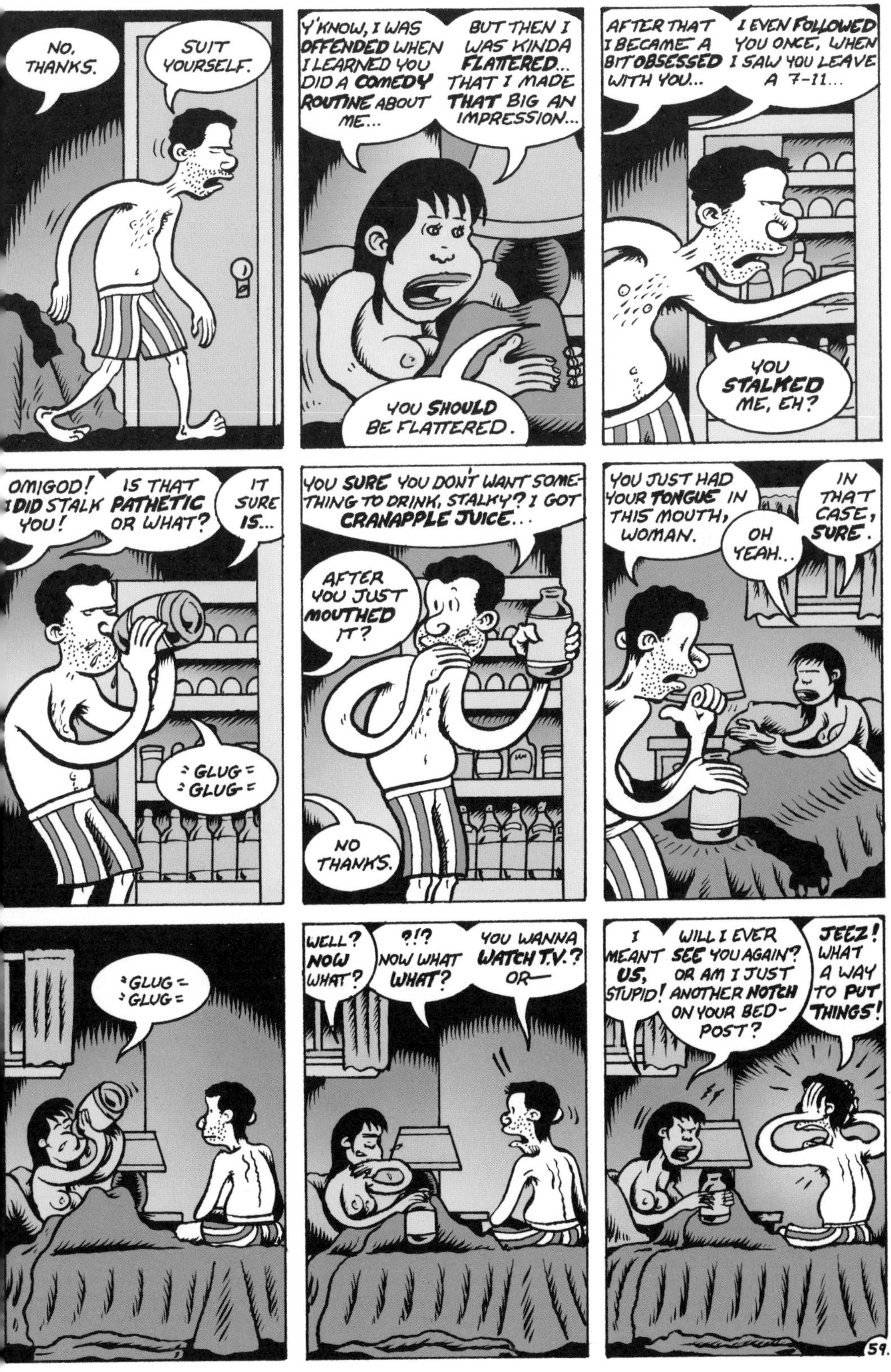
NO. THANKS.
SUIT YOURSELF.
Y'KNOW, I WAS OFFENDED WHEN I LEARNED YOU DID A COMEDY ROUTINE ABOUT ME...
BUT THEN I WAS KINDA FLATTERED... THAT I MADE THAT BIG AN IMPRESSION...
YOU SHOULD BE FLATTERED.
AFTER THAT I BECAME A BIT OBSESSED WITH YOU...
I EVEN FOLLOWED YOU ONCE, WHEN I SAW YOU LEAVE A 7-11...
YOU STALKED ME, EH?
OMIGOD! I DID STALK YOU!
IS THAT PATHETIC OR WHAT?
IT SURE IS...
GLUG GLUG
YOU SURE YOU DON'T WANT SOMETHING TO DRINK, STALKY? I GOT CRANAPPLE JUICE...
AFTER YOU JUST MOUTHED IT?
NO THANKS.
YOU JUST HAD YOUR TONGUE IN THIS MOUTH, WOMAN.
OH YEAH...
IN THAT CASE, SURE.
GLUG GLUG
WELL? NOW WHAT?
?!? NOW WHAT WHAT?
YOU WANNA WATCH T.V.? OR—
I MEANT US, STUPID!
WILL I EVER SEE YOU AGAIN? OR AM I JUST ANOTHER NOTCH ON YOUR BED-POST?
JEEZ! WHAT A WAY TO PUT THINGS!

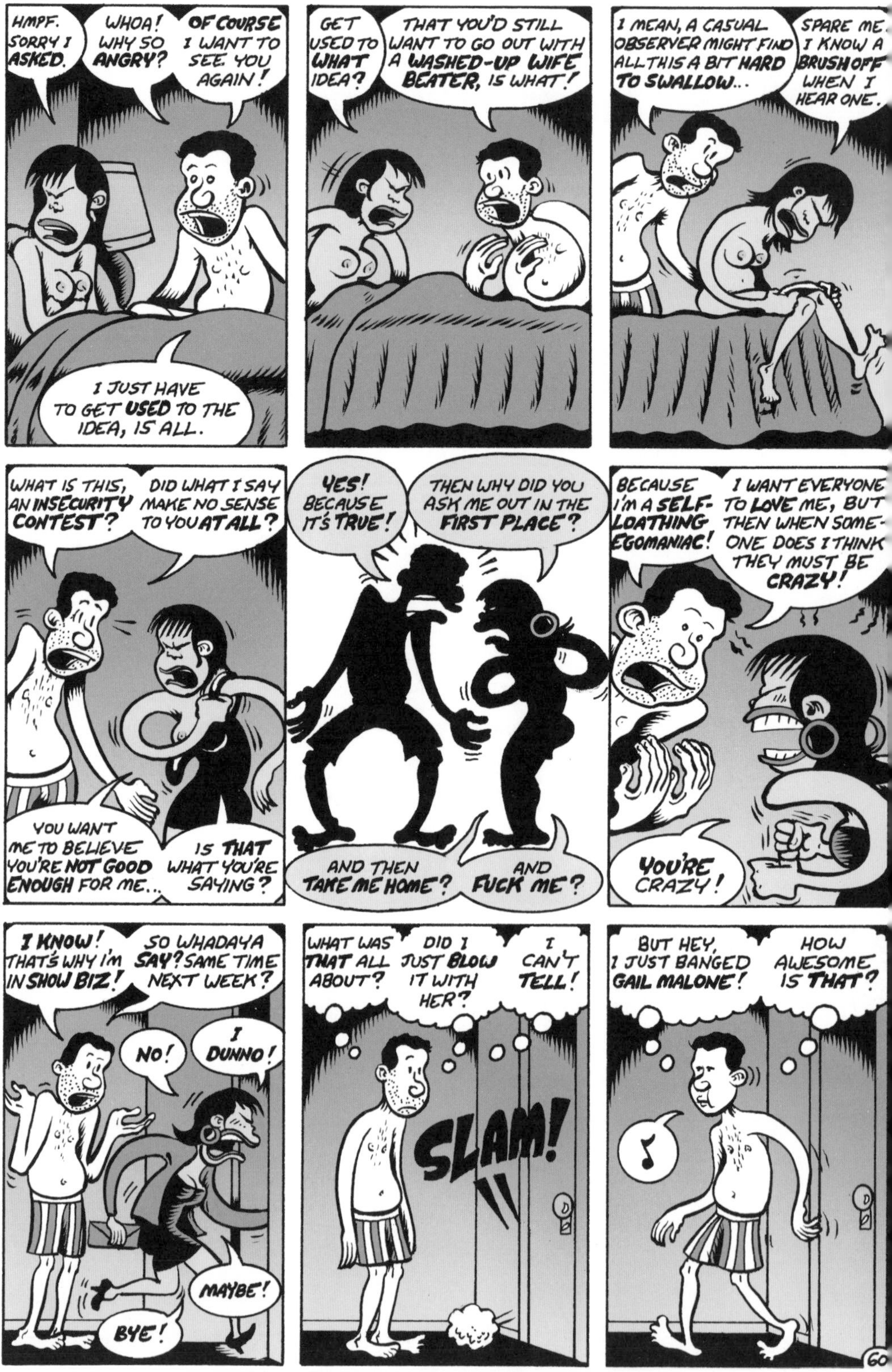
HMPF. SORRY I ASKED.
WHOA! WHY SO ANGRY?
OF COURSE I WANT TO SEE YOU AGAIN!
I JUST HAVE TO GET USED TO THE IDEA, IS ALL.
GET USED TO WHAT IDEA?
THAT YOU'D STILL WANT TO GO OUT WITH A WASHED-UP WIFE BEATER, IS WHAT!
I MEAN, A CASUAL OBSERVER MIGHT FIND ALL THIS A BIT HARD TO SWALLOW...
SPARE ME. I KNOW A BRUSHOFF WHEN I HEAR ONE.
WHAT IS THIS, AN INSECURITY CONTEST?
DID WHAT I SAY MAKE NO SENSE TO YOU AT ALL?
YOU WANT ME TO BELIEVE YOU'RE NOT GOOD ENOUGH FOR ME...
IS THAT WHAT YOU'RE SAYING?
YES! BECAUSE IT'S TRUE!
THEN WHY DID YOU ASK ME OUT IN THE FIRST PLACE?
AND THEN TAKE ME HOME?
AND FUCK ME?
BECAUSE I'M A SELF-LOATHING EGOMANIAC!
I WANT EVERYONE TO LOVE ME, BUT THEN WHEN SOME-ONE DOES I THINK THEY MUST BE CRAZY!
YOU'RE CRAZY!
I KNOW! THAT'S WHY I'M IN SHOW BIZ!
SO WHADAYA SAY? SAME TIME NEXT WEEK?
NO!
I DUNNO!
MAYBE!
BYE!
WHAT WAS THAT ALL ABOUT?
DID I JUST BLOW IT WITH HER?
I CAN'T TELL!
SLAM!
BUT HEY, I JUST BANGED GAIL MALONE!
HOW AWESOME IS THAT?

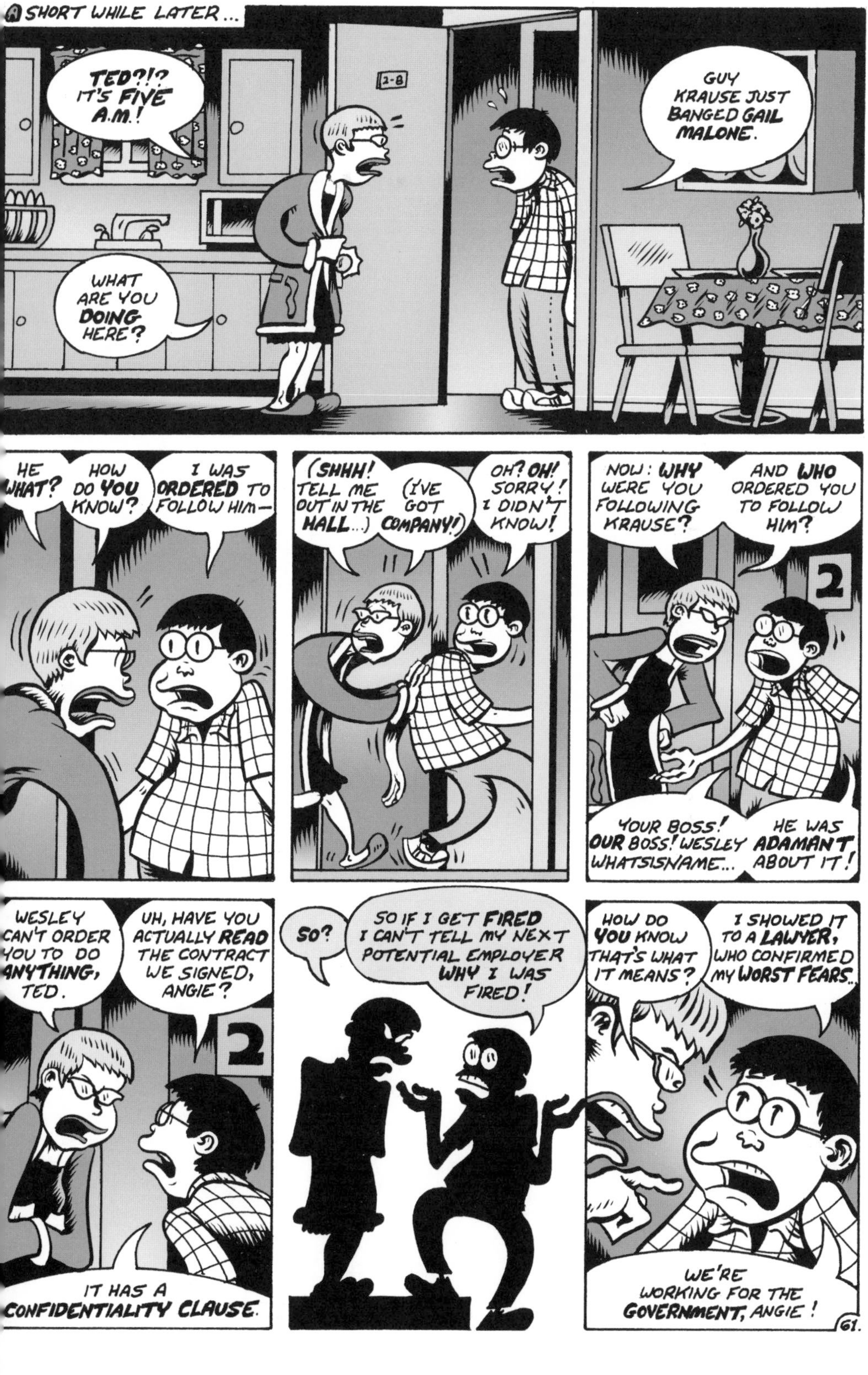
A SHORT WHILE LATER...
TED?!? IT'S FIVE A.M.!
WHAT ARE YOU DOING HERE?
GUY KRAUSE JUST BANGED GAIL MALONE.
2-8
HE WHAT?
HOW DO YOU KNOW?
I WAS ORDERED TO FOLLOW HIM—
(SHHH! TELL ME OUT IN THE HALL...)
(I'VE GOT COMPANY!)
OH? OH! SORRY! I DIDN'T KNOW!
NOW: WHY WERE YOU FOLLOWING KRAUSE?
AND WHO ORDERED YOU TO FOLLOW HIM?
2
YOUR BOSS! OUR BOSS! WESLEY WHATSISNAME...
HE WAS ADAMANT ABOUT IT!
WESLEY CAN'T ORDER YOU TO DO ANYTHING, TED.
UH, HAVE YOU ACTUALLY READ THE CONTRACT WE SIGNED, ANGIE?
2
IT HAS A CONFIDENTIALITY CLAUSE.
SO?
SO IF I GET FIRED I CAN'T TELL MY NEXT POTENTIAL EMPLOYER WHY I WAS FIRED!
HOW DO YOU KNOW THAT'S WHAT IT MEANS?
I SHOWED IT TO A LAWYER, WHO CONFIRMED MY WORST FEARS...
WE'RE WORKING FOR THE GOVERNMENT, ANGIE!

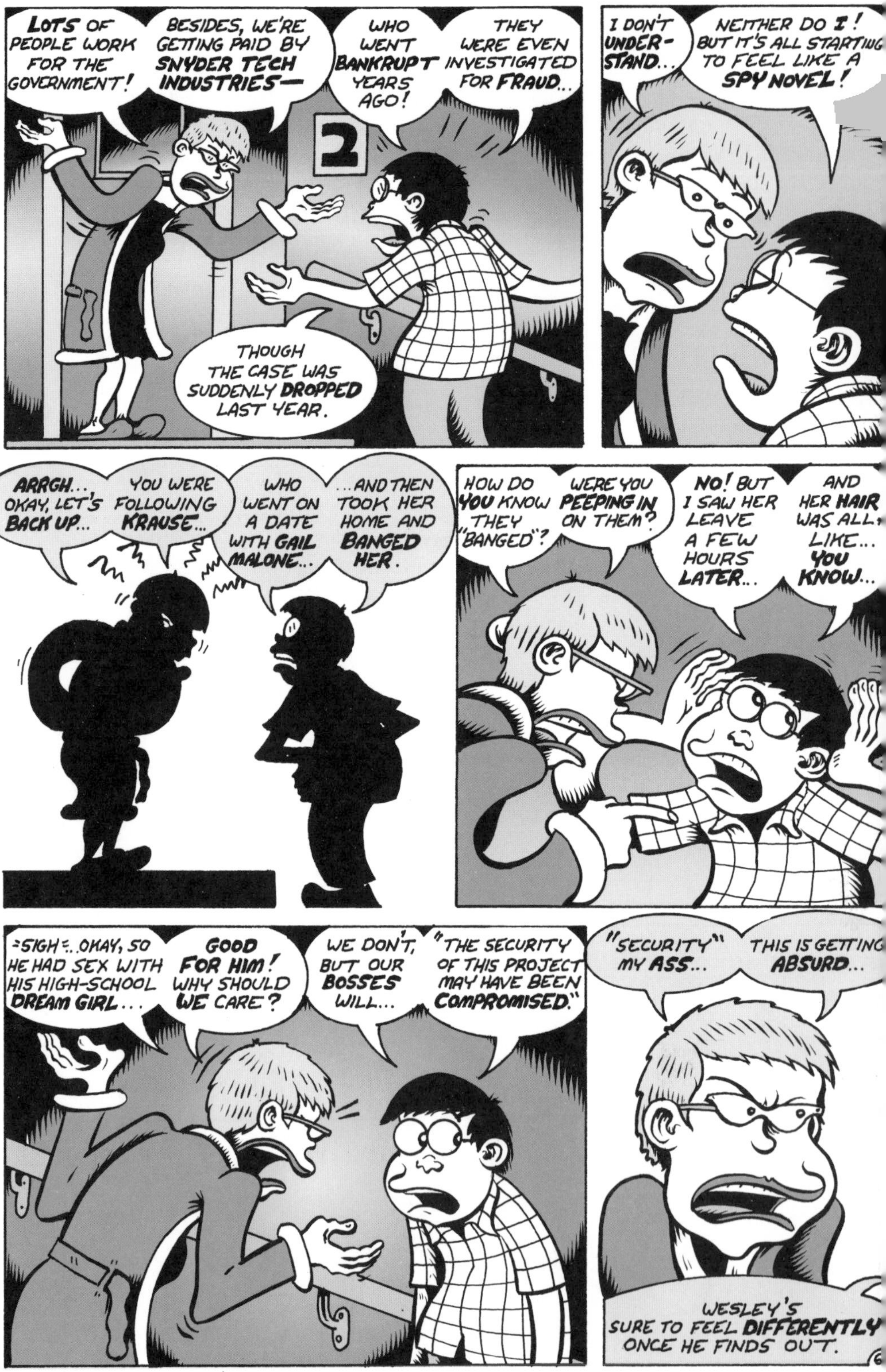

LOTS OF PEOPLE WORK FOR THE GOVERNMENT!
BESIDES, WE'RE GETTING PAID BY SNYDER TECH INDUSTRIES—
WHO WENT BANKRUPT YEARS AGO!
THEY WERE EVEN INVESTIGATED FOR FRAUD...
THOUGH THE CASE WAS SUDDENLY DROPPED LAST YEAR.
2
I DON'T UNDER-STAND...
NEITHER DO I! BUT IT'S ALL STARTING TO FEEL LIKE A SPY NOVEL!
ARRGH... OKAY, LET'S BACK UP...
YOU WERE FOLLOWING KRAUSE...
WHO WENT ON A DATE WITH GAIL MALONE...
...AND THEN TOOK HER HOME AND BANGED HER.
HOW DO YOU KNOW THEY "BANGED"?
WERE YOU PEEPING IN ON THEM?
NO! BUT I SAW HER LEAVE A FEW HOURS LATER...
AND HER HAIR WAS ALL, LIKE... YOU KNOW...
=SIGH=.. OKAY, SO HE HAD SEX WITH HIS HIGH-SCHOOL DREAM GIRL...
GOOD FOR HIM! WHY SHOULD WE CARE?
WE DON'T, BUT OUR BOSSES WILL...
"THE SECURITY OF THIS PROJECT MAY HAVE BEEN COMPROMISED."
"SECURITY" MY ASS...
THIS IS GETTING ABSURD...
WESLEY'S SURE TO FEEL DIFFERENTLY ONCE HE FINDS OUT.

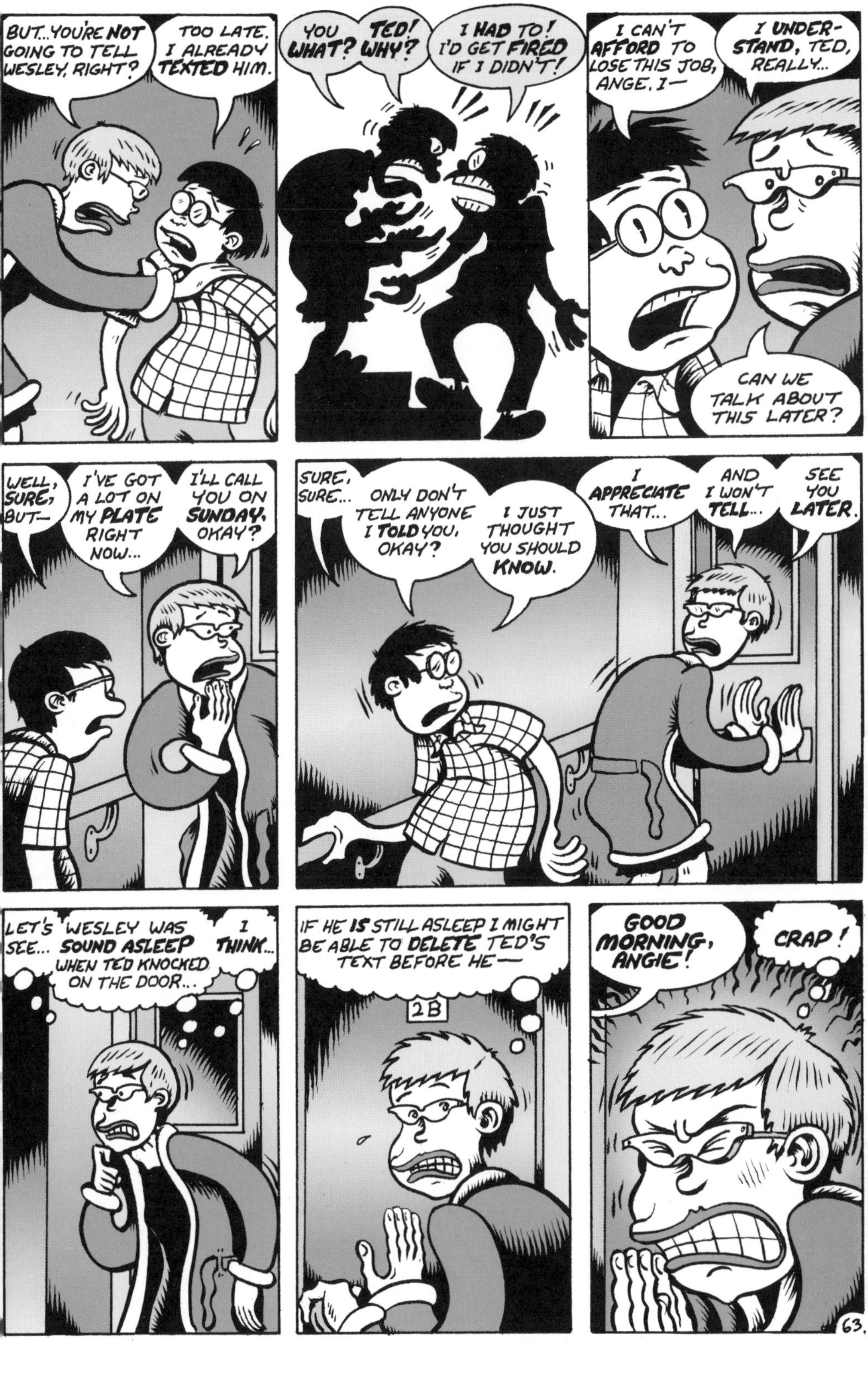
BUT... YOU'RE NOT GOING TO TELL WESLEY, RIGHT?
TOO LATE. I ALREADY TEXTED HIM.
YOU WHAT?
TED! WHY?
I HAD TO! I'D GET FIRED IF I DIDN'T!
I CAN'T AFFORD TO LOSE THIS JOB, ANGE. I—
I UNDERSTAND, TED, REALLY...
CAN WE TALK ABOUT THIS LATER?
WELL, SURE, BUT—
I'VE GOT A LOT ON MY PLATE RIGHT NOW...
I'LL CALL YOU ON SUNDAY, OKAY?
SURE, SURE...
ONLY DON'T TELL ANYONE I TOLD YOU, OKAY?
I JUST THOUGHT YOU SHOULD KNOW.
I APPRECIATE THAT...
AND I WON'T TELL...
SEE YOU LATER.
LET'S SEE...
WESLEY WAS SOUND ASLEEP WHEN TED KNOCKED ON THE DOOR...
I THINK...
IF HE IS STILL ASLEEP I MIGHT BE ABLE TO DELETE TED'S TEXT BEFORE HE—
2B
GOOD MORNING, ANGIE!
CRAP!

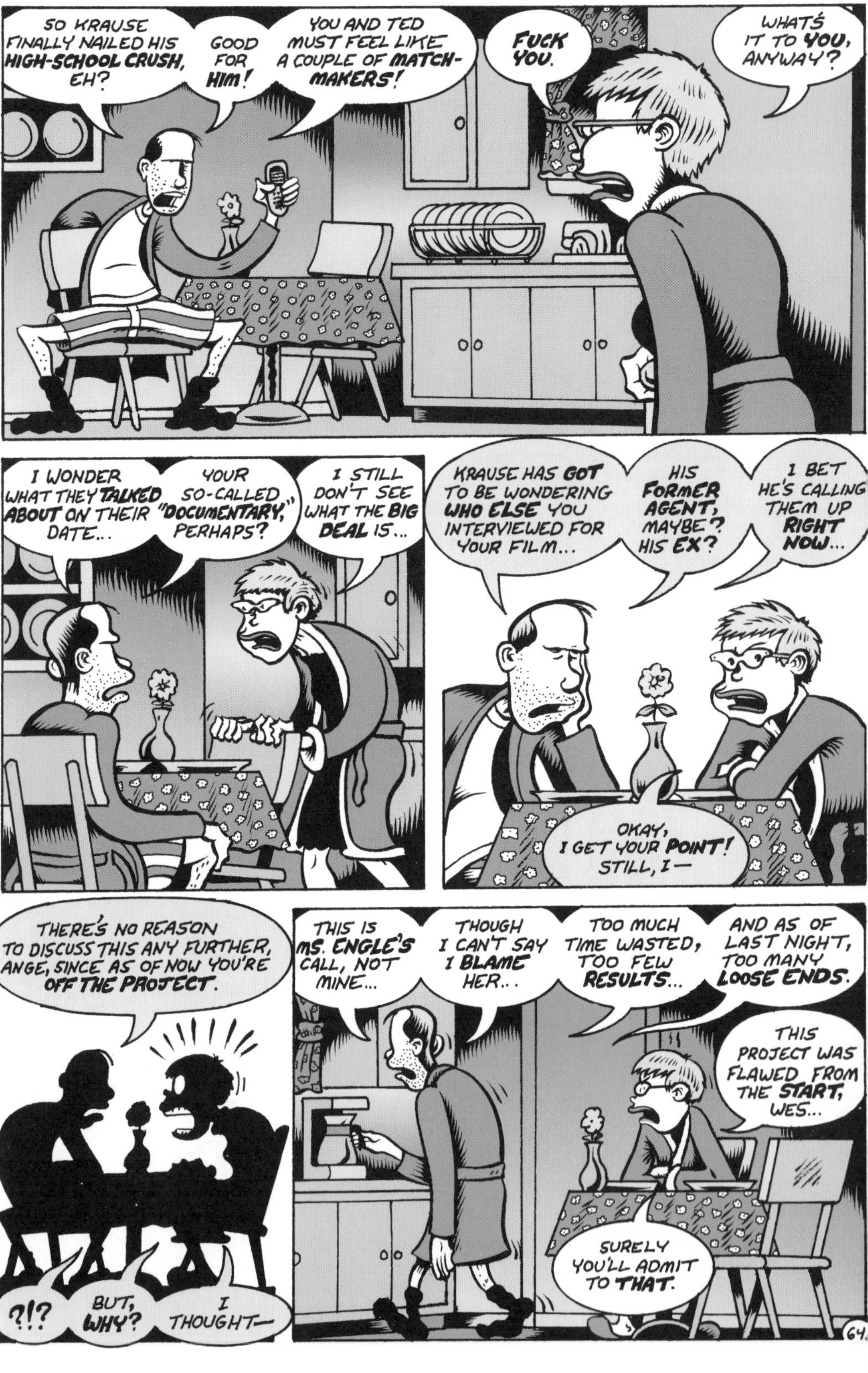

SO KRAUSE FINALLY NAILED HIS HIGH-SCHOOL CRUSH, EH?
GOOD FOR HIM!
YOU AND TED MUST FEEL LIKE A COUPLE OF MATCH-MAKERS!
FUCK YOU.
WHAT'S IT TO YOU, ANYWAY?
I WONDER WHAT THEY TALKED ABOUT ON THEIR DATE...
YOUR SO-CALLED "DOCUMENTARY," PERHAPS?
I STILL DON'T SEE WHAT THE BIG DEAL IS...
KRAUSE HAS GOT TO BE WONDERING WHO ELSE YOU INTERVIEWED FOR YOUR FILM...
HIS FORMER AGENT, MAYBE? HIS EX?
I BET HE'S CALLING THEM UP RIGHT NOW...
OKAY, I GET YOUR POINT! STILL, I—
THERE'S NO REASON TO DISCUSS THIS ANY FURTHER, ANGE, SINCE AS OF NOW YOU'RE OFF THE PROJECT.
?!?
BUT, WHY?
I THOUGHT—
THIS IS MS. ENGLE'S CALL, NOT MINE...
THOUGH I CAN'T SAY I BLAME HER...
TOO MUCH TIME WASTED, TOO FEW RESULTS...
AND AS OF LAST NIGHT, TOO MANY LOOSE ENDS.
THIS PROJECT WAS FLAWED FROM THE START, WES...
SURELY YOU'LL ADMIT TO THAT.

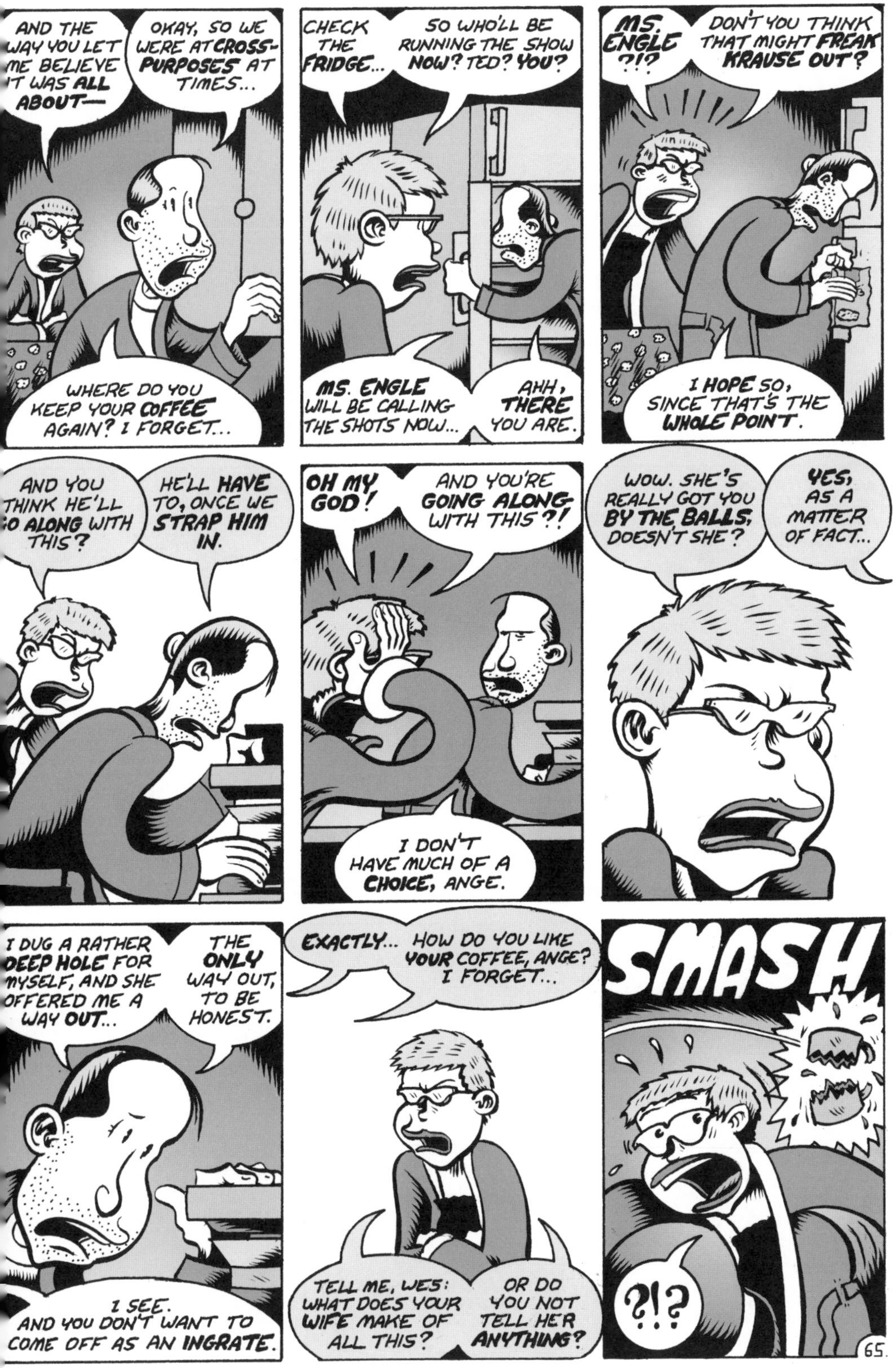

AND THE WAY YOU LET ME BELIEVE IT WAS ALL ABOUT—
OKAY, SO WE WERE AT CROSS-PURPOSES AT TIMES...
WHERE DO YOU KEEP YOUR COFFEE AGAIN? I FORGET...
CHECK THE FRIDGE...
SO WHO'LL BE RUNNING THE SHOW NOW? TED? YOU?
MS. ENGLE WILL BE CALLING THE SHOTS NOW...
AHH, THERE YOU ARE.
MS. ENGLE ?!?
DON'T YOU THINK THAT MIGHT FREAK KRAUSE OUT?
I HOPE SO, SINCE THAT'S THE WHOLE POINT.
AND YOU THINK HE'LL GO ALONG WITH THIS?
HE'LL HAVE TO, ONCE WE STRAP HIM IN.
OH MY GOD!
AND YOU'RE GOING ALONG WITH THIS?!
I DON'T HAVE MUCH OF A CHOICE, ANGE.
WOW. SHE'S REALLY GOT YOU BY THE BALLS, DOESN'T SHE?
YES, AS A MATTER OF FACT...
I DUG A RATHER DEEP HOLE FOR MYSELF, AND SHE OFFERED ME A WAY OUT...
THE ONLY WAY OUT, TO BE HONEST.
I SEE. AND YOU DON'T WANT TO COME OFF AS AN INGRATE.
EXACTLY...
HOW DO YOU LIKE YOUR COFFEE, ANGE? I FORGET...
TELL ME, WES: WHAT DOES YOUR WIFE MAKE OF ALL THIS?
OR DO YOU NOT TELL HER ANYTHING?
SMASH
?!?

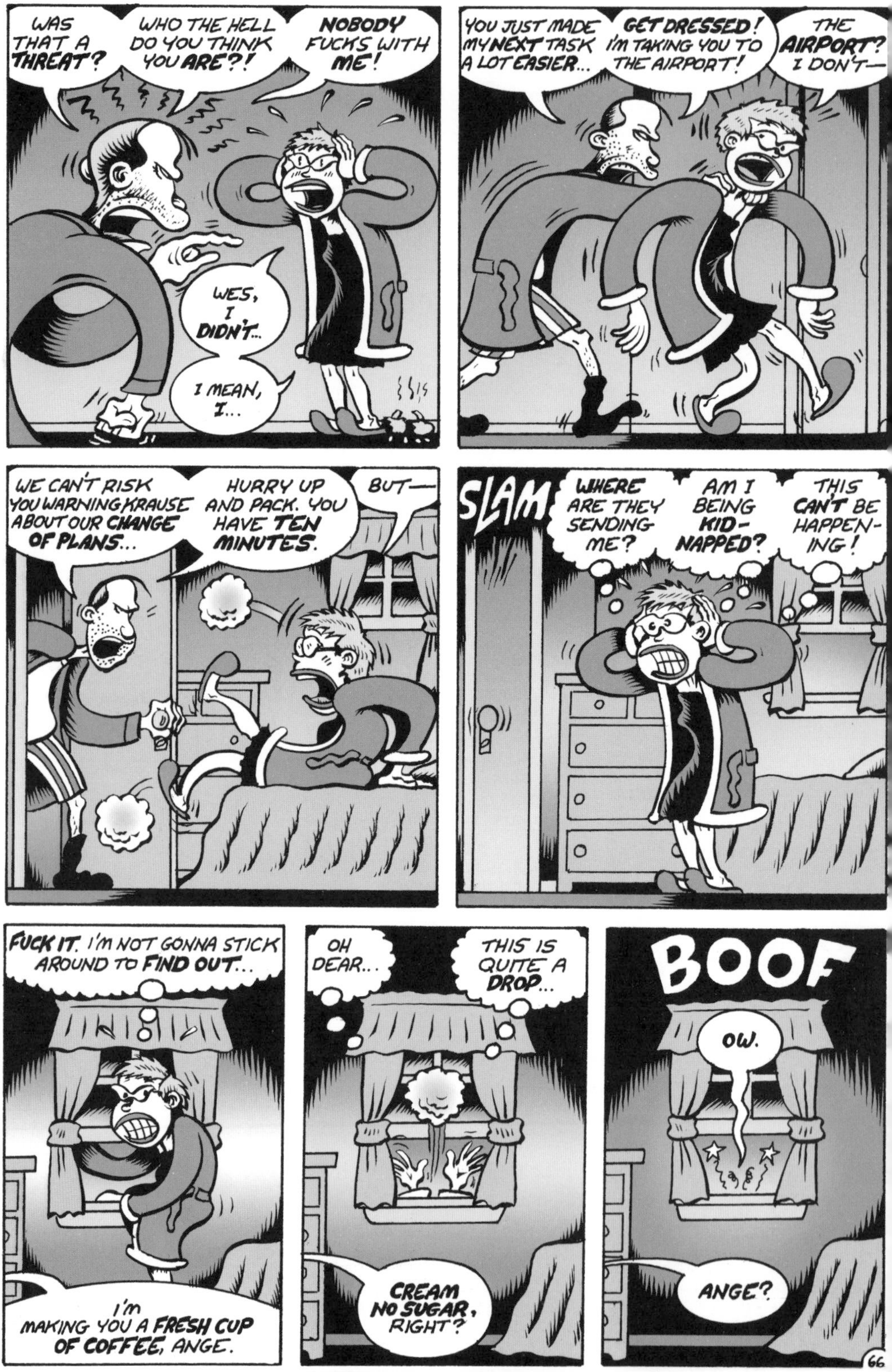
WAS THAT A THREAT?
WHO THE HELL DO YOU THINK YOU ARE?!
NOBODY FUCKS WITH ME!
WES, I DIDN'T...
I MEAN, I...
YOU JUST MADE MY NEXT TASK A LOT EASIER...
GET DRESSED! I'M TAKING YOU TO THE AIRPORT!
THE AIRPORT? I DON'T—
WE CAN'T RISK YOU WARNING KRAUSE ABOUT OUR CHANGE OF PLANS...
HURRY UP AND PACK. YOU HAVE TEN MINUTES.
BUT—
SLAM
WHERE ARE THEY SENDING ME?
AM I BEING KID-NAPPED?
THIS CAN'T BE HAPPEN-ING!
FUCK IT. I'M NOT GONNA STICK AROUND TO FIND OUT...
I'M MAKING YOU A FRESH CUP OF COFFEE, ANGE.
OH DEAR...
THIS IS QUITE A DROP...
CREAM NO SUGAR, RIGHT?
BOOF
OW.
ANGE?

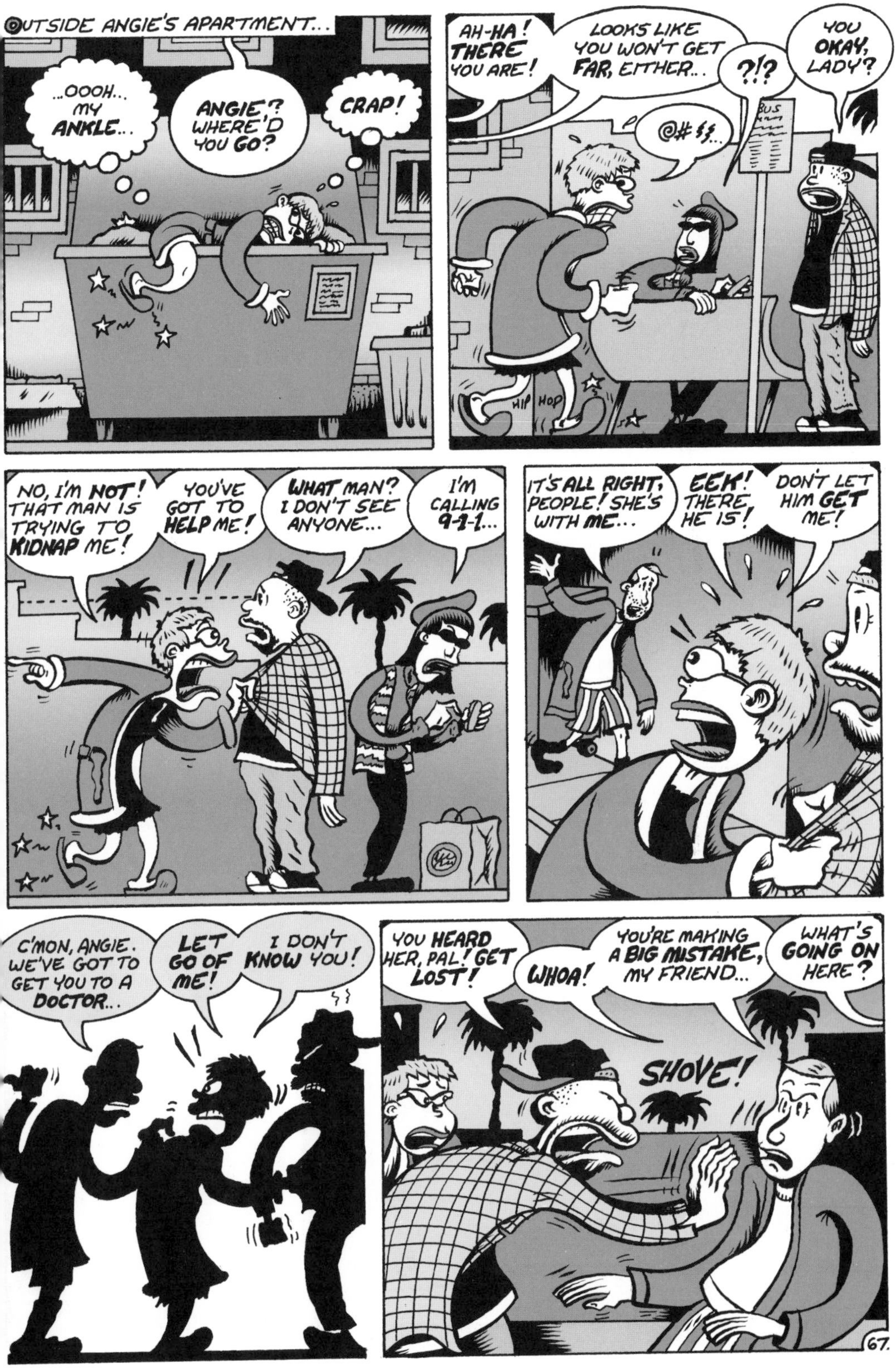
OUTSIDE ANGIE'S APARTMENT...
...OOOH... MY ANKLE...
ANGIE? WHERE'D YOU GO?
CRAP!
AH-HA! THERE YOU ARE!
LOOKS LIKE YOU WON'T GET FAR, EITHER...
?!?
YOU OKAY, LADY?
@#$$...
BUS
HIP HOP
NO, I'M NOT! THAT MAN IS TRYING TO KIDNAP ME!
YOU'VE GOT TO HELP ME!
WHAT MAN? I DON'T SEE ANYONE...
I'M CALLING 9-1-1...
IT'S ALL RIGHT, PEOPLE! SHE'S WITH ME...
EEK! THERE HE IS!
DON'T LET HIM GET ME!
C'MON, ANGIE. WE'VE GOT TO GET YOU TO A DOCTOR...
LET GO OF ME!
I DON'T KNOW YOU!
YOU HEARD HER, PAL! GET LOST!
WHOA!
YOU'RE MAKING A BIG MISTAKE, MY FRIEND...
WHAT'S GOING ON HERE?
SHOVE!

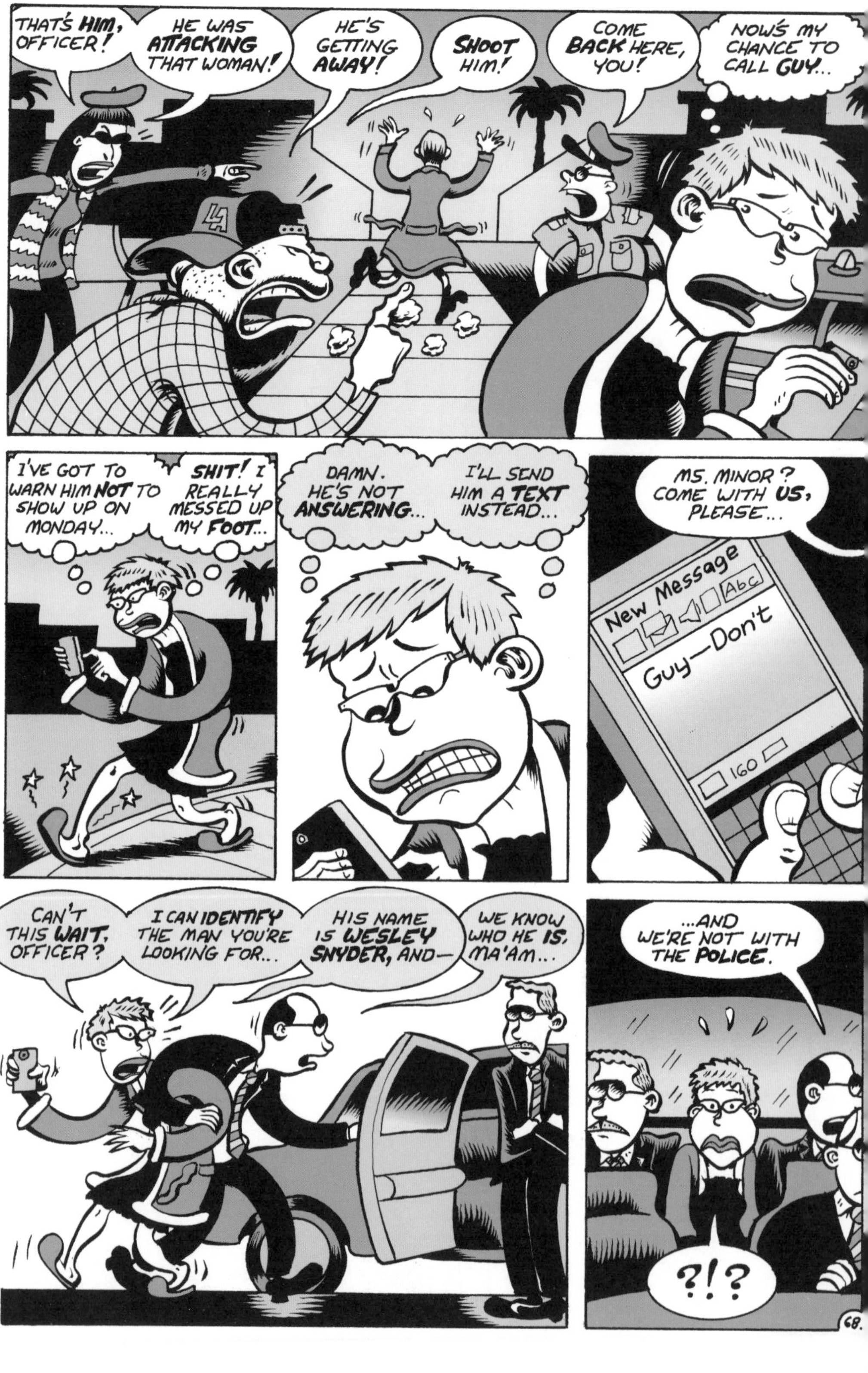
THAT'S HIM, OFFICER!
HE WAS ATTACKING THAT WOMAN!
HE'S GETTING AWAY!
SHOOT HIM!
COME BACK HERE, YOU!
NOW'S MY CHANCE TO CALL GUY...
I'VE GOT TO WARN HIM NOT TO SHOW UP ON MONDAY...
SHIT! I REALLY MESSED UP MY FOOT...
DAMN. HE'S NOT ANSWERING...
I'LL SEND HIM A TEXT INSTEAD...
MS. MINOR? COME WITH US, PLEASE...
New Message
Abc
Guy—Don't
160
CAN'T THIS WAIT, OFFICER?
I CAN IDENTIFY THE MAN YOU'RE LOOKING FOR...
HIS NAME IS WESLEY SNYDER, AND—
WE KNOW WHO HE IS, MA'AM...
...AND WE'RE NOT WITH THE POLICE.
?!?

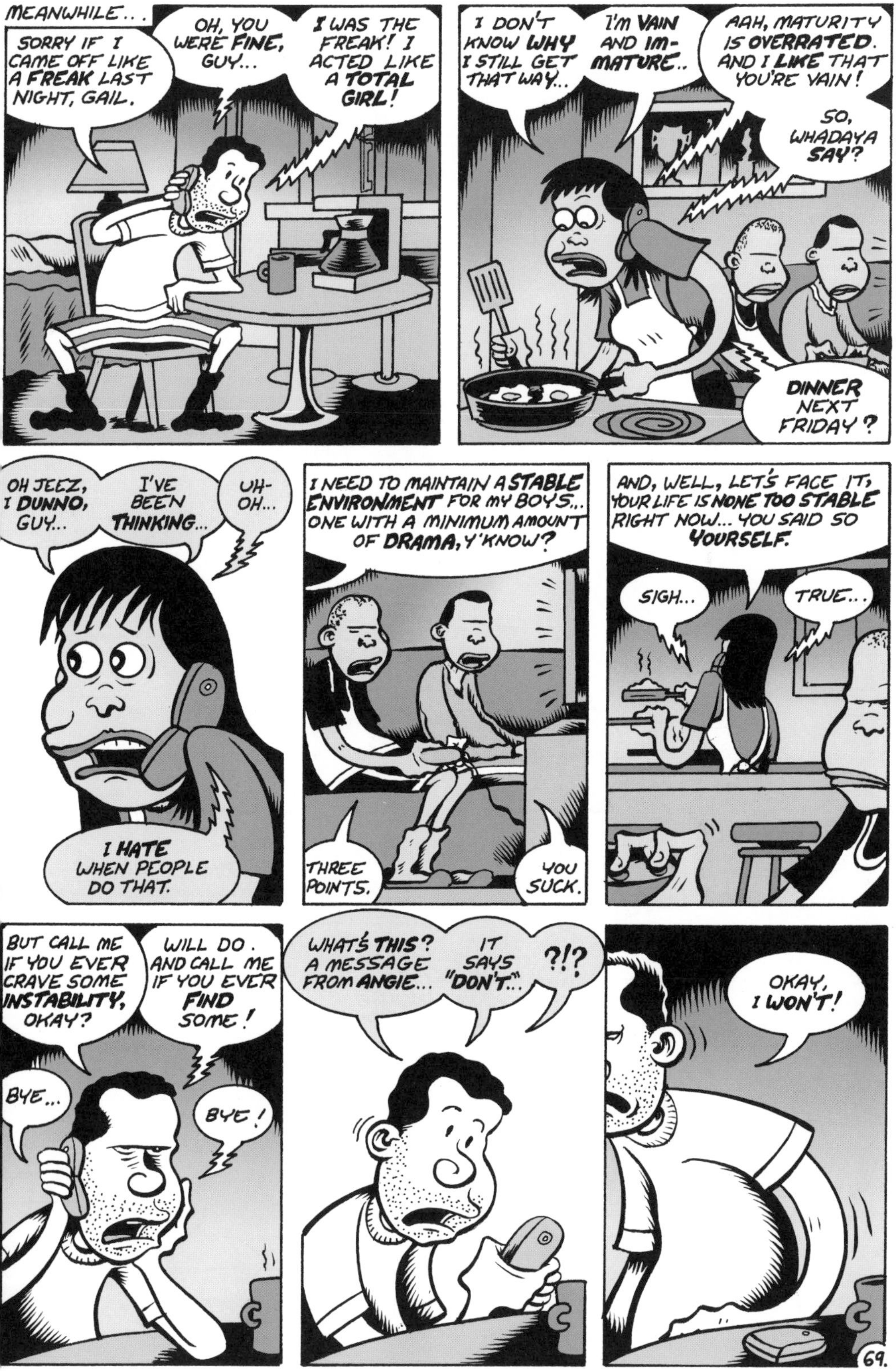
MEANWHILE...
SORRY IF I CAME OFF LIKE A FREAK LAST NIGHT, GAIL.
OH, YOU WERE FINE, GUY...
I WAS THE FREAK! I ACTED LIKE A TOTAL GIRL!
I DON'T KNOW WHY I STILL GET THAT WAY...
I'M VAIN AND IMMATURE...
AAH, MATURITY IS OVERRATED. AND I LIKE THAT YOU'RE VAIN!
SO, WHADAYA SAY?
DINNER NEXT FRIDAY?
OH JEEZ, I DUNNO, GUY...
I'VE BEEN THINKING...
UH-OH...
I HATE WHEN PEOPLE DO THAT.
I NEED TO MAINTAIN A STABLE ENVIRONMENT FOR MY BOYS... ONE WITH A MINIMUM AMOUNT OF DRAMA, Y'KNOW?
THREE POINTS.
YOU SUCK.
AND, WELL, LET'S FACE IT, YOUR LIFE IS NONE TOO STABLE RIGHT NOW... YOU SAID SO YOURSELF.
SIGH...
TRUE...
BUT CALL ME IF YOU EVER CRAVE SOME INSTABILITY, OKAY?
WILL DO. AND CALL ME IF YOU EVER FIND SOME!
BYE...
BYE!
WHAT'S THIS? A MESSAGE FROM ANGIE...
IT SAYS "DON'T."
?!?
OKAY, I WON'T!

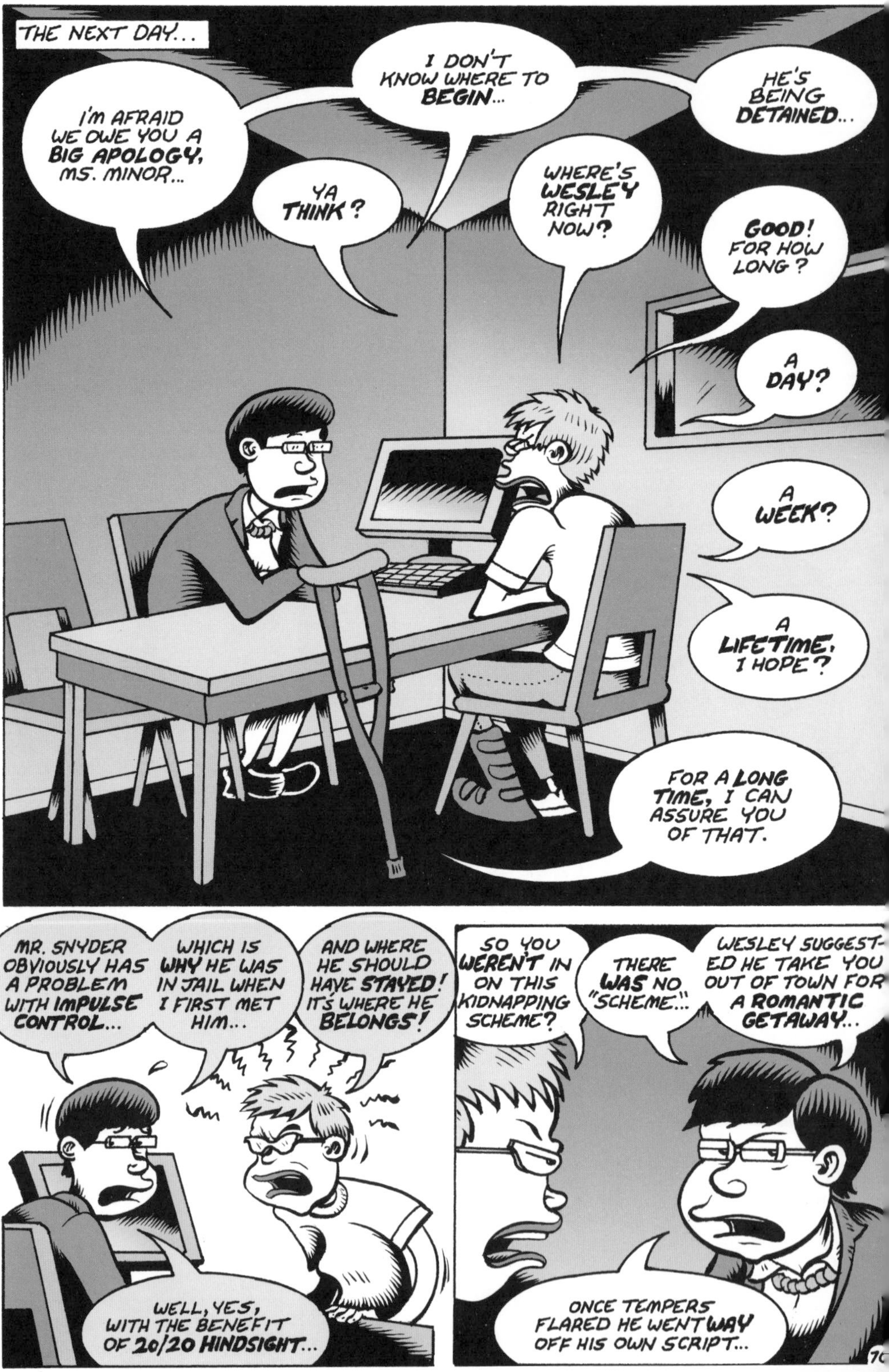
THE NEXT DAY...
I'M AFRAID WE OWE YOU A BIG APOLOGY, MS. MINOR...
YA THINK?
I DON'T KNOW WHERE TO BEGIN...
WHERE'S WESLEY RIGHT NOW?
HE'S BEING DETAINED...
GOOD! FOR HOW LONG?
A DAY?
A WEEK?
A LIFETIME, I HOPE?
FOR A LONG TIME, I CAN ASSURE YOU OF THAT.
MR. SNYDER OBVIOUSLY HAS A PROBLEM WITH IMPULSE CONTROL...
WHICH IS WHY HE WAS IN JAIL WHEN I FIRST MET HIM...
AND WHERE HE SHOULD HAVE STAYED! IT'S WHERE HE BELONGS!
WELL, YES, WITH THE BENEFIT OF 20/20 HINDSIGHT...
SO YOU WEREN'T IN ON THIS KIDNAPPING SCHEME?
THERE WAS NO "SCHEME."
WESLEY SUGGESTED HE TAKE YOU OUT OF TOWN FOR A ROMANTIC GETAWAY...
ONCE TEMPERS FLARED HE WENT WAY OFF HIS OWN SCRIPT...

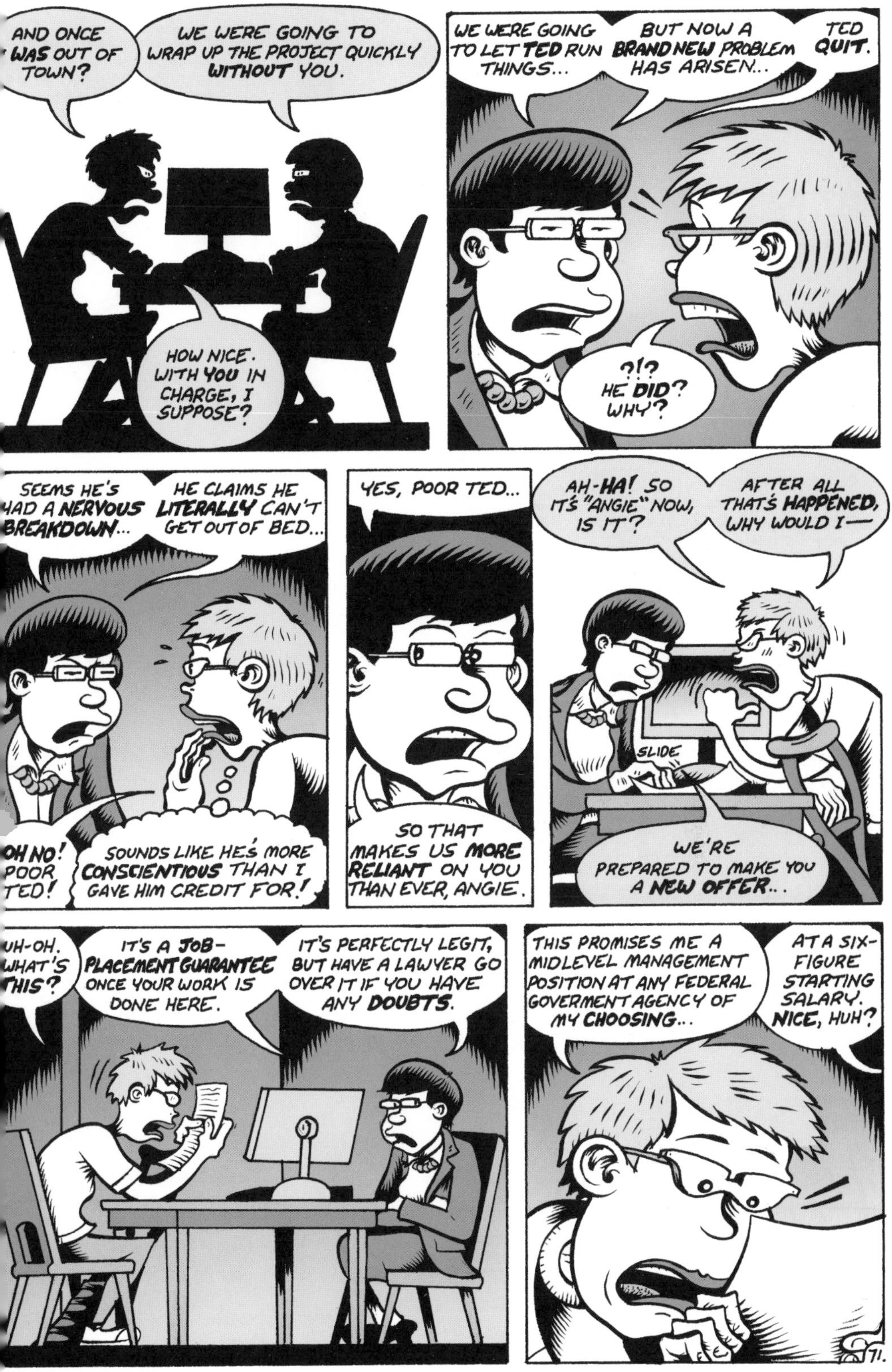
AND ONCE WAS OUT OF TOWN?
WE WERE GOING TO WRAP UP THE PROJECT QUICKLY WITHOUT YOU.
HOW NICE. WITH YOU IN CHARGE, I SUPPOSE?
WE WERE GOING TO LET TED RUN THINGS...
BUT NOW A BRAND NEW PROBLEM HAS ARISEN...
TED QUIT.
?!? HE DID? WHY?
SEEMS HE'S HAD A NERVOUS BREAKDOWN...
HE CLAIMS HE LITERALLY CAN'T GET OUT OF BED...
OH NO! POOR TED!
SOUNDS LIKE HE'S MORE CONSCIENTIOUS THAN I GAVE HIM CREDIT FOR!
YES, POOR TED...
SO THAT MAKES US MORE RELIANT ON YOU THAN EVER, ANGIE.
AH-HA! SO IT'S "ANGIE" NOW, IS IT?
AFTER ALL THAT'S HAPPENED, WHY WOULD I—
SLIDE
WE'RE PREPARED TO MAKE YOU A NEW OFFER...
UH-OH. WHAT'S THIS?
IT'S A JOB-PLACEMENT GUARANTEE ONCE YOUR WORK IS DONE HERE.
IT'S PERFECTLY LEGIT, BUT HAVE A LAWYER GO OVER IT IF YOU HAVE ANY DOUBTS.
THIS PROMISES ME A MIDLEVEL MANAGEMENT POSITION AT ANY FEDERAL GOVERMENT AGENCY OF MY CHOOSING...
AT A SIX-FIGURE STARTING SALARY. NICE, HUH?
71.

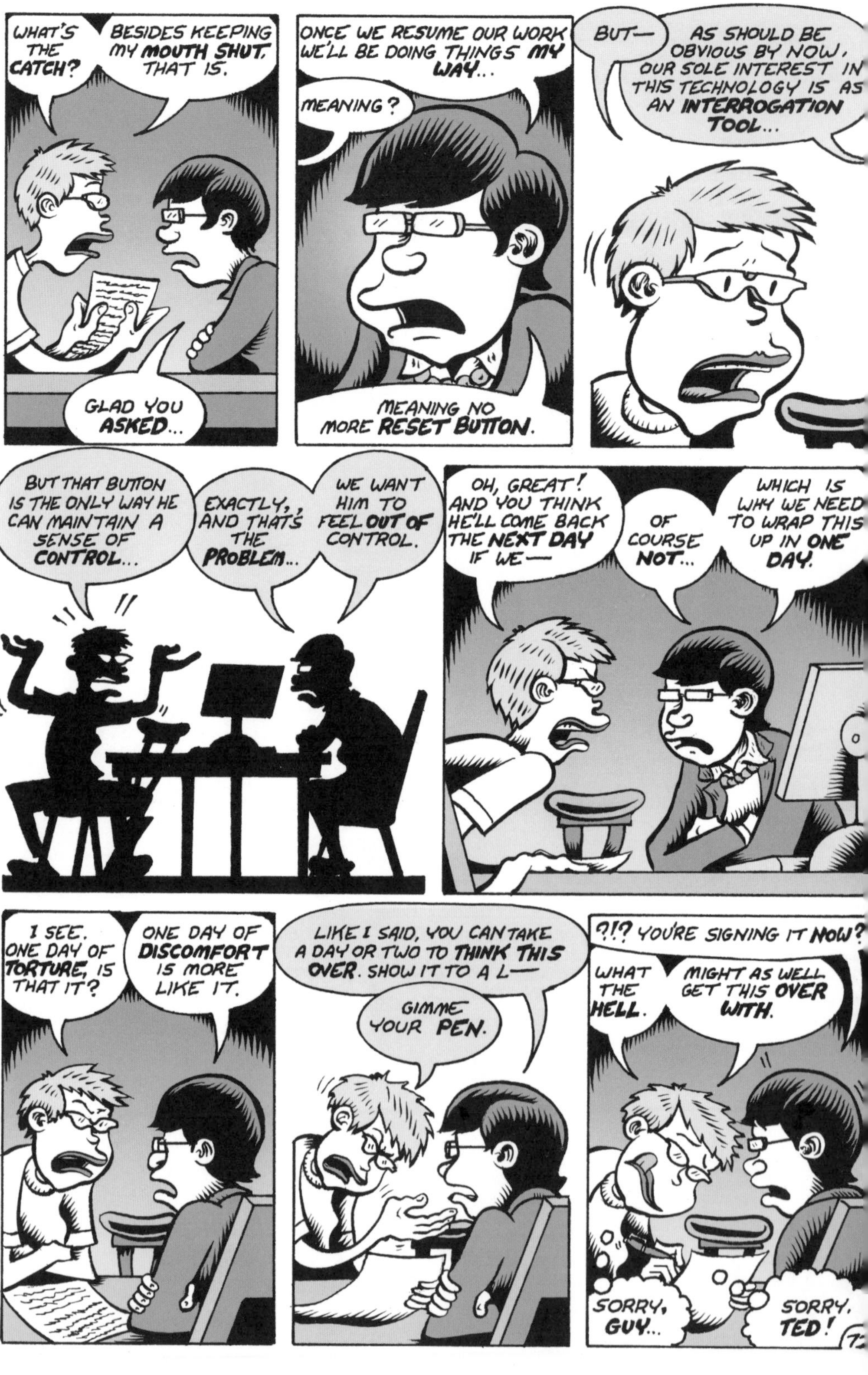
WHAT'S THE CATCH?
BESIDES KEEPING MY MOUTH SHUT, THAT IS.
GLAD YOU ASKED...
ONCE WE RESUME OUR WORK WE'LL BE DOING THINGS MY WAY...
MEANING?
MEANING NO MORE RESET BUTTON.
BUT—
AS SHOULD BE OBVIOUS BY NOW, OUR SOLE INTEREST IN THIS TECHNOLOGY IS AS AN INTERROGATION TOOL...
BUT THAT BUTTON IS THE ONLY WAY HE CAN MAINTAIN A SENSE OF CONTROL...
EXACTLY,, AND THAT'S THE PROBLEM...
WE WANT HIM TO FEEL OUT OF CONTROL.
OH, GREAT! AND YOU THINK HE'LL COME BACK THE NEXT DAY IF WE—
OF COURSE NOT...
WHICH IS WHY WE NEED TO WRAP THIS UP IN ONE DAY.
I SEE. ONE DAY OF TORTURE, IS THAT IT?
ONE DAY OF DISCOMFORT IS MORE LIKE IT.
LIKE I SAID, YOU CAN TAKE A DAY OR TWO TO THINK THIS OVER. SHOW IT TO A L—
GIMME YOUR PEN.
?!? YOU'RE SIGNING IT NOW?
WHAT THE HELL.
MIGHT AS WELL GET THIS OVER WITH.
SORRY, GUY...
SORRY, TED!

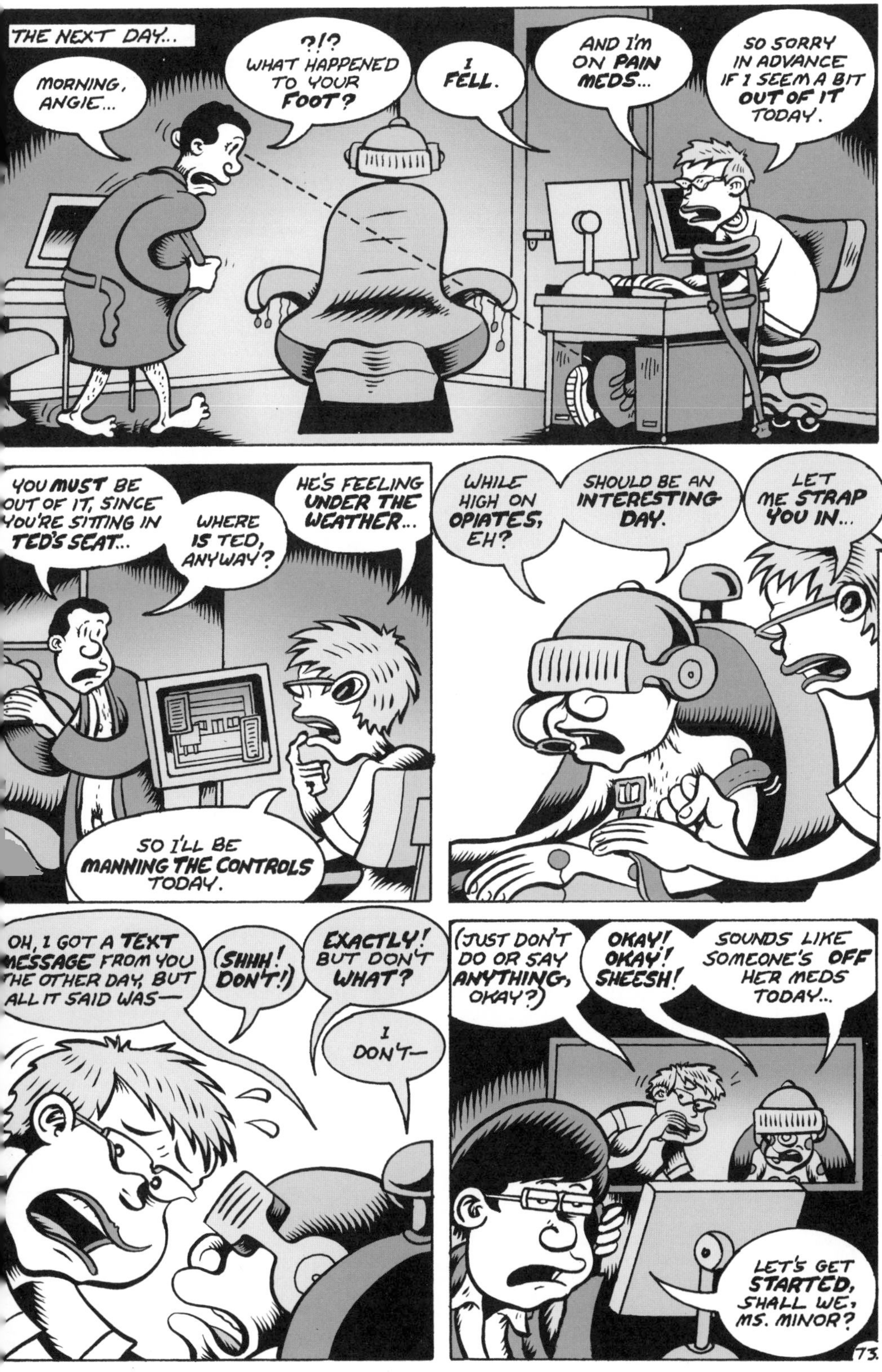
THE NEXT DAY...
MORNING, ANGIE...
?!? WHAT HAPPENED TO YOUR FOOT?
I FELL.
AND I'M ON PAIN MEDS...
SO SORRY IN ADVANCE IF I SEEM A BIT OUT OF IT TODAY.
YOU MUST BE OUT OF IT, SINCE YOU'RE SITTING IN TED'S SEAT...
WHERE IS TED, ANYWAY?
HE'S FEELING UNDER THE WEATHER...
SO I'LL BE MANNING THE CONTROLS TODAY.
WHILE HIGH ON OPIATES, EH?
SHOULD BE AN INTERESTING DAY.
LET ME STRAP YOU IN...
OH, I GOT A TEXT MESSAGE FROM YOU THE OTHER DAY, BUT ALL IT SAID WAS—
(SHHH! DON'T!)
EXACTLY! BUT DON'T WHAT?
I DON'T—
(JUST DON'T DO OR SAY ANYTHING, OKAY?)
OKAY! OKAY! SHEESH!
SOUNDS LIKE SOMEONE'S OFF HER MEDS TODAY...
LET'S GET STARTED, SHALL WE, MS. MINOR?
73.

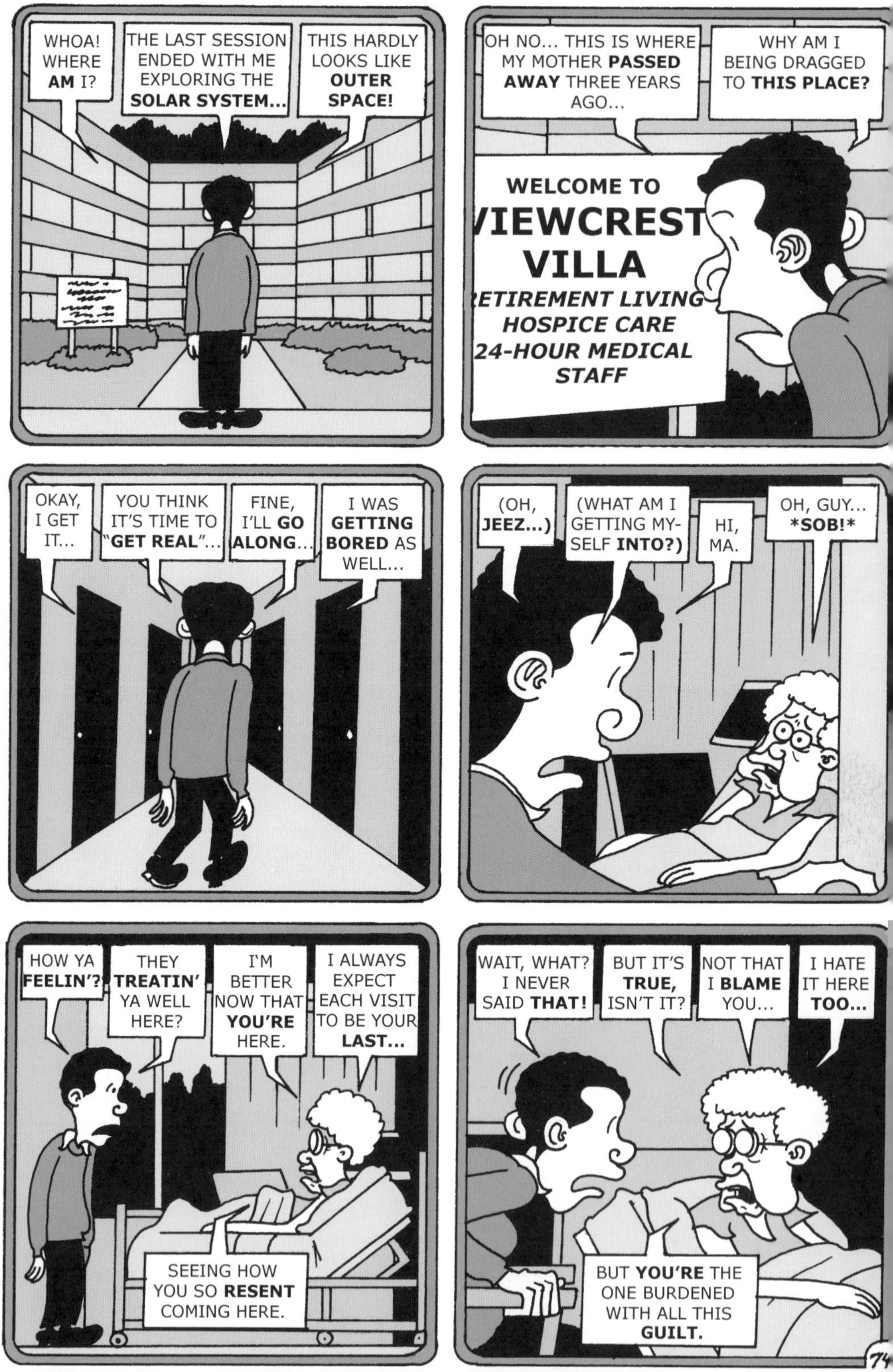
WHOA! WHERE **AM** I?
THE LAST SESSION ENDED WITH ME EXPLORING THE **SOLAR SYSTEM...**
THIS HARDLY LOOKS LIKE **OUTER SPACE!**
OH NO... THIS IS WHERE MY MOTHER **PASSED AWAY** THREE YEARS AGO...
WHY AM I BEING DRAGGED TO **THIS PLACE?**
WELCOME TO
VIEWCREST VILLA
RETIREMENT LIVING
HOSPICE CARE
24-HOUR MEDICAL STAFF
OKAY, I GET IT...
YOU THINK IT'S TIME TO "**GET REAL**"...
FINE, I'LL **GO ALONG**...
I WAS **GETTING BORED** AS WELL...
(OH, **JEEZ...**)
(WHAT AM I GETTING MY-SELF **INTO?**)
HI, MA.
OH, GUY... ***SOB!***
HOW YA **FEELIN'?**
THEY **TREATIN'** YA WELL HERE?
I'M BETTER NOW THAT **YOU'RE** HERE.
I ALWAYS EXPECT EACH VISIT TO BE YOUR **LAST...**
SEEING HOW YOU SO **RESENT** COMING HERE.
WAIT, WHAT? I NEVER SAID **THAT!**
BUT IT'S **TRUE,** ISN'T IT?
NOT THAT I **BLAME** YOU...
I HATE IT HERE **TOO...**
BUT **YOU'RE** THE ONE BURDENED WITH ALL THIS **GUILT.**
74

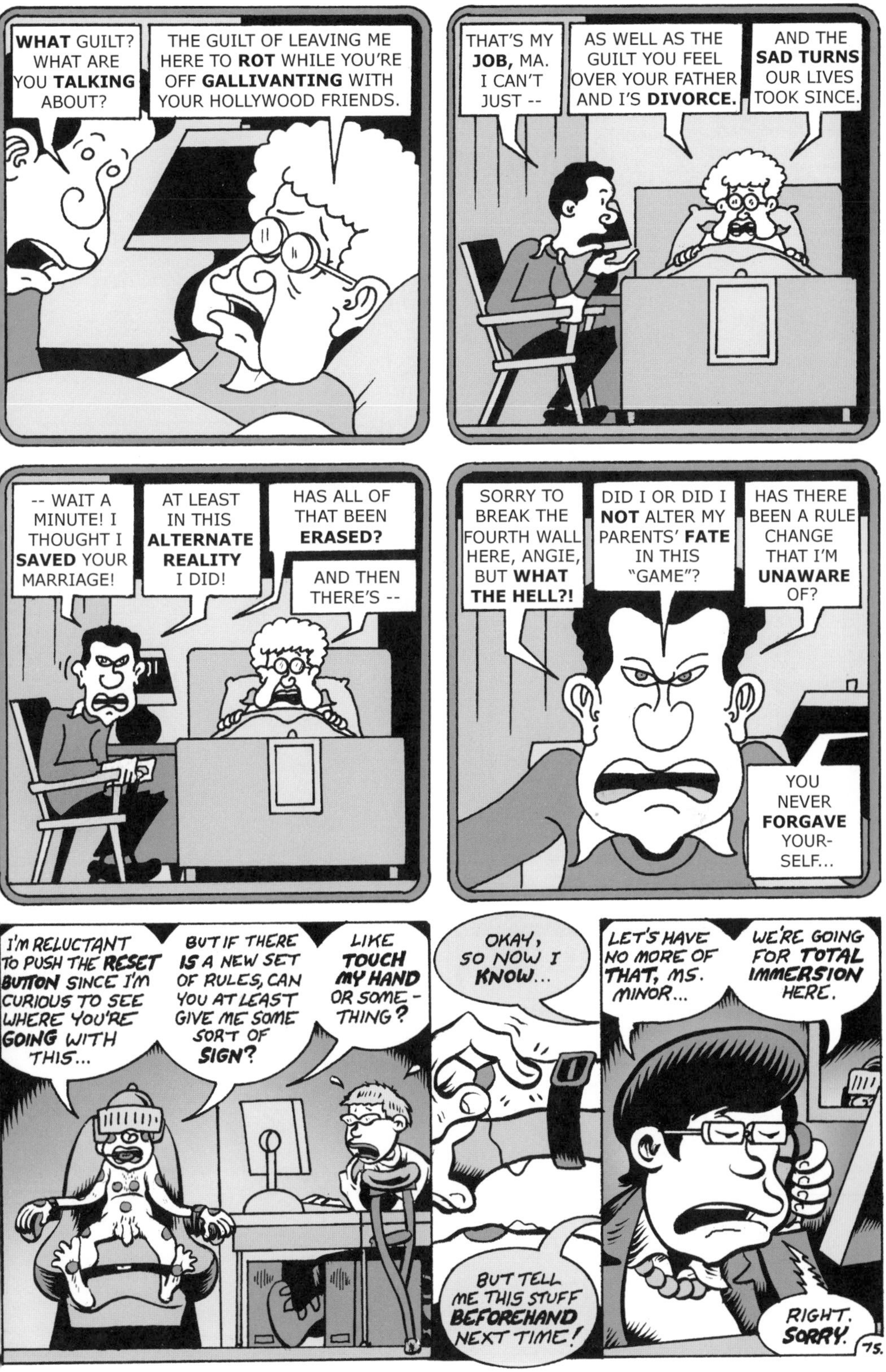
WHAT GUILT? WHAT ARE YOU TALKING ABOUT?
THE GUILT OF LEAVING ME HERE TO ROT WHILE YOU'RE OFF GALLIVANTING WITH YOUR HOLLYWOOD FRIENDS.
THAT'S MY JOB, MA. I CAN'T JUST --
AS WELL AS THE GUILT YOU FEEL OVER YOUR FATHER AND I'S DIVORCE.
AND THE SAD TURNS OUR LIVES TOOK SINCE.
-- WAIT A MINUTE! I THOUGHT I SAVED YOUR MARRIAGE!
AT LEAST IN THIS ALTERNATE REALITY I DID!
HAS ALL OF THAT BEEN ERASED?
AND THEN THERE'S --
SORRY TO BREAK THE FOURTH WALL HERE, ANGIE, BUT WHAT THE HELL?!
DID I OR DID I NOT ALTER MY PARENTS' FATE IN THIS "GAME"?
HAS THERE BEEN A RULE CHANGE THAT I'M UNAWARE OF?
YOU NEVER FORGAVE YOUR-SELF...
I'M RELUCTANT TO PUSH THE RESET BUTTON SINCE I'M CURIOUS TO SEE WHERE YOU'RE GOING WITH THIS...
BUT IF THERE IS A NEW SET OF RULES, CAN YOU AT LEAST GIVE ME SOME SORT OF SIGN?
LIKE TOUCH MY HAND OR SOME-THING?
OKAY, SO NOW I KNOW...
BUT TELL ME THIS STUFF BEFOREHAND NEXT TIME!
LET'S HAVE NO MORE OF THAT, MS. MINOR...
WE'RE GOING FOR TOTAL IMMERSION HERE.
RIGHT. SORRY.

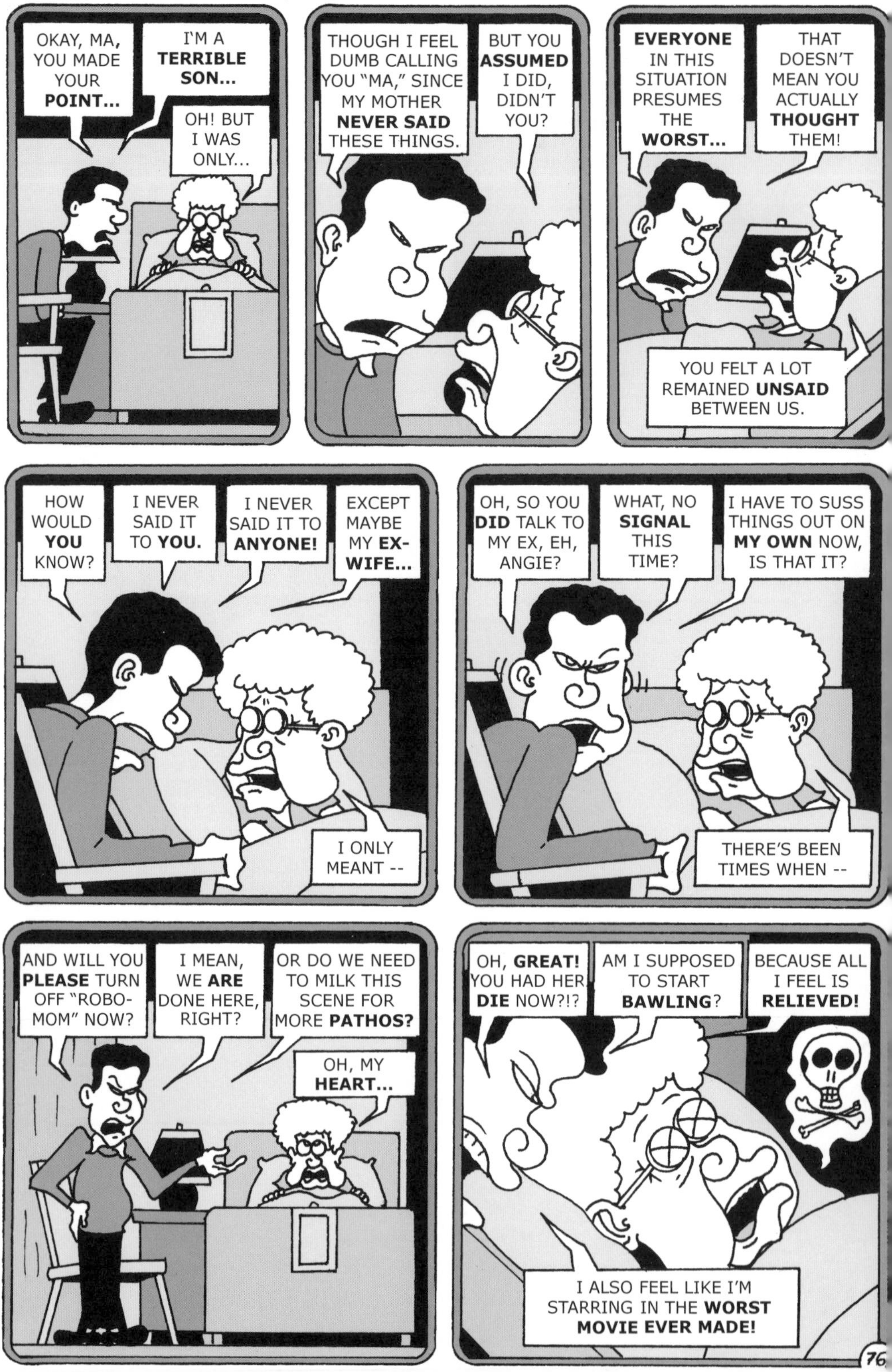

OKAY, MA, YOU MADE YOUR POINT...
I'M A TERRIBLE SON...
OH! BUT I WAS ONLY...
THOUGH I FEEL DUMB CALLING YOU "MA," SINCE MY MOTHER NEVER SAID THESE THINGS.
BUT YOU ASSUMED I DID, DIDN'T YOU?
EVERYONE IN THIS SITUATION PRESUMES THE WORST...
THAT DOESN'T MEAN YOU ACTUALLY THOUGHT THEM!
YOU FELT A LOT REMAINED UNSAID BETWEEN US.
HOW WOULD YOU KNOW?
I NEVER SAID IT TO YOU.
I NEVER SAID IT TO ANYONE!
EXCEPT MAYBE MY EX-WIFE...
I ONLY MEANT --
OH, SO YOU DID TALK TO MY EX, EH, ANGIE?
WHAT, NO SIGNAL THIS TIME?
I HAVE TO SUSS THINGS OUT ON MY OWN NOW, IS THAT IT?
THERE'S BEEN TIMES WHEN --
AND WILL YOU PLEASE TURN OFF "ROBO-MOM" NOW?
I MEAN, WE ARE DONE HERE, RIGHT?
OR DO WE NEED TO MILK THIS SCENE FOR MORE PATHOS?
OH, MY HEART...
OH, GREAT! YOU HAD HER DIE NOW?!?
AM I SUPPOSED TO START BAWLING?
BECAUSE ALL I FEEL IS RELIEVED!
I ALSO FEEL LIKE I'M STARRING IN THE WORST MOVIE EVER MADE!

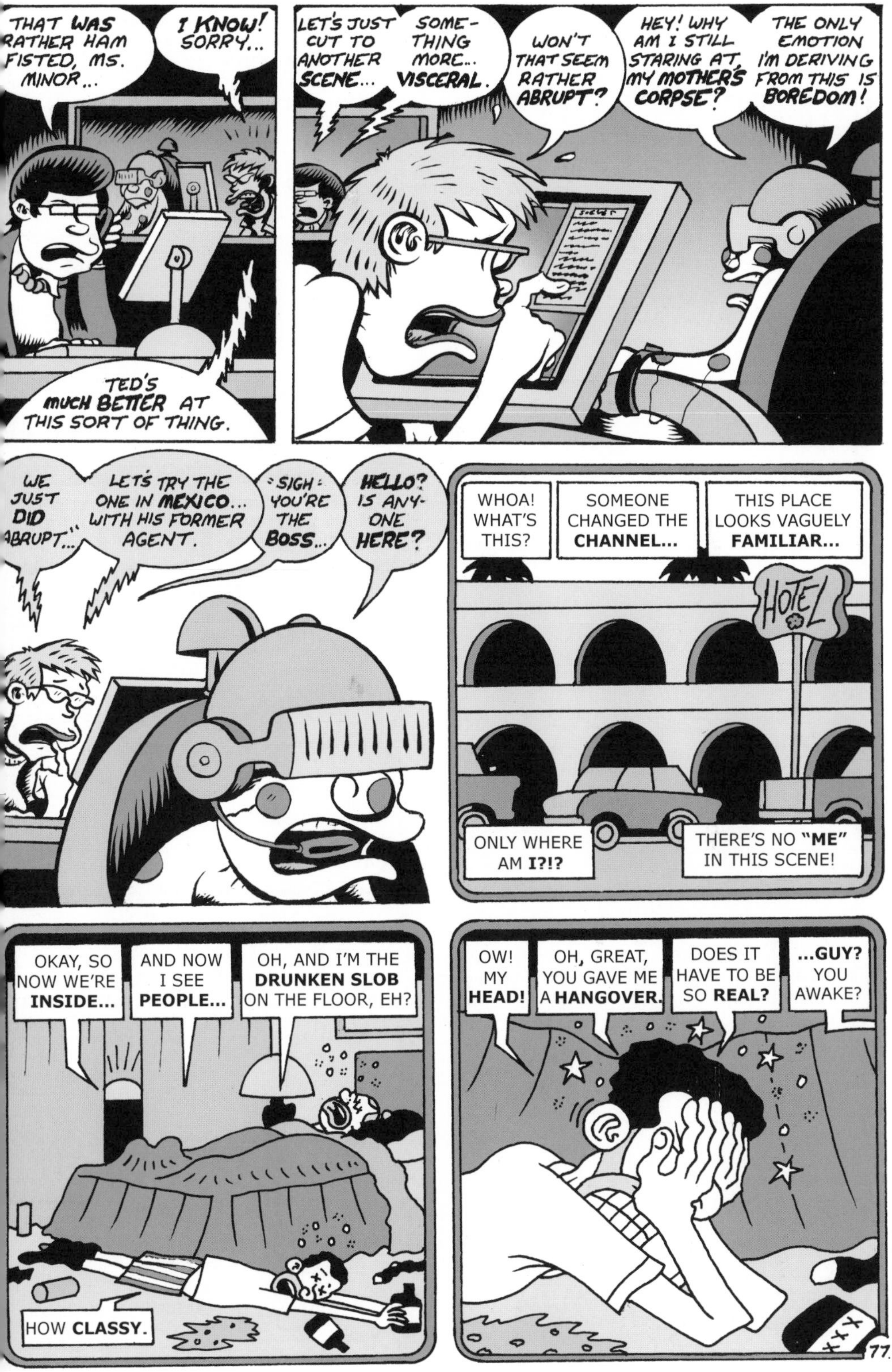
THAT WAS RATHER HAM FISTED, MS. MINOR...
I KNOW! SORRY...
TED'S MUCH BETTER AT THIS SORT OF THING.
LET'S JUST CUT TO ANOTHER SCENE...
SOME-THING MORE... VISCERAL.
WON'T THAT SEEM RATHER ABRUPT?
HEY! WHY AM I STILL STARING AT MY MOTHER'S CORPSE?
THE ONLY EMOTION I'M DERIVING FROM THIS IS BOREDOM!
WE JUST DID ABRUPT...
LET'S TRY THE ONE IN MEXICO... WITH HIS FORMER AGENT.
:SIGH: YOU'RE THE BOSS...
HELLO? IS ANY-ONE HERE?
WHOA! WHAT'S THIS?
SOMEONE CHANGED THE CHANNEL...
THIS PLACE LOOKS VAGUELY FAMILIAR...
HOTEL
ONLY WHERE AM I?!?
THERE'S NO "ME" IN THIS SCENE!
OKAY, SO NOW WE'RE INSIDE...
AND NOW I SEE PEOPLE...
OH, AND I'M THE DRUNKEN SLOB ON THE FLOOR, EH?
HOW CLASSY.
OW! MY HEAD!
OH, GREAT, YOU GAVE ME A HANGOVER.
DOES IT HAVE TO BE SO REAL?
...GUY? YOU AWAKE?
XXX

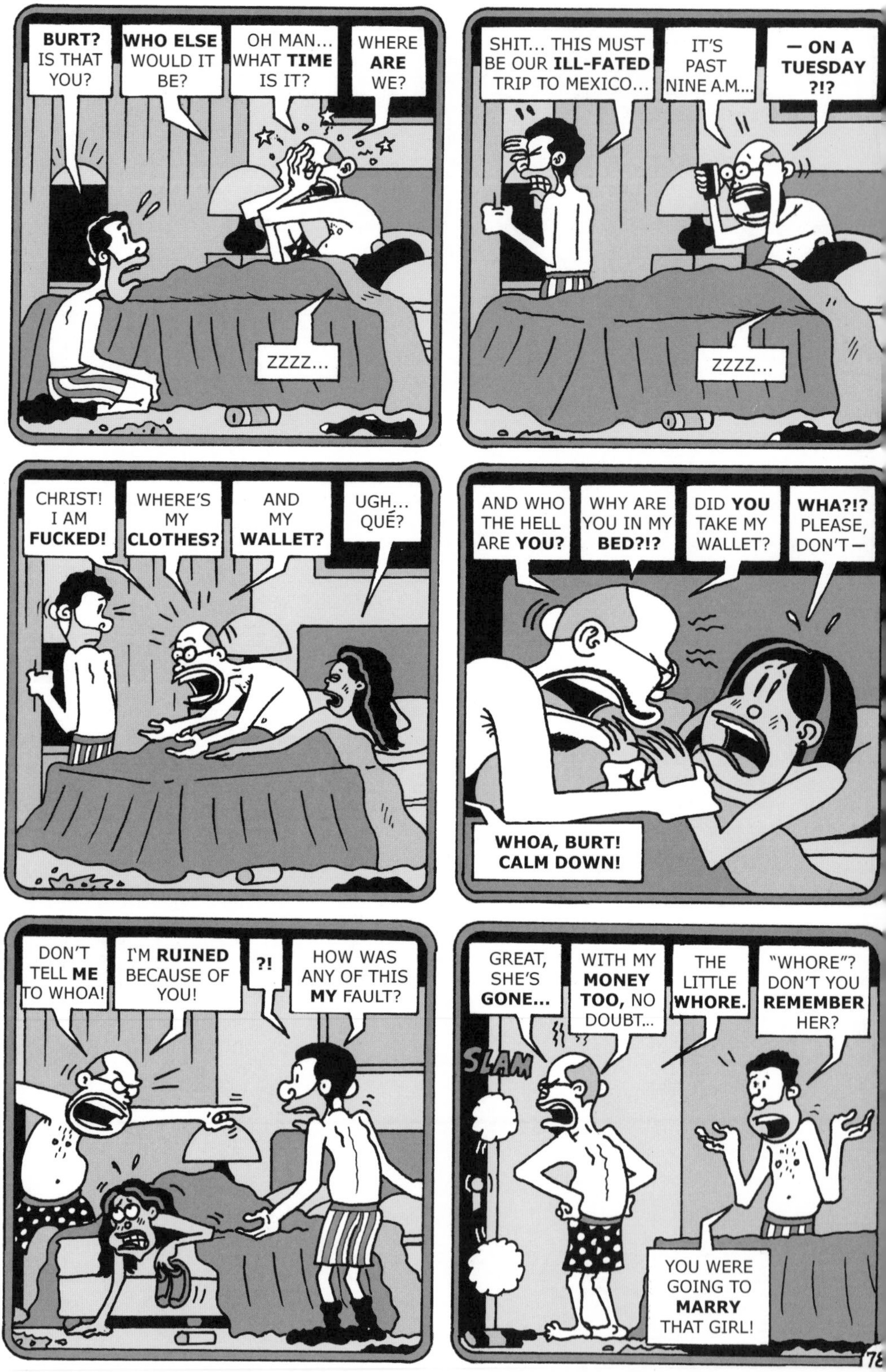
BURT? IS THAT YOU?
WHO ELSE WOULD IT BE?
OH MAN... WHAT TIME IS IT?
WHERE ARE WE?
ZZZZ...
SHIT... THIS MUST BE OUR ILL-FATED TRIP TO MEXICO...
IT'S PAST NINE A.M....
— ON A TUESDAY ?!?
ZZZZ...
CHRIST! I AM FUCKED!
WHERE'S MY CLOTHES?
AND MY WALLET?
UGH... QUÉ?
AND WHO THE HELL ARE YOU?
WHY ARE YOU IN MY BED?!?
DID YOU TAKE MY WALLET?
WHA?!? PLEASE, DON'T—
WHOA, BURT! CALM DOWN!
DON'T TELL ME TO WHOA!
I'M RUINED BECAUSE OF YOU!
?!
HOW WAS ANY OF THIS MY FAULT?
SLAM
GREAT, SHE'S GONE...
WITH MY MONEY TOO, NO DOUBT...
THE LITTLE WHORE.
"WHORE"? DON'T YOU REMEMBER HER?
YOU WERE GOING TO MARRY THAT GIRL!

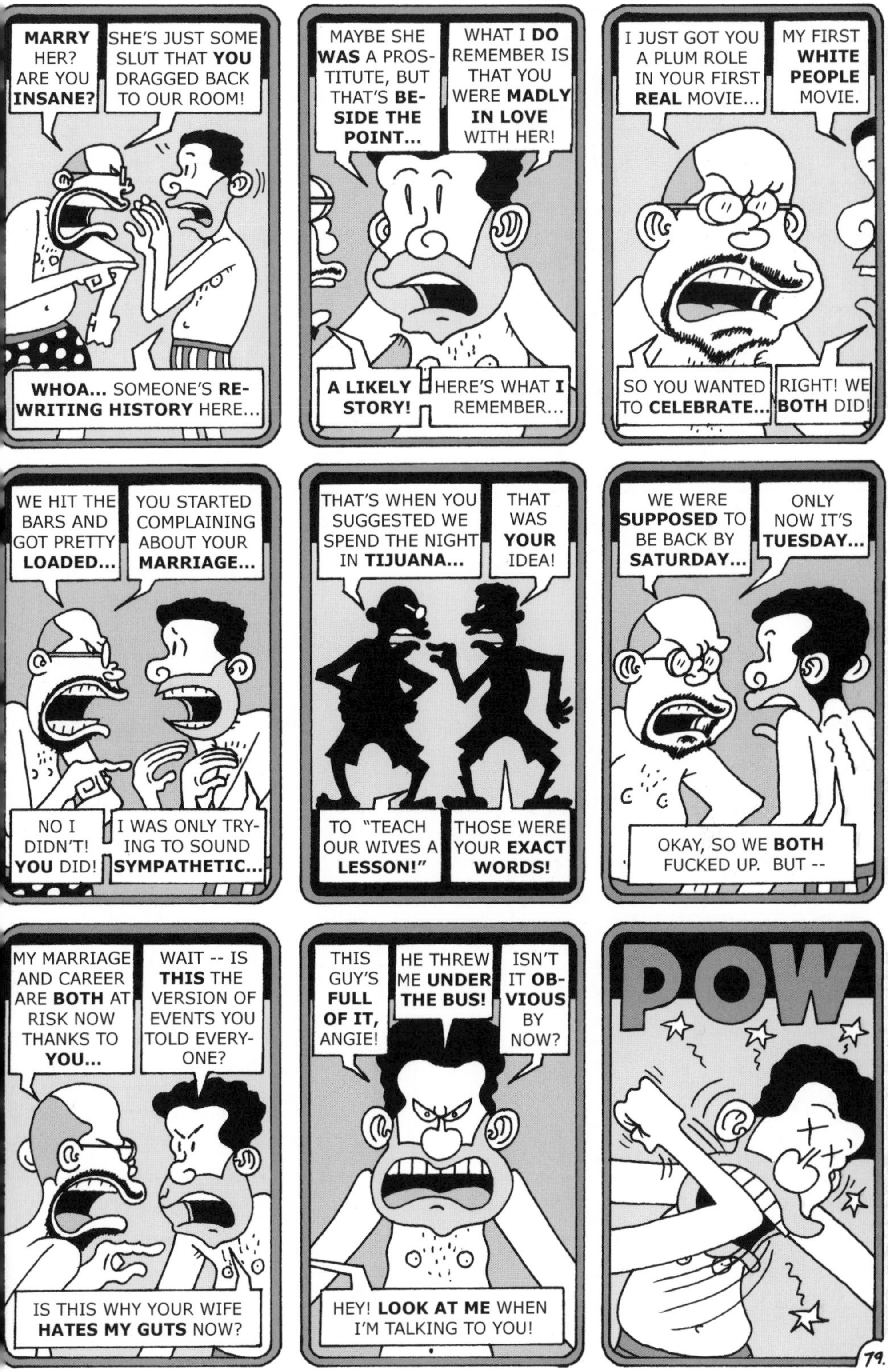
MARRY HER? ARE YOU INSANE?
SHE'S JUST SOME SLUT THAT YOU DRAGGED BACK TO OUR ROOM!
WHOA... SOMEONE'S RE-WRITING HISTORY HERE...
MAYBE SHE WAS A PROS-TITUTE, BUT THAT'S BE-SIDE THE POINT...
WHAT I DO REMEMBER IS THAT YOU WERE MADLY IN LOVE WITH HER!
A LIKELY STORY!
HERE'S WHAT I REMEMBER...
I JUST GOT YOU A PLUM ROLE IN YOUR FIRST REAL MOVIE...
MY FIRST WHITE PEOPLE MOVIE.
SO YOU WANTED TO CELEBRATE...
RIGHT! WE BOTH DID!
WE HIT THE BARS AND GOT PRETTY LOADED...
YOU STARTED COMPLAINING ABOUT YOUR MARRIAGE...
NO I DIDN'T! YOU DID!
I WAS ONLY TRY-ING TO SOUND SYMPATHETIC...
THAT'S WHEN YOU SUGGESTED WE SPEND THE NIGHT IN TIJUANA...
THAT WAS YOUR IDEA!
TO "TEACH OUR WIVES A LESSON!"
THOSE WERE YOUR EXACT WORDS!
WE WERE SUPPOSED TO BE BACK BY SATURDAY...
ONLY NOW IT'S TUESDAY...
OKAY, SO WE BOTH FUCKED UP. BUT --
MY MARRIAGE AND CAREER ARE BOTH AT RISK NOW THANKS TO YOU...
WAIT -- IS THIS THE VERSION OF EVENTS YOU TOLD EVERY-ONE?
IS THIS WHY YOUR WIFE HATES MY GUTS NOW?
THIS GUY'S FULL OF IT, ANGIE!
HE THREW ME UNDER THE BUS!
ISN'T IT OB-VIOUS BY NOW?
HEY! LOOK AT ME WHEN I'M TALKING TO YOU!
POW

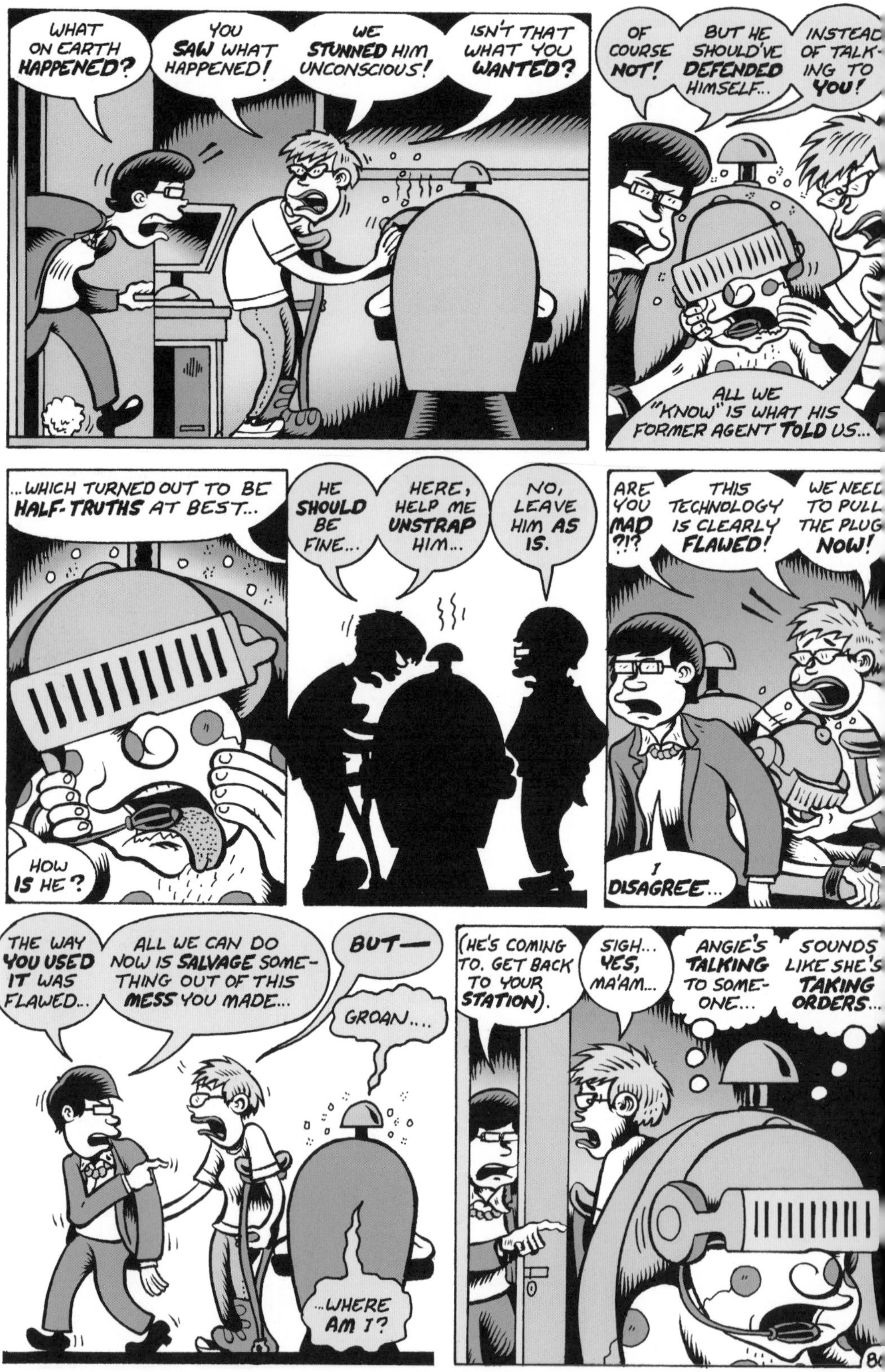
WHAT ON EARTH HAPPENED?
YOU SAW WHAT HAPPENED!
WE STUNNED HIM UNCONSCIOUS!
ISN'T THAT WHAT YOU WANTED?
OF COURSE NOT!
BUT HE SHOULD'VE DEFENDED HIMSELF...
INSTEAD OF TALK-ING TO YOU!
ALL WE "KNOW" IS WHAT HIS FORMER AGENT TOLD US...
...WHICH TURNED OUT TO BE HALF-TRUTHS AT BEST...
HOW IS HE?
HE SHOULD BE FINE...
HERE, HELP ME UNSTRAP HIM...
NO, LEAVE HIM AS IS.
ARE YOU MAD ?!?
THIS TECHNOLOGY IS CLEARLY FLAWED!
WE NEED TO PULL THE PLUG NOW!
I DISAGREE...
THE WAY YOU USED IT WAS FLAWED...
ALL WE CAN DO NOW IS SALVAGE SOME-THING OUT OF THIS MESS YOU MADE...
BUT—
GROAN....
...WHERE AM I?
(HE'S COMING TO. GET BACK TO YOUR STATION).
SIGH... YES, MA'AM...
ANGIE'S TALKING TO SOME-ONE...
SOUNDS LIKE SHE'S TAKING ORDERS...

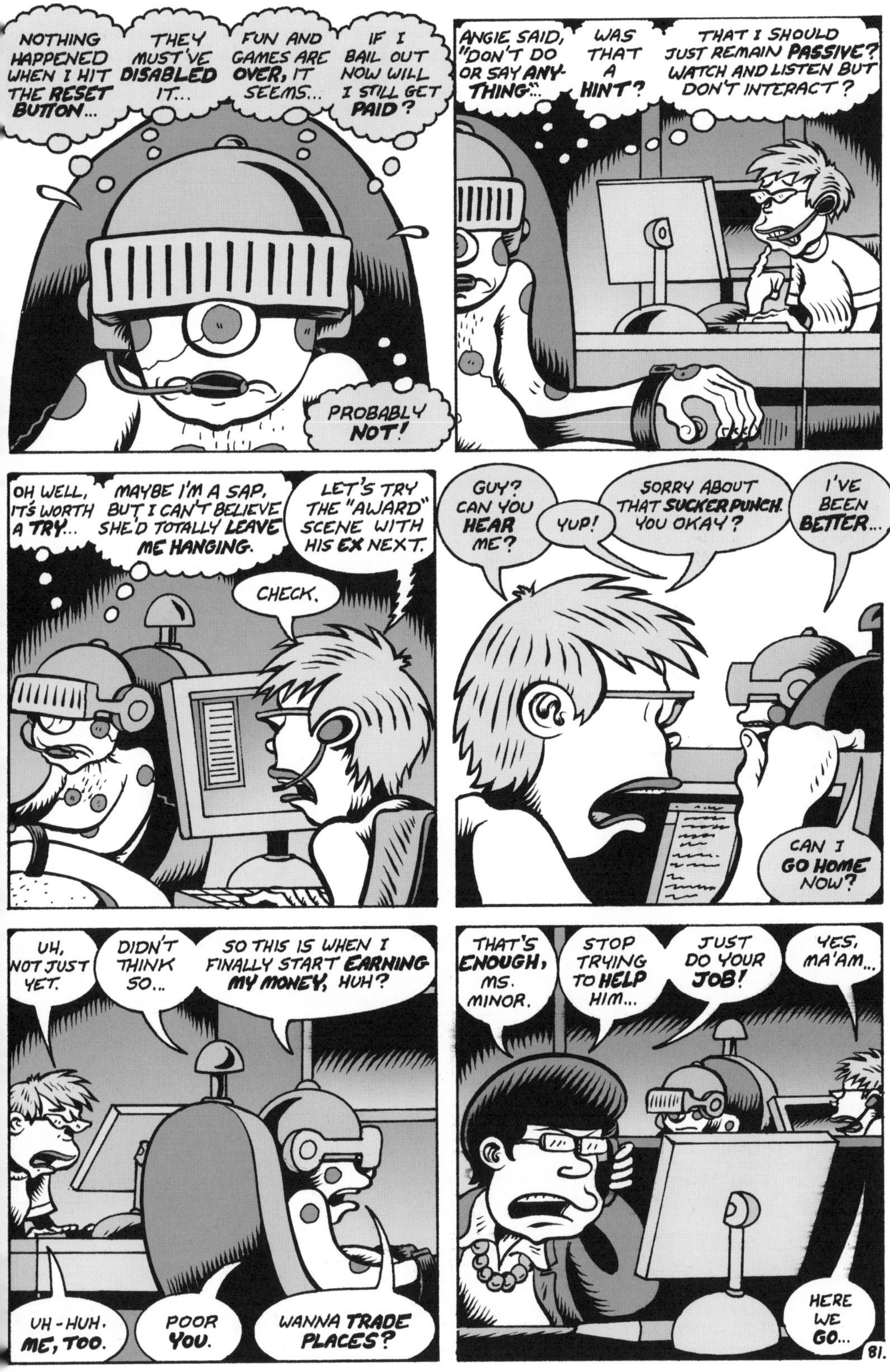
NOTHING HAPPENED WHEN I HIT THE RESET BUTTON...
THEY MUST'VE DISABLED IT...
FUN AND GAMES ARE OVER, IT SEEMS...
IF I BAIL OUT NOW WILL I STILL GET PAID?
PROBABLY NOT!
ANGIE SAID, "DON'T DO OR SAY ANYTHING"...
WAS THAT A HINT?
THAT I SHOULD JUST REMAIN PASSIVE? WATCH AND LISTEN BUT DON'T INTERACT?
OH WELL, IT'S WORTH A TRY...
MAYBE I'M A SAP, BUT I CAN'T BELIEVE SHE'D TOTALLY LEAVE ME HANGING.
LET'S TRY THE "AWARD" SCENE WITH HIS EX NEXT.
CHECK.
GUY? CAN YOU HEAR ME?
YUP!
SORRY ABOUT THAT SUCKER PUNCH. YOU OKAY?
I'VE BEEN BETTER...
CAN I GO HOME NOW?
UH, NOT JUST YET.
DIDN'T THINK SO...
SO THIS IS WHEN I FINALLY START EARNING MY MONEY, HUH?
UH-HUH. ME, TOO.
POOR YOU.
WANNA TRADE PLACES?
THAT'S ENOUGH, MS. MINOR.
STOP TRYING TO HELP HIM...
JUST DO YOUR JOB!
YES, MA'AM...
HERE WE GO...

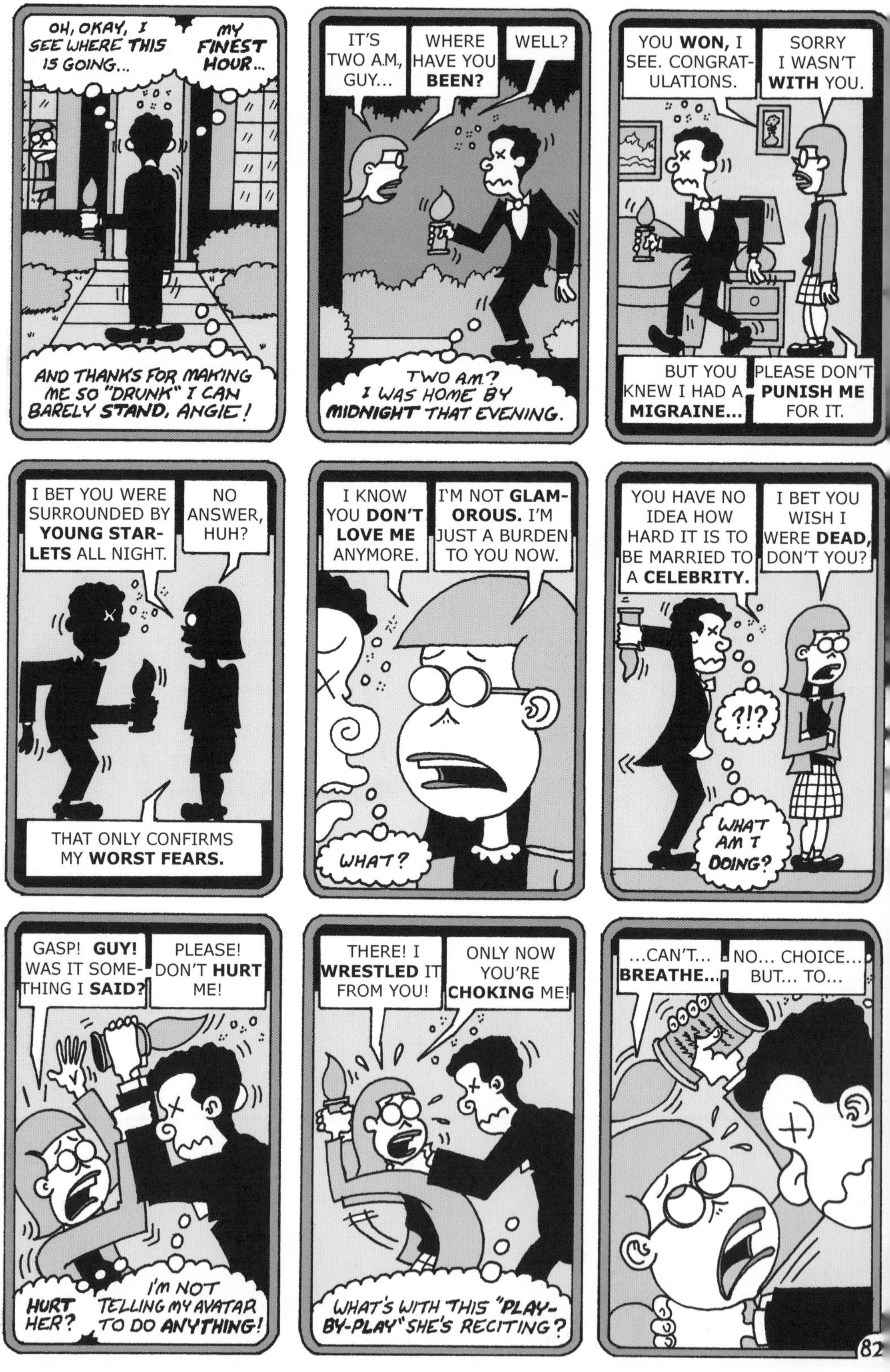
OH, OKAY, I SEE WHERE THIS IS GOING...
MY FINEST HOUR...
AND THANKS FOR MAKING ME SO "DRUNK" I CAN BARELY STAND, ANGIE!
IT'S TWO A.M., GUY...
WHERE HAVE YOU BEEN?
WELL?
TWO AM? I WAS HOME BY MIDNIGHT THAT EVENING.
YOU WON, I SEE. CONGRATULATIONS.
SORRY I WASN'T WITH YOU.
BUT YOU KNEW I HAD A MIGRAINE...
PLEASE DON'T PUNISH ME FOR IT.
I BET YOU WERE SURROUNDED BY YOUNG STARLETS ALL NIGHT.
NO ANSWER, HUH?
THAT ONLY CONFIRMS MY WORST FEARS.
I KNOW YOU DON'T LOVE ME ANYMORE.
I'M NOT GLAMOROUS. I'M JUST A BURDEN TO YOU NOW.
WHAT?
YOU HAVE NO IDEA HOW HARD IT IS TO BE MARRIED TO A CELEBRITY.
I BET YOU WISH I WERE DEAD, DON'T YOU?
?!?
WHAT AM I DOING?
GASP! GUY! WAS IT SOMETHING I SAID?
PLEASE! DON'T HURT ME!
HURT HER?
I'M NOT TELLING MY AVATAR TO DO ANYTHING!
THERE! I WRESTLED IT FROM YOU!
ONLY NOW YOU'RE CHOKING ME!
WHAT'S WITH THIS "PLAY-BY-PLAY" SHE'S RECITING?
...CAN'T... BREATHE...
NO... CHOICE... BUT... TO...

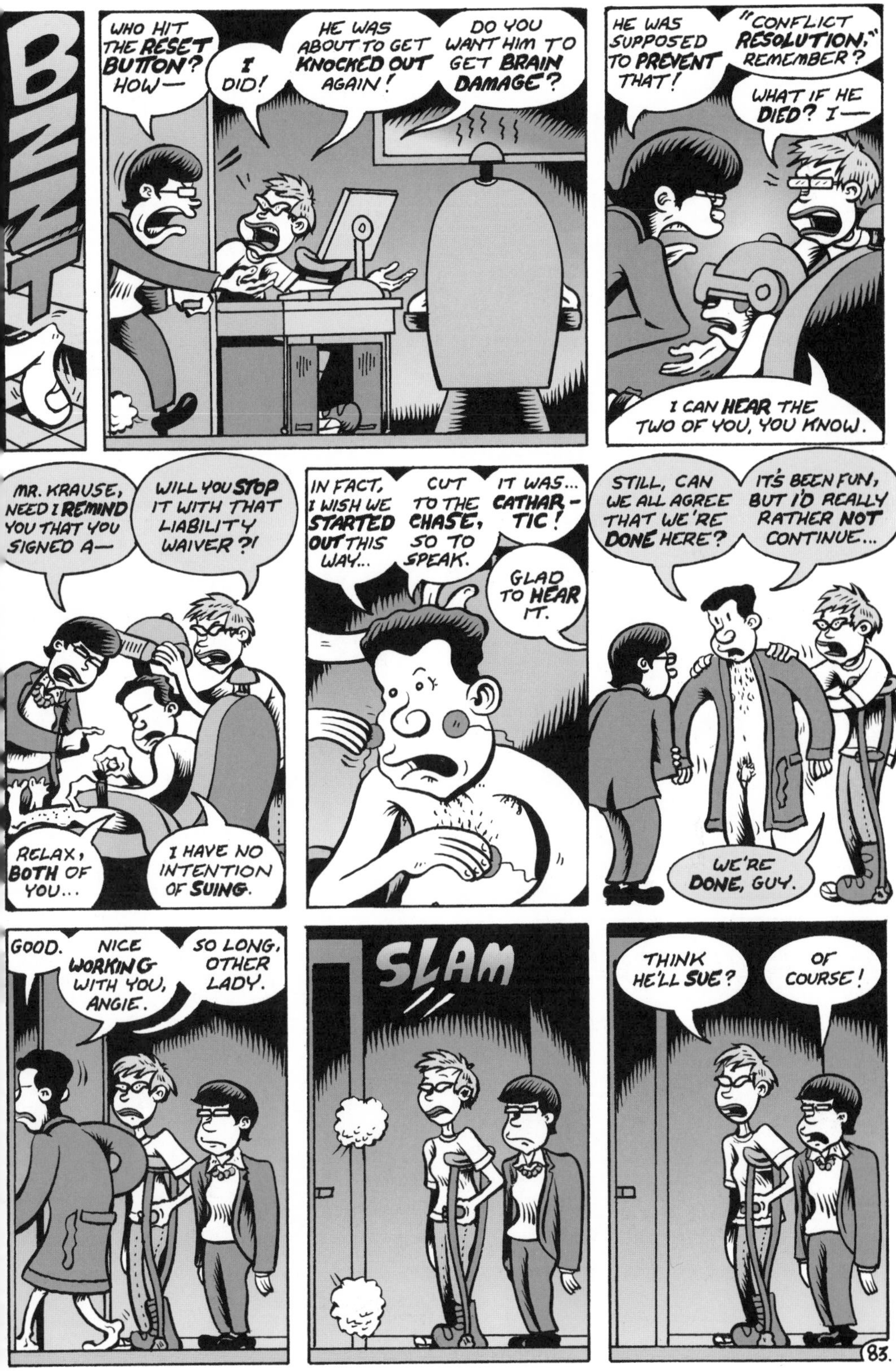
BZZT
WHO HIT THE RESET BUTTON? HOW—
I DID!
HE WAS ABOUT TO GET KNOCKED OUT AGAIN!
DO YOU WANT HIM TO GET BRAIN DAMAGE?
HE WAS SUPPOSED TO PREVENT THAT!
"CONFLICT RESOLUTION," REMEMBER?
WHAT IF HE DIED? I—
I CAN HEAR THE TWO OF YOU, YOU KNOW.
MR. KRAUSE, NEED I REMIND YOU THAT YOU SIGNED A—
WILL YOU STOP IT WITH THAT LIABILITY WAIVER?!
RELAX, BOTH OF YOU...
I HAVE NO INTENTION OF SUING.
IN FACT, I WISH WE STARTED OUT THIS WAY...
CUT TO THE CHASE, SO TO SPEAK.
IT WAS... CATHAR-TIC!
GLAD TO HEAR IT.
STILL, CAN WE ALL AGREE THAT WE'RE DONE HERE?
IT'S BEEN FUN, BUT I'D REALLY RATHER NOT CONTINUE...
WE'RE DONE, GUY.
GOOD.
NICE WORKING WITH YOU, ANGIE.
SO LONG, OTHER LADY.
SLAM
THINK HE'LL SUE?
OF COURSE!

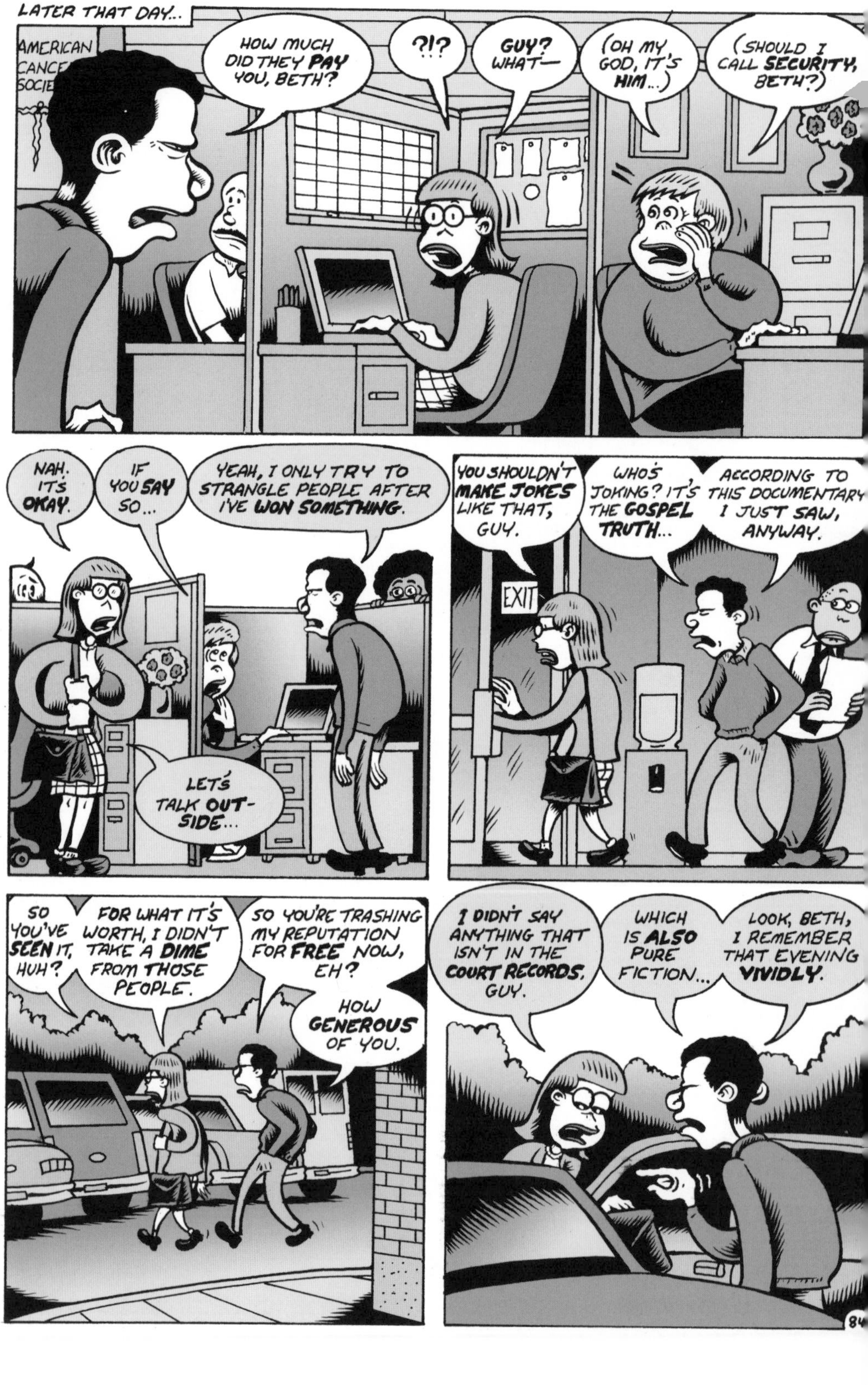
LATER THAT DAY...
AMERICAN CANCE SOCIE
HOW MUCH DID THEY PAY YOU, BETH?
?!?
GUY? WHAT—
(OH MY GOD, IT'S HIM...)
(SHOULD I CALL SECURITY, BETH?)
NAH. IT'S OKAY.
IF YOU SAY SO...
YEAH, I ONLY TRY TO STRANGLE PEOPLE AFTER I'VE WON SOMETHING.
LET'S TALK OUT-SIDE...
YOU SHOULDN'T MAKE JOKES LIKE THAT, GUY.
WHO'S JOKING? IT'S THE GOSPEL TRUTH...
ACCORDING TO THIS DOCUMENTARY I JUST SAW, ANYWAY.
EXIT
SO YOU'VE SEEN IT, HUH?
FOR WHAT IT'S WORTH, I DIDN'T TAKE A DIME FROM THOSE PEOPLE.
SO YOU'RE TRASHING MY REPUTATION FOR FREE NOW, EH?
HOW GENEROUS OF YOU.
I DIDN'T SAY ANYTHING THAT ISN'T IN THE COURT RECORDS, GUY.
WHICH IS ALSO PURE FICTION...
LOOK, BETH, I REMEMBER THAT EVENING VIVIDLY.

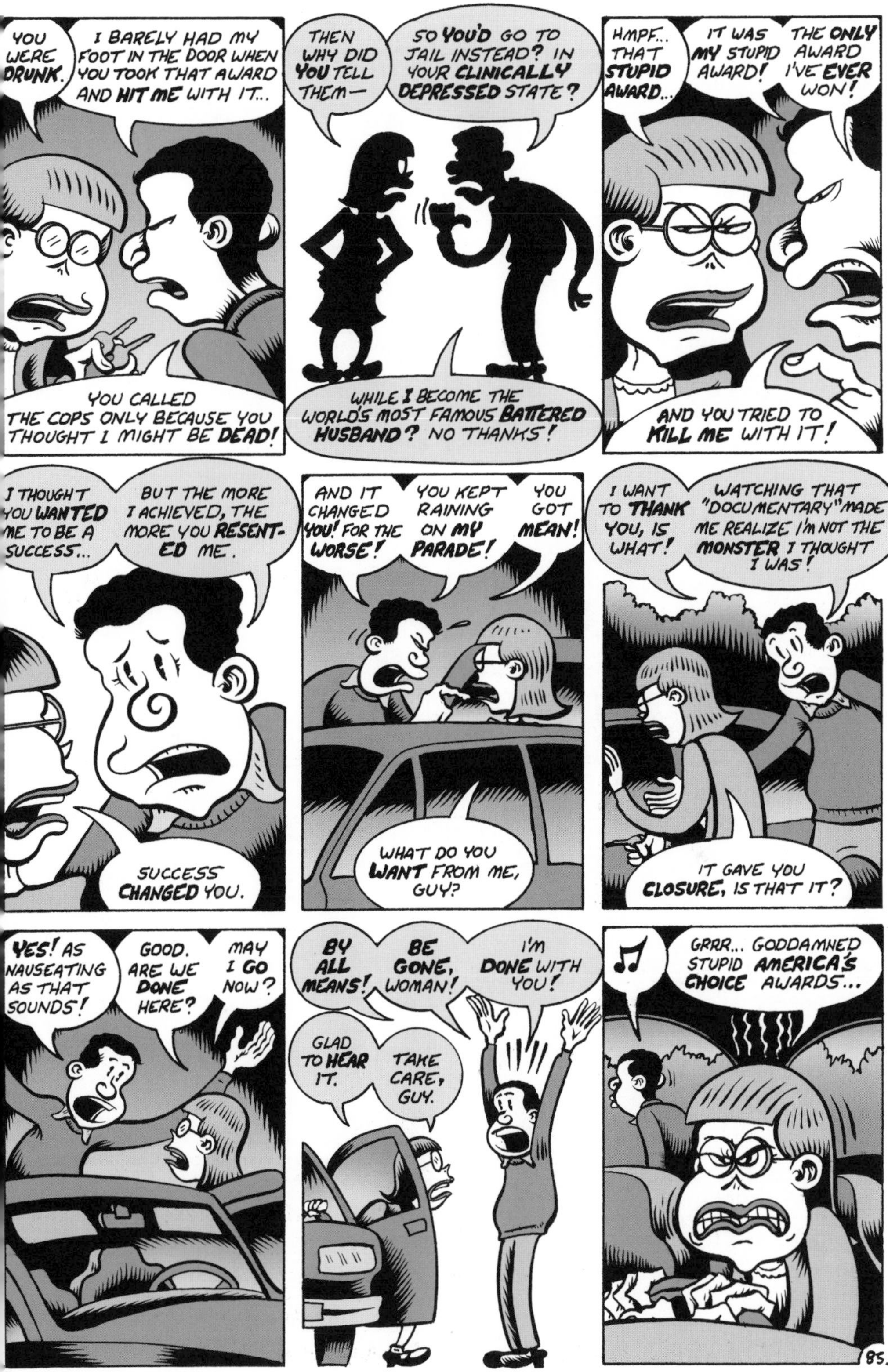
YOU WERE DRUNK.
I BARELY HAD MY FOOT IN THE DOOR WHEN YOU TOOK THAT AWARD AND HIT ME WITH IT...
YOU CALLED THE COPS ONLY BECAUSE YOU THOUGHT I MIGHT BE DEAD!
THEN WHY DID YOU TELL THEM—
SO YOU'D GO TO JAIL INSTEAD? IN YOUR CLINICALLY DEPRESSED STATE?
WHILE I BECOME THE WORLD'S MOST FAMOUS BATTERED HUSBAND? NO THANKS!
HMPF... THAT STUPID AWARD...
IT WAS MY STUPID AWARD!
THE ONLY AWARD I'VE EVER WON!
AND YOU TRIED TO KILL ME WITH IT!
I THOUGHT YOU WANTED ME TO BE A SUCCESS...
BUT THE MORE I ACHIEVED, THE MORE YOU RESENTED ME.
SUCCESS CHANGED YOU.
AND IT CHANGED YOU! FOR THE WORSE!
YOU KEPT RAINING ON MY PARADE!
YOU GOT MEAN!
WHAT DO YOU WANT FROM ME, GUY?
I WANT TO THANK YOU, IS WHAT!
WATCHING THAT "DOCUMENTARY" MADE ME REALIZE I'M NOT THE MONSTER I THOUGHT I WAS!
IT GAVE YOU CLOSURE, IS THAT IT?
YES! AS NAUSEATING AS THAT SOUNDS!
GOOD. ARE WE DONE HERE?
MAY I GO NOW?
BY ALL MEANS!
BE GONE, WOMAN!
I'M DONE WITH YOU!
GLAD TO HEAR IT.
TAKE CARE, GUY.
♫
GRRR... GODDAMNED STUPID AMERICA'S CHOICE AWARDS...

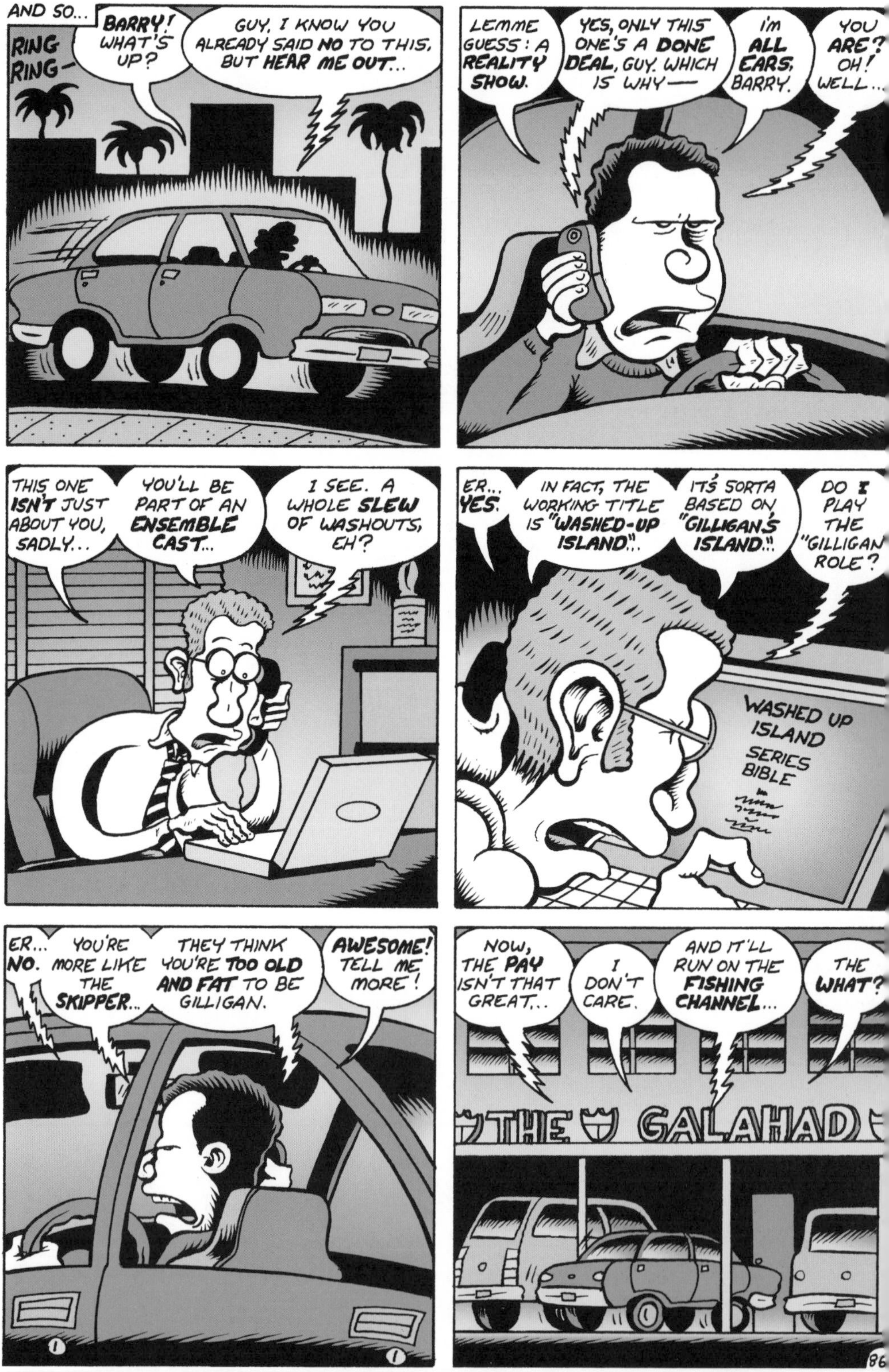
AND SO...
RING RING—
BARRY! WHAT'S UP?
GUY, I KNOW YOU ALREADY SAID NO TO THIS, BUT HEAR ME OUT...
LEMME GUESS: A REALITY SHOW.
YES, ONLY THIS ONE'S A DONE DEAL, GUY. WHICH IS WHY—
I'M ALL EARS, BARRY.
YOU ARE? OH! WELL...
THIS ONE ISN'T JUST ABOUT YOU, SADLY...
YOU'LL BE PART OF AN ENSEMBLE CAST...
I SEE. A WHOLE SLEW OF WASHOUTS, EH?
ER... YES.
IN FACT, THE WORKING TITLE IS "WASHED-UP ISLAND"...
IT'S SORTA BASED ON "GILLIGAN'S ISLAND."
DO I PLAY THE "GILLIGAN" ROLE?
WASHED UP ISLAND SERIES BIBLE
ER... NO.
YOU'RE MORE LIKE THE SKIPPER...
THEY THINK YOU'RE TOO OLD AND FAT TO BE GILLIGAN.
AWESOME! TELL ME MORE!
NOW, THE PAY ISN'T THAT GREAT...
I DON'T CARE.
AND IT'LL RUN ON THE FISHING CHANNEL...
THE WHAT?
THE GALAHAD

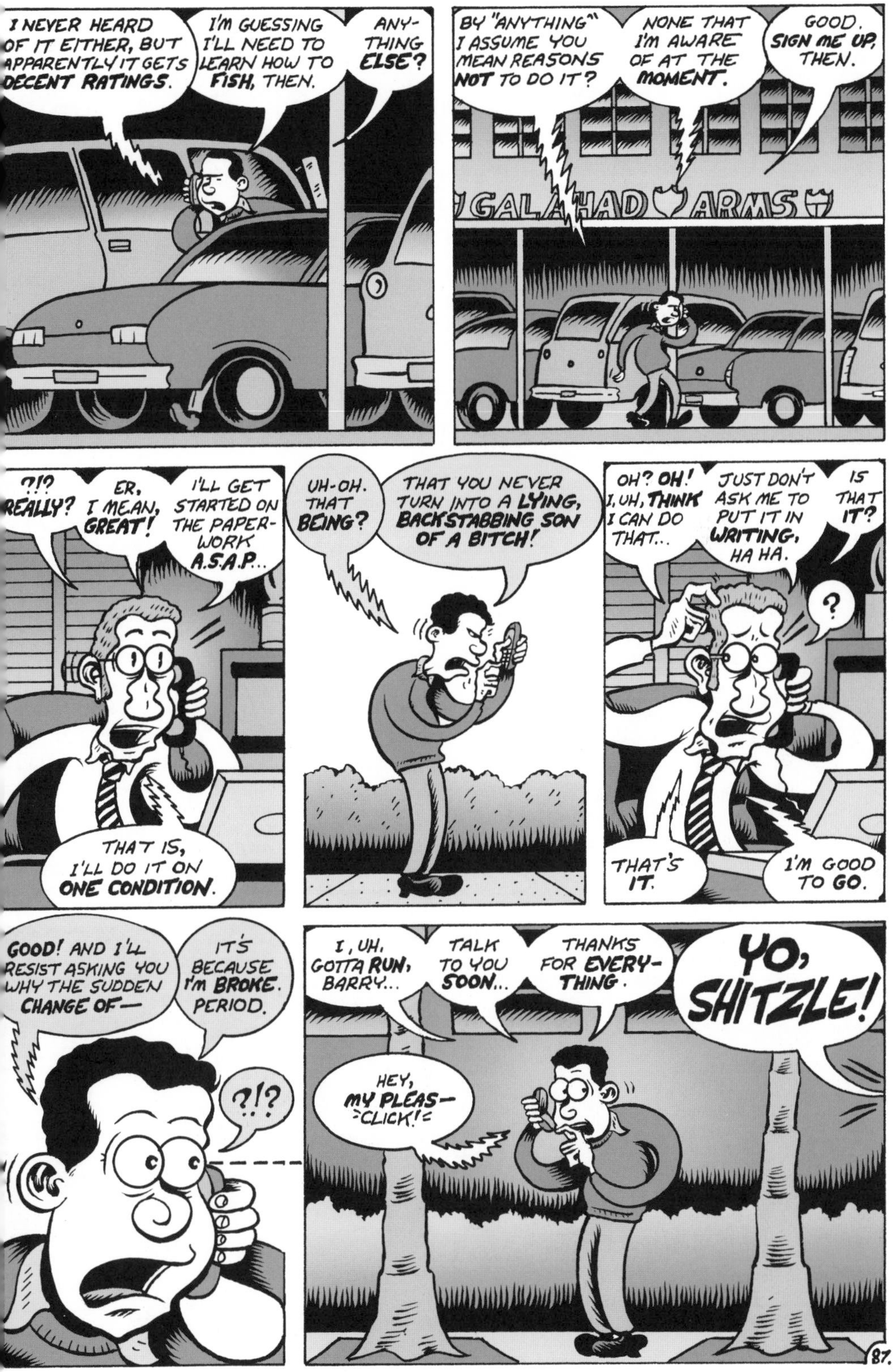

I NEVER HEARD OF IT EITHER, BUT APPARENTLY IT GETS DECENT RATINGS.
I'M GUESSING I'LL NEED TO LEARN HOW TO FISH, THEN.
ANY-THING ELSE?
BY "ANYTHING" I ASSUME YOU MEAN REASONS NOT TO DO IT?
NONE THAT I'M AWARE OF AT THE MOMENT.
GOOD. SIGN ME UP, THEN.
GALAHAD ARMS
?!?
REALLY?
ER, I MEAN, GREAT!
I'LL GET STARTED ON THE PAPER-WORK A.S.A.P...
THAT IS, I'LL DO IT ON ONE CONDITION.
UH-OH. THAT BEING?
THAT YOU NEVER TURN INTO A LYING, BACKSTABBING SON OF A BITCH!
OH? OH! I, UH, THINK I CAN DO THAT...
JUST DON'T ASK ME TO PUT IT IN WRITING, HA HA.
IS THAT IT?
?
THAT'S IT.
I'M GOOD TO GO.
GOOD! AND I'LL RESIST ASKING YOU WHY THE SUDDEN CHANGE OF—
IT'S BECAUSE I'M BROKE. PERIOD.
?!?
I, UH, GOTTA RUN, BARRY...
TALK TO YOU SOON...
THANKS FOR EVERY-THING.
YO, SHITZLE!
HEY, MY PLEAS- =CLICK!=

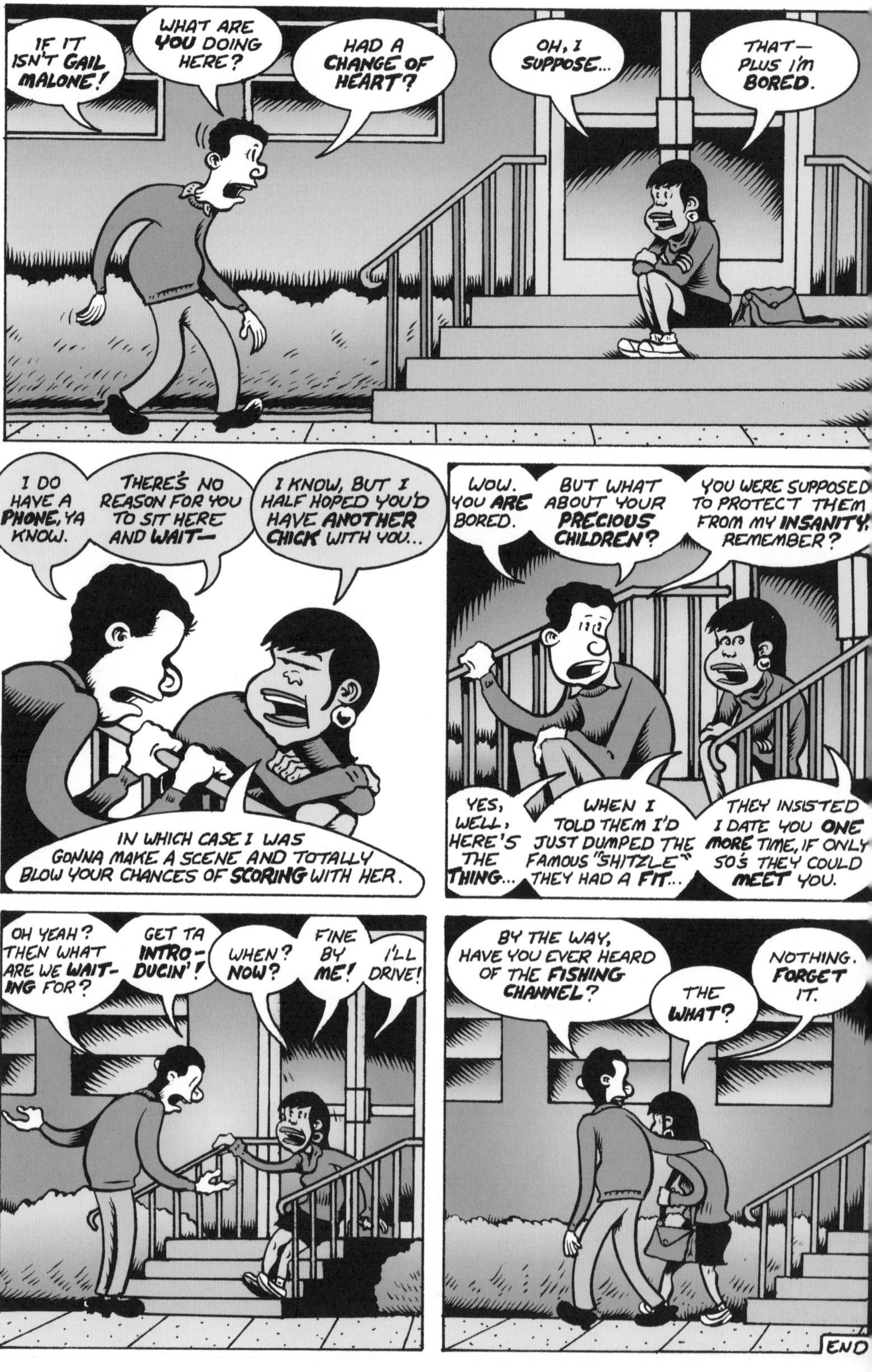
IF IT ISN'T GAIL MALONE!
WHAT ARE YOU DOING HERE?
HAD A CHANGE OF HEART?
OH, I SUPPOSE...
THAT— PLUS I'M BORED.
I DO HAVE A PHONE, YA KNOW.
THERE'S NO REASON FOR YOU TO SIT HERE AND WAIT—
I KNOW, BUT I HALF HOPED YOU'D HAVE ANOTHER CHICK WITH YOU...
IN WHICH CASE I WAS GONNA MAKE A SCENE AND TOTALLY BLOW YOUR CHANCES OF SCORING WITH HER.
WOW. YOU ARE BORED.
BUT WHAT ABOUT YOUR PRECIOUS CHILDREN?
YOU WERE SUPPOSED TO PROTECT THEM FROM MY INSANITY, REMEMBER?
YES, WELL, HERE'S THE THING...
WHEN I TOLD THEM I'D JUST DUMPED THE FAMOUS "SHITZLE" THEY HAD A FIT...
THEY INSISTED I DATE YOU ONE MORE TIME, IF ONLY SO'S THEY COULD MEET YOU.
OH YEAH? THEN WHAT ARE WE WAITING FOR?
GET TA INTRO-DUCIN'!
WHEN? NOW?
FINE BY ME!
I'LL DRIVE!
BY THE WAY, HAVE YOU EVER HEARD OF THE FISHING CHANNEL?
THE WHAT?
NOTHING. FORGET IT.
END

Reset #1 cover art/April 2012

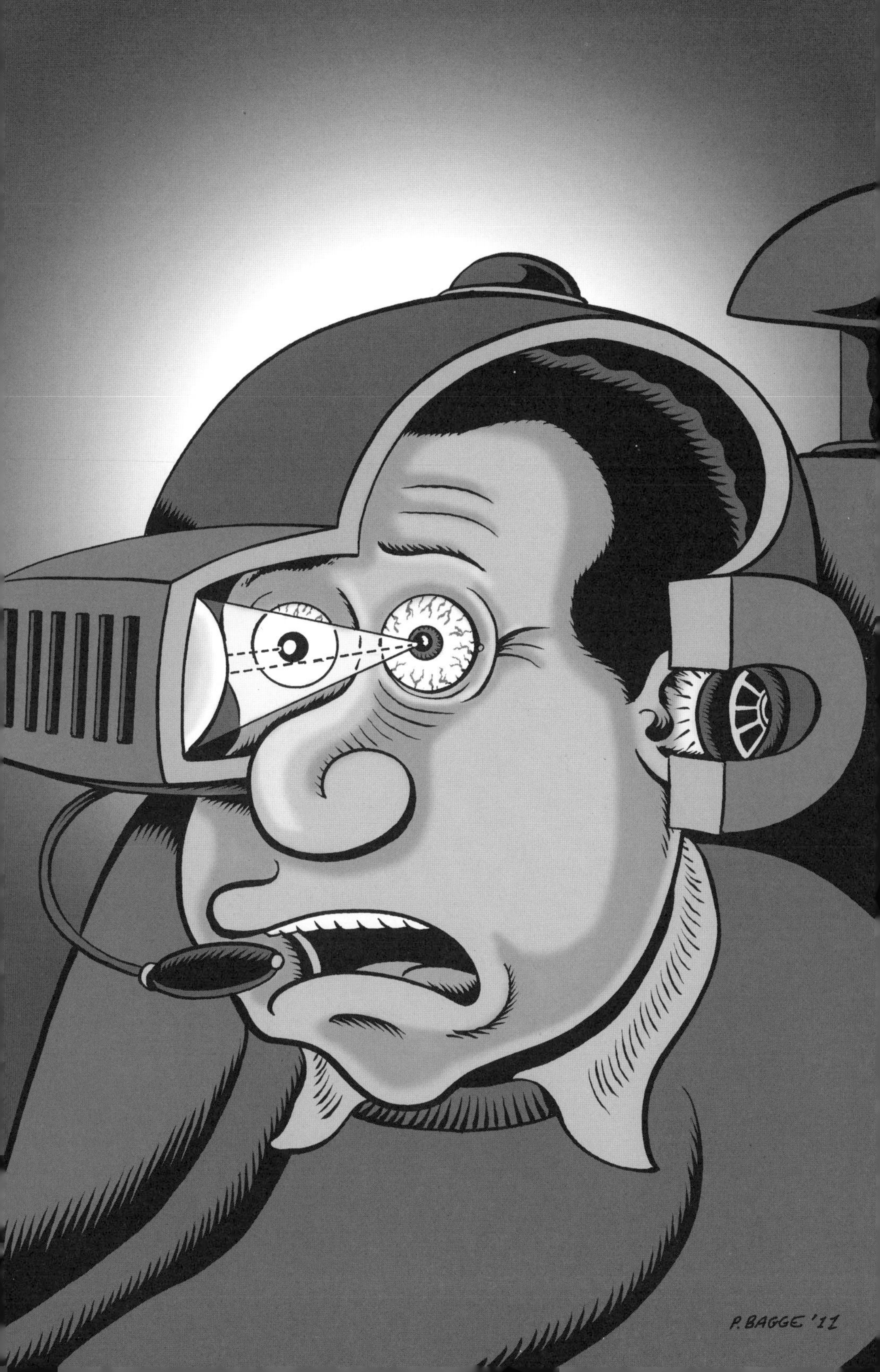
P. BAGGE '11

Reset #2 cover art/May 2012

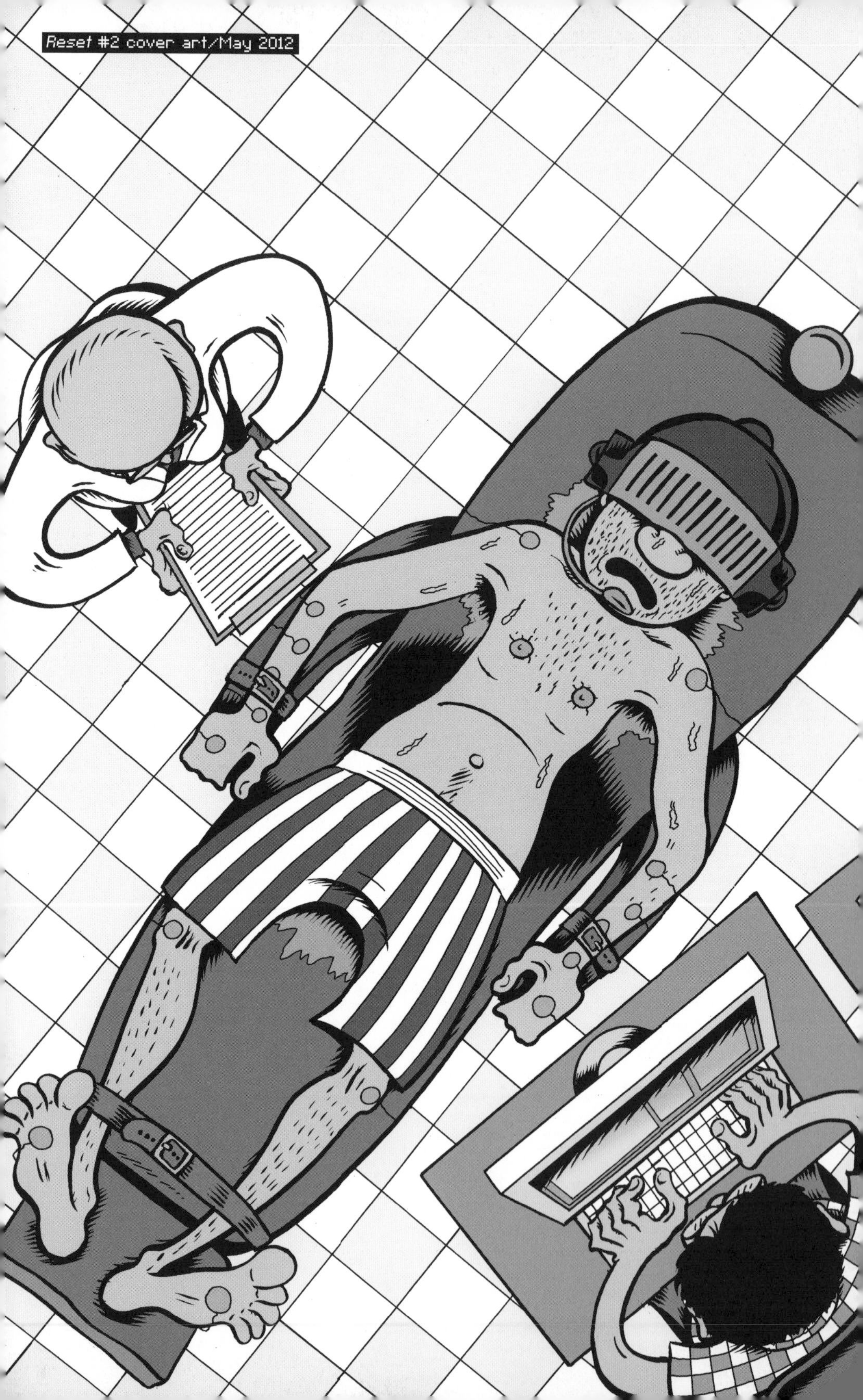

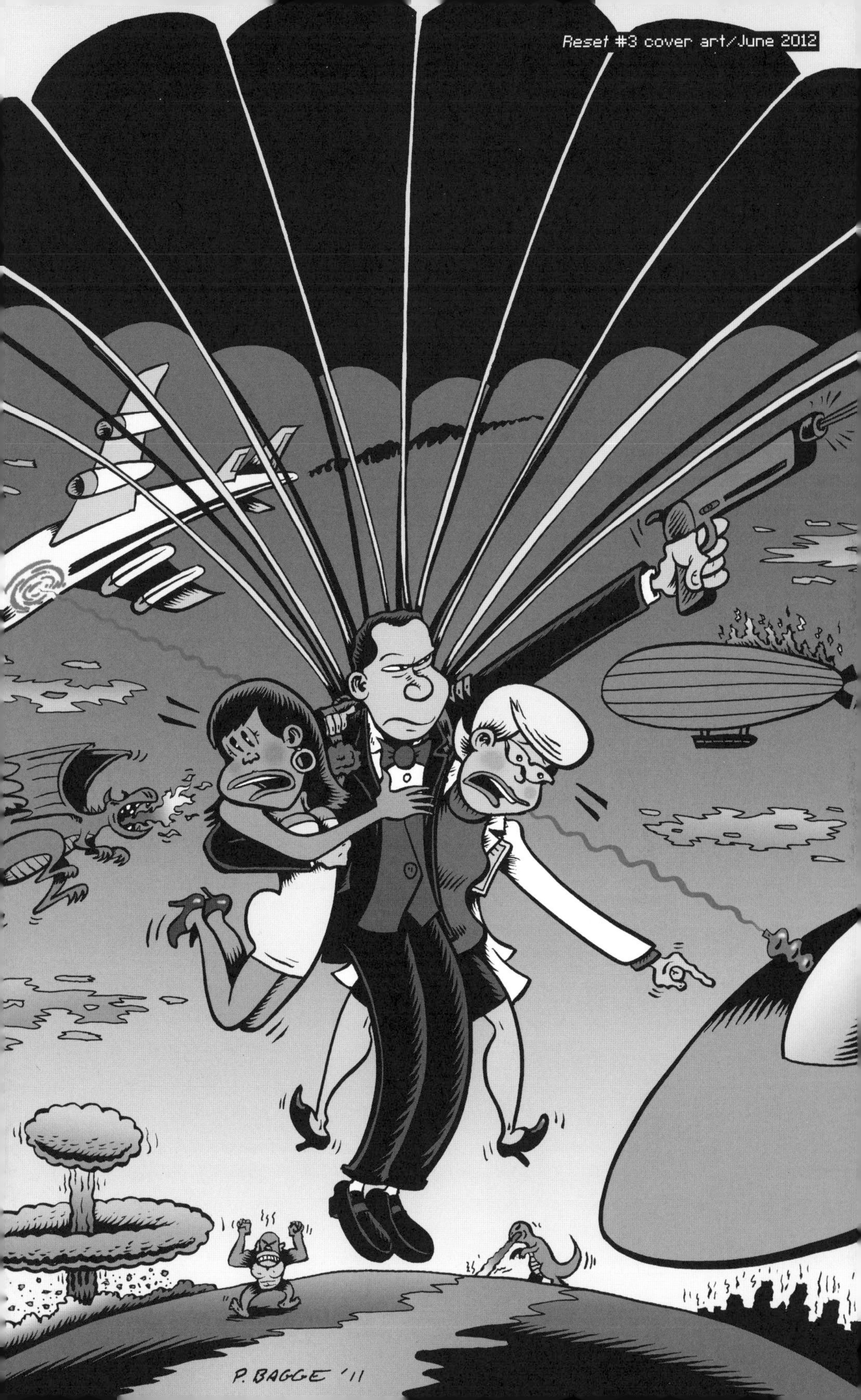
P. BAGGE '11
Reset #3 cover art/June 2012

Reset #4 cover art/July 2012

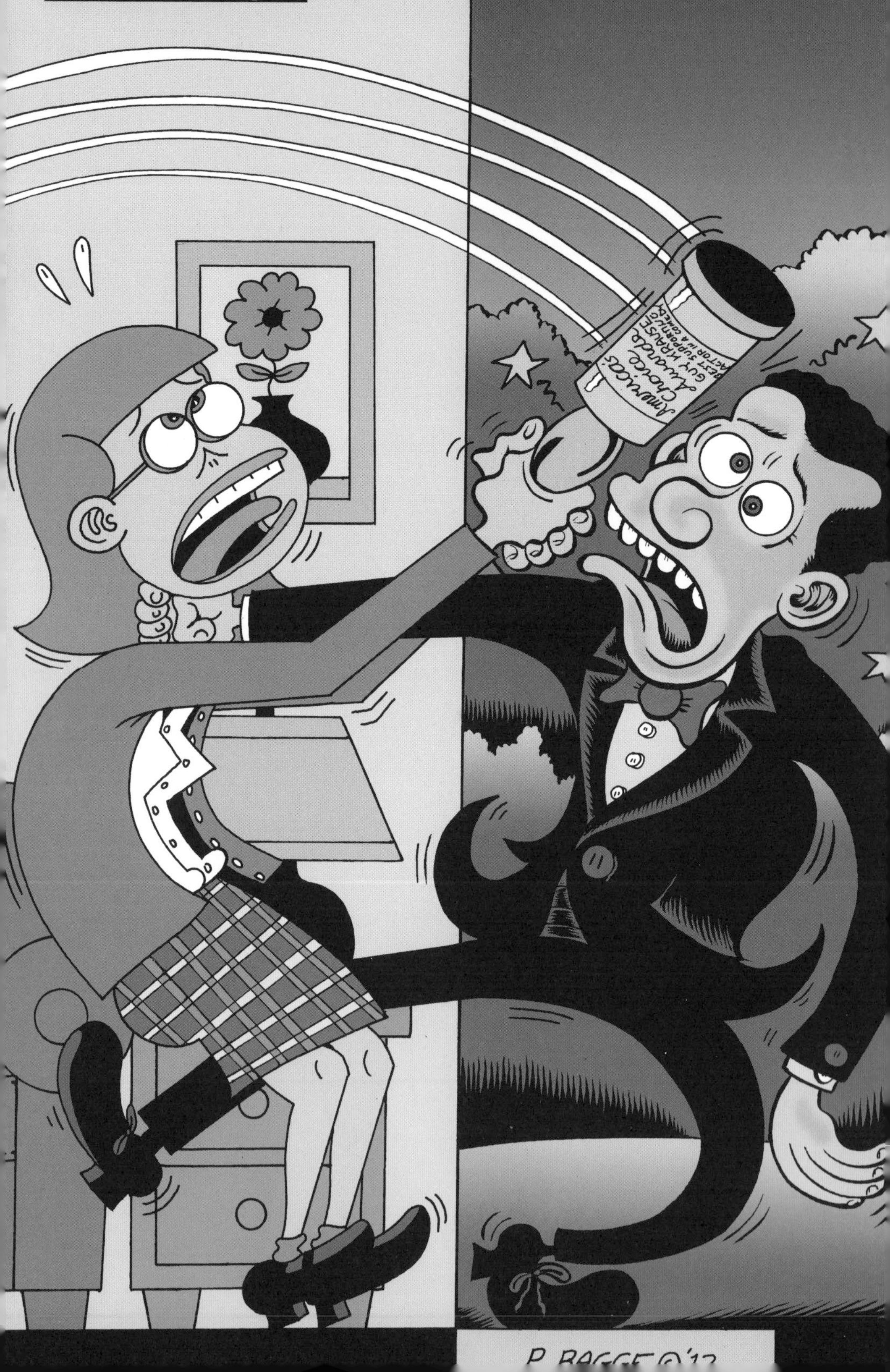
America's Choice Awards
GUY KRAUSE
BEST SUPPORTING ACTOR in a COMEDY
P. BAGGE ©'12